Change the World With

C000044924

Change the World Without Taking Power
New Edition

John Holloway

Instituto de Ciencias Sociales y Humanidades
Benemérita Universidad Autónoma de Puebla

Pluto Press
LONDON • ANN ARBOR, MI

First published 2002 and 2005 by Pluto Press
345 Archway Road, London N6 5AA
and 839 Greene Street, Ann Arbor, MI 48106

www.plutobooks.com

British Library Cataloguing in Publication Data
A catalogue record for this book is available from the British Library

ISBN 0 7453 2466 5 paperback

10   9   8   7   6   5   4   3   2   1

Designed and produced for Pluto Press by
Chase Publishing Services Ltd, Fortescue, Sidmouth EX10 9QG
Typeset from disk by Stanford DTP Services, Northampton
Printed in the European Union by Antony Rowe, Chippenham, England

Contents

Acknowledgements

There are an awful lot of people to thank for their help in producing this book.

First, my thanks to Eloína Peláez, whose mephistophelean presence moves through every word, dot and comma of the book, and without whom I could never even have imagined the unity of constitution and existence: not duration, but nunc stans.

To Werner Bonefeld, Richard Gunn and now Sergio Tischler I owe a great deal for countless shared seminars and discussions over the years, for their support and for their very valuable comments on various stages of this text.

I have been very fortunate in being able to discuss both the text in detail and related ideas with the members of the seminar group on Subjectivity and Critical Theory in the Instituto de Ciencias Sociales y Humanidades in Puebla: to all involved, very many thanks. Two trips to Argentina have also played an important part in helping me to crystallise the ideas contained in this book: the first, to give a seminar in the Instituto Argentino de Desarrollo Económico, organised by Gustavo Roux and Eliseo Giai; the second to give a week-long intensive seminar on the first draft of the book in the Facultad de Filosofía y Letras in Rosario, organised by Gladys Rimini and Gustavo Guevara: to the organisers and all the participants my deepest thanks. And, while in Argentina, a very special thanks to Alberto Bonnet, Marcela Zangaro and Néstor López for their constant help and encouragement. Jumping from the other side of the world, from Argentina to Scotland, I owe much to the long-term inspiration and encouragement of George Wilson, Eileen Simpson, Maggie Sinclair, Rod MacKenzie, Vassiliki Kolocotroni and Olga Taxidou.

My sincerest thanks too to those others who have been kind enough to comment, often in great detail, on drafts of this book: Simon Susen, Ana Dinerstein, Jorge Luis Acanda, Chris Wright, José Manuel Martínez, Cyril Smith, Massimo de Angelis, Rowan Wilson, Ana Esther Ceceña, Enrique Rajchenberg, Patricia King, Javier Villanueva and Lars Stubbe. To Steve Wright, thanks for last-minute help with a quotation.

To Roberto Vélez Pliego, Director of the Instituto de Ciencias Sociales of the Benemérita Universidad Autónoma de Puebla, heartfelt thanks for his support and for helping to make the Institute an exceptional place to work.

To Aidan, Anna-Maeve and Mariana Holloway, thanks for making the abandonment of hope unthinkable.

To the many others who have helped and encouraged, but whom I do not mention here, please accept my thanks and remember that identification is domination.

Preface to the First Edition

This book was already in the publishing process before the attacks on the World Trade Center occurred, before the bombing of Afghanistan began.

The scream with which the book begins has become louder and more anguished since that date as we witness the arrogant stupidity of those who kill, those who bomb, those who would destroy the human race. The call to think about how we can change the world without entering into the pursuit of power is more urgent than ever.

Most terrible of all is the feeling of helplessness as we watch the televised bombs falling and the bodies being pulled from the rubble. How, in spite of everything, can we understand our own force, our own capacity to create a different world? That is the issue that this book seeks to address.

The deepening world recession is the other phenomenon which has changed since I submitted the manuscript to Pluto Press. I have done nothing to add new data to the discussion of crisis in Chapter 10, but the argument is given extra force by current developments. Again the central issue is: how do we overcome the feeling of help-lessness that seems now to pervade everything? How do we understand that, in relation to the crisis as in relation to the war, we are not victims but subjects, the only subjects?

Preface to the New Edition

I did not expect that so many people would want to talk about revolution. Yet the response to the book has shown that they do.

The response is not so much a reflection of the merits of the book (although I certainly would not deny those) as of the situation in which we live. It becomes clearer everyday that capitalism is a catastrophe for humanity, but we do not know how to get rid of it. There has been an upsurge of struggles of all sorts in recent years, often loosely connected to the social forum movement, but without any ideological or political centre. The most exciting thing about the response to this book has been to feel the book caught up in this cacophony of movements, carried on a wave of discussion that goes far beyond me and far beyond the words printed on these pages. It is like being hit by a big wave at the seaside and being turned over and over and feeling the exhilaration of being swept off one's feet. This is not alienation but the realisation that the discussion around the book is part of a much wider movement.

I am delighted that the book is being published now in this new expanded edition, which gives me the opportunity to step back from the waves and reflect upon the discussion generated by the book. I have added an epilogue which has the aim not of providing the answer to the question of the book but of taking that question forward.

1 The Scream

In the beginning is the scream. We scream.

When we write or when we read, it is easy to forget that the beginning is not the word, but the scream. Faced with the mutilation of human lives by capitalism, a scream of sadness, a scream of horror, a scream of anger, a scream of refusal: NO.

The starting point of theoretical reflection is opposition, negativity, struggle. It is from rage that thought is born, not from the pose of reason, not from the reasoned-sitting-back-and-reflecting-on-the-mysteries-of-existence that is the conventional image of 'the thinker'.

We start from negation, from dissonance. The dissonance can take many shapes. An inarticulate mumble of discontent, tears of frustration, a scream of rage, a confident roar. An unease, a confusion, a longing, a critical vibration.

Our dissonance comes from our experience, but that experience varies. Sometimes it is the direct experience of exploitation in the factory, or of oppression in the home, of stress in the office, of hunger and poverty, or of state violence or discrimination. Sometimes it is the less direct experience through television, newspapers or books that moves us to rage. Millions of children live on the streets of the world. In some cities, street children are systematically murdered as the only way of enforcing respect for private property. In 1998 the assets of the 358 richest people were worth more than the total annual income of 45 per cent of the world's people (over 2.5 billion). The gap between rich and poor is growing, not just between countries but within countries. The stock market rises every time there is an increase in unemployment. Students are imprisoned for struggling for free education while those who are actively responsible for the misery of millions are heaped with honours and given titles of distinction: General, Secretary of Defence, President. The list goes on and on. It is impossible to read a newspaper without feeling rage, without feeling pain. You can think of your own examples. Our anger changes each day, as outrage piles upon outrage.[1]

Dimly perhaps, we feel that these things that anger us are not isolated phenomena, that there is a connection between them, that they are all part of a world that is flawed, a world that is wrong in some fundamental way. We see more and more people begging on the street while the stock markets break new records and company directors' salaries rise to ever dizzier heights, and we feel that the wrongs of the world are not chance injustices but part of a system that is profoundly wrong. Even Hollywood films (surprisingly, perhaps) almost always start from the portrayal of a fundamentally unjust world – before going on to reassure us (less surprisingly) that justice for the individual can be won through individual effort. Our anger is directed not just against particular happenings but against a more general wrongness, a feeling that the world is askew, that the world is in some way untrue. When we experience something particularly horrific, we hold up our hands in horror and say 'that cannot be! it cannot be true!' We know that it is true, but feel that it is the truth of an untrue world.[2]

What would a true world look like? We may have a vague idea: it would be a world of justice, a world in which people could relate to each other as people and not as things, a world in which people would shape their own lives. But we do not need to have a picture of what a true world would be like in order to feel that there is something radically wrong with the world that exists. Feeling that the world is wrong does not necessarily mean that we have a picture of a utopia to put in its place. Nor does it necessarily mean a romantic, some-day-my-prince-will-come idea that, although things are wrong now, one day we shall come to a true world, a promised land, a happy ending. We need no promise of a happy ending to justify our rejection of a world we feel to be wrong.

That is our starting point: rejection of a world that we feel to be wrong, negation of a world we feel to be negative. This is what we must cling to.

II

'Cling to', indeed, for there is so much to stifle our negativity, to smother our scream. Our anger is constantly fired by experience, but any attempt to express that anger is met by a wall of absorbent cotton wool. We are met with so many arguments that seem quite reasonable. There are so many ways of bouncing our scream back against us, of looking at us and asking why we scream. Is it because of our age, our social background, or just some psychological maladjustment that we are so negative? Are we hungry, did we sleep badly or is it just pre-menstrual tension? Do we not understand the complexity of the world, the practical difficulties of implementing radical change? Do we not know that it is unscientific to scream?

And so they urge us (and we feel the need) to study society, and to study social and political theory. And a strange thing happens. The more we study society, the more our negativity is dissipated or sidelined as being irrelevant. There is no room for the scream in academic discourse. More than that: academic study provides us with a language and a way of thinking that makes it very difficult for us to express our scream. The scream, if it appears at all, appears as something to be explained, not as something to be articulated. The scream, from being the subject of our questions about society, becomes the object of analysis. Why is it that we scream? Or rather, since *we* are now social scientists, why is it that *they* scream? How do we explain social revolt, social discontent? The scream is systematically disqualified by dissolving it into its context. It is because of infantile experiences that they scream, because of their modernist conception of the subject, because of their unhealthy diet, because of the weakening of family structures: all of these explanations are backed up by statistically supported research. The scream is not entirely denied, but it is robbed of all validity. By being torn from 'us' and projected on to a 'they', the scream is excluded from the scientific method. When we become social scientists, we learn that the way to understand is to pursue objectivity, to put our own feelings on one side. It is not so much *what* we learn as *how* we learn that seems to smother our scream. It is a whole structure of thought that disarms us.

And yet none of the things which made us so angry to start off with have disappeared. We have learnt, perhaps, how they fit together as parts of a system of social domination, but somehow our negativity has been erased from the picture. The horrors of the world continue. That is why it is necessary to do what is considered scientifically taboo: to scream like a child, to lift the scream from all its structural explanations, to say 'We don't care what the psychiatrist says, we don't care if our subjectivity is a social construct: this is our scream, this is our pain, these are our tears. We will not let our rage be diluted into reality: it is reality rather that must yield to our scream. Call us childish or adolescent if you like, but this is our starting point: we scream.'[3]

III

Who are 'we' anyway, this 'we' that assert ourselves so forcefully at the start of what is meant to be a serious book?

Serious books on social theory usually start in the third person, not with the assertion of an undefined 'we'. 'We' is a dangerous word, open to attack from all sides. Some readers will already be saying 'You scream if you like, mate, but don't count me as part of your "we"! Don't say "we" when you really mean "I", because then you are just using "we" to impose your views on the readers.' Others will no doubt object that it is quite illegitimate to start from an innocent 'we' as though the world had just been born. The subject, we are told, is not a legitimate place to start, since the subject is itself a result, not a beginning. It is quite wrong to start from 'we scream' because first we must understand the processes that lead to the social construction of this 'we' and to the constitution of our scream.

And yet where else can we possibly start? In so far as writing/reading is a creative act, it is inevitably the act of a 'we'. To start in the third person is not a neutral starting point, since it already presupposes the suppression of the 'we', of the subject of the writing and reading. 'We' are here as the starting point because we cannot honestly start anywhere else. We cannot start anywhere other than with our own thoughts and our own reactions. The fact that 'we' and our conception of 'we' are the product of a whole history of the subjection of the subject[4] changes nothing. We can only start from where we are, from where we are but do not want to be, from where we scream.

For the moment, this 'we' of ours is a confused 'we'. We are an indistinct first-person plural, a blurred and possibly discordant mixture between the 'I' of the writer and the 'I' or 'we' of the readers. But we start from 'we', not from 'I', because 'I' already pre-supposes an individualisation, a claim to individuality in thoughts and feelings, whereas the act of writing or reading is based on the assumption of some sort of community, however contradictory or confused. The 'we' of our starting point is very much a question rather than an answer: it affirms the social character of the scream, but poses the nature of that sociality as a question. The merit of starting with a 'we' rather than with an 'it' is that we are then openly confronted with the question that must underlie any theoretical assertion, but which is rarely addressed: who are we that make the assertion?

Of course this 'we' is not a pure, transcendent Subject: we are not Man or Woman or the Working Class, not for the moment at least. We are much too confused for that. We are an antagonistic 'we' grown from an antagonistic society. What we feel is not necessarily correct, but it is a starting point to be respected and criticised, not just to be put aside in favour of objectivity. We are undoubtedly self-contradictory: not only in the sense that the reader may not feel the same as the writer (nor each reader the same as the others), but also in the sense that our feelings are contradictory. The dissonance we feel at work or when we read the newspapers may give way to a feeling of contentment as we relax after a meal. The dissonance is not an external 'us' against 'the world': inevitably it is a dissonance that reaches into us as well, that divides us against ourselves. 'We' are a question that will continue to rumble throughout this book.

We are flies caught in a spider's web. We start from a tangled mess, because there is no other place to start. We cannot start by pretending to stand outside the dissonance of our own experience, for to do so would be a lie. Flies caught in a web of social relations beyond our control, we can only try to free ourselves by hacking at the strands that imprison us. We can only try to emancipate ourselves, to move outwards, negatively, critically, from where we are. It is not because we are maladjusted that we criticise, it is not because we want to be difficult. It is just that the negative situation in which we exist leaves us no option: to live, to think, is to negate in whatever way we can the negativeness of our existence. 'Why so negative?' says the spider to the fly. 'Be objective, forget your prejudices.' But there is no way the fly can be objective, however much she may want to be: 'to look at the web objectively, from the outside – what a dream', muses the fly, 'what an empty, deceptive dream'. For the moment, however, any study of the web that does not start from the fly's entrapment in it is quite simply untrue.[5]

We are unbalanced, unstable. We scream not because we are sitting back in an armchair, but because we are falling over the edge of a cliff. The thinker in the armchair assumes that the world around her is stable, that disruptions of the equilibrium are anomalies to be explained. To speak of someone as unbalanced or unstable is then a pejorative term, a term that disqualifies what they say. For us who are falling off the edge of the cliff (and here 'we' includes all of humanity, perhaps) it is just the opposite: we see all as blurred movement. The world is a world of disequilibrium and it is equilibrium and the assumption of equilibrium that must be explained.

IV

Our scream is not just a scream of horror. We scream not because we face certain death in the spider's web, but because we dream of freeing ourselves. We scream as we fall over the cliff not because we are resigned to being dashed on the rocks below but because we still hope that it might be otherwise.

Our scream is a refusal to accept. A refusal to accept that the spider will eat us, a refusal to accept that we shall be killed on the rocks, a refusal to accept the unacceptable. A refusal to accept the inevitability of increasing inequality, misery, exploitation and violence. A refusal to accept the truth of the untrue, a refusal to accept closure. Our scream is a refusal to wallow in being victims of oppression, a refusal to immerse ourselves in that 'left-wing melancholy'[6] which is so characteristic of oppositional thought. It is a refusal to accept the role of Cassandra so readily adopted by left-wing intellectuals: predicting the downfall of the world while accepting that there is nothing we can do about it. Our scream is a scream to break windows, a refusal to be contained, an overflowing, a going beyond the pale, beyond the bounds of polite society.

Our refusal to accept tells us nothing of the future, nor does it depend for its validity on any particular outcome. The fact that we scream as we fall over the cliff does not give us any guarantee of a safe landing, nor does the legitimacy of the scream depend on a happy ending. Gone is the certainty of the old revolutionaries that history (or God) was on our side: such certainty is historically dead and buried, blasted into the grave by the bomb that fell on Hiroshima. There is certainly no inevitable happy ending, but, even as we plunge downwards, even in the moments of darkest despair, we refuse to accept that such a happy ending is impossible. The scream clings to the possibility of an opening, refuses to accept the closure of the possibility of radical otherness.

Our scream, then, is two-dimensional: the scream of rage that arises from present experience carries within itself a hope, a projection of possible otherness. The scream is ecstatic, in the literal sense of standing out ahead of itself towards an open future.[7] We who scream exist ecstatically. We stand out beyond ourselves, we exist in two dimensions. The scream implies a tension between that which exists and that which might conceivably exist, between the indicative (that which is) and the subjunctive (that which might be). We live in an unjust society but we wish it were not so: the two parts of the sentence are inseparable and exist in constant tension with each other. The scream does not require to be justified by the fulfilment of what might be: it is simply the recognition of the dual dimension of reality. The second part of the sentence (we wish it were not so) is no less real than the first. It is the tension between the two parts of the sentence that gives meaning to the scream. If the second part of the sentence (the subjunctive wish) is seen as being less real than the first, then the scream too is disqualified. What is then seen as real is that we live in an unjust society: what we might wish for is our private affair, of secondary importance. And since the adjective 'unjust' really makes sense only in reference to a possible just society, that too falls away, leaving us with 'we live in an x society'. And if we scream because we live in an x society, then we must be mad.

From the time of Machiavelli, social theory has been concerned to break the unbreakable sentence in half. Machiavelli lays the basis for a new realism when he says that he is concerned only with what is, not with things as we might wish them to be.[8] Reality refers to the first part of the sentence, to what is. The second part of the sentence, what ought to be, is clearly distinguished from what is, and is not regarded as part of reality. The 'ought' is not entirely discarded: it becomes the theme of 'normative' social theory. What is completely broken is the *unity* of the two parts of the sentence. With that step alone, the scream of rejection-and-longing is disqualified.

Our scream implies a two-dimensionality which insists on the conjunction of tension between the two dimensions. We are, but we exist in an arc of tension towards that which we are not, or are not yet. Society is, but it exists in an arc of tension towards that which is not, or is not yet. There is identity, but identity exists in an arc of tension towards non-identity. The double dimensionality is the antagonistic presence (that is, movement) of the not-yet within the Is, of non-identity within identity. The scream is an explosion of the tension: the explosion of the Not-Yet contained-in-but-bursting-from the Is, the explosion of non-identity contained-in-but-bursting-from identity. The scream is an expression of the present existence of that which is denied, the present existence of the not-yet, of non-identity. The theoretical force of the scream depends not on the future existence of the not-yet (who knows if there will ever be a society based on the mutual recognition of dignity?) but on its present existence as possibility. To start from the scream is simply to insist on the centrality of dialectics, which is no more than 'the consistent sense of non-identity' (Adorno 1990, p. 5).

Our scream is a scream of horror-and-hope. If the two sides of the scream are separated, they become banal. The horror arises from the 'bitterness of history',[9] but if there is no transcendence of that bitterness, the one-dimensional horror leads only to political depression and theoretical closure. Similarly, if the hope is not grounded firmly in that same bitterness of history, it becomes just a one-dimensional and silly expression of optimism. Precisely such a separation of horror and hope is expressed in the oft-quoted Gramscian aphorism, 'pessimism of the intelligence, optimism of the will'.[10] The challenge is rather to unite pessimism and optimism, horror and hope, in a theoretical understanding of the two-dimensionality of the world. Optimism not just of the spirit but of the intellect is the aim. It is the very horror of the world that obliges us to learn to hope.[11]

V

The aim of this book is to strengthen negativity, to take the side of the fly in the web, to make the scream more strident. We quite consciously start from the subject, or at least from an undefined subjectivity, aware of all the problems that this implies. We start there because to start anywhere else is simply an untruth. The challenge is to develop a way of thinking that builds critically upon the initial negative standpoint, a way of understanding that negates the untruth of the world. This is not just a question of seeing things from below, or from the bottom up, for that too often implies the adoption of pre-existing categories, a mere reversal of negative and positive signs. What must be tackled is not just a top-down perspective, but the whole mode of thinking that derives from and supports such a perspective. In trying to hack our way through the social theory which is part of the strands which bind us, there is only one compass to guide us: the force of our own 'no!' in all its two-dimensionality: the rejection of what is and the projection of what might be.

Negative thought is as old as the scream. The most powerful current of negative thought is undoubtedly the Marxist tradition. However, the development of the Marxist tradition, both because of its particular history and because of the transformation of negative thought into a defining 'ism', has created a framework that has often limited and obstructed the force of negativity. This book is therefore not a Marxist book in the sense of taking Marxism as a defining framework of reference, nor is the force of its argument to be judged by whether it is 'Marxist' or not: far less is it neo-Marxist or post-Marxist. The aim is rather to locate those issues that are often described as 'Marxist' in the problematic of negative thought, in the hope of giving body to negative thought and of sharpening the Marxist critique of capitalism.[12]

This is not a book that tries to depict the horrors of capitalism. There are many books that do that, and, besides, we have our daily experience to tell us the story. Here we take that for granted. The loss of hope for a more human society is not the result of people being blind to the horrors of capitalism, it is just that there does not seem to be anywhere else to go, any otherness to turn to. The most sensible thing seems to be to forget our negativity, to discard it as a fantasy of youth. And yet the world gets worse, the inequalities become more strident, the self-destruction of humanity seems to come closer. So perhaps we should not abandon our negativity but, on the contrary, try to theorise the world from the perspective of the scream.

And what if the reader feels no dissonance? What if you feel no negativity, if you are content to say 'we are, and the world is'? It is hard to believe that anyone is so at home with the world that they do not feel revulsion at the hunger, violence and inequality that surrounds them. It is much more likely that the revulsion or dissonance is consciously or unconsciously suppressed, either in the interests of a quiet life or, much more simply, because pretending not to see or feel the horrors of the world carries direct material benefits. In order to protect our jobs, our visas, our profits, our chances of receiving good grades, our sanity, we pretend not to see, we sanitise our own perception, filtering out the pain, pretending that it is not here but out there, far away, in Africa, in Russia, a hundred years ago, in an otherness that, by being alien, cleanses our own experience of all negativity. It is on such a sanitised perception that the idea of an objective, value-free social science is built. The negativity, the revulsion at exploitation and violence, is buried completely, drowned in the concrete of the foundation blocks of social science just as surely as, in some parts of the world, the bodies of sacrificed animals are buried by builders in the foundation blocks of houses or bridges. Such theory is, as Adorno puts it, 'in the nature of the musical accompaniment with which the SS liked to drown out the screams of its victims' (1990, p. 365). It is against such suppression of pain that this book is directed.

But what is the point? Our scream is a scream of frustration, the discontent of the powerless. But if we are powerless, there is nothing we can do. And if we manage to become powerful, by building a party or taking up arms or winning an election, then we shall be no different from all the other powerful in history. So there is no way out, no breaking the circularity of power. What can we do?

Change the world without taking power.

Ha! Ha! Very funny.

2   Beyond the State?

In the beginning was the scream. And then what?

The scream implies an anguished enthusiasm for changing the world. But how can we do it? What can we do to make the world a better, more human place? What can we do to put an end to all the misery and exploitation?

I

There is an answer ready at hand. *Do it through the state*. Join a political party, help it to win governmental power, change the country in that way. Or, if you are more impatient, more angry, more doubtful about what can be achieved through parliamentary means, join a revolutionary organisation, help it to conquer state power, by violent or non-violent means, and then use the revolutionary state to change society.

Change the world through the state: this is the paradigm that has dominated revolutionary thought for more than a century. The debate between Rosa Luxemburg and Eduard Bernstein[1] a hundred years ago on the issue of 'reform or revolution' established clearly the terms that were to dominate thinking about revolution for most of the twentieth century. On the one hand reform, on the other side revolution. Reform was a gradual transition to socialism, to be achieved by winning elections and introducing change by parliamentary means; revolution was a much more rapid transition, to be achieved by the taking of state power and the quick introduction of radical change by the new state. The intensity of the disagreements concealed a basic point of agreement: both approaches focus on the state as the vantage point from which society can be changed. Despite all their differences, both aim at the winning of state power. This is not exclusive, of course. In the revolutionary perspective and also in the more radical parliamentary approaches, the winning of state power is seen as part of an upsurge of social upheaval. Nevertheless the winning of state power is seen as the centrepiece of the revolutionary process, the hub from which revolutionary change will

11

radiate. Approaches that fall outside this dichotomy between reform and revolution were stigmatised as being anarchist (a sharp distinction that was consolidated at about the same time as the Bernstein–Luxemburg debate).[2] Until recently, theoretical and political debate, at least in the Marxist tradition, has been dominated by these three classifications: Revolutionary, Reformist, Anarchist.

The state paradigm, that is, the assumption that the winning of state power is central to radical change, dominated not just theory but also the revolutionary experience throughout most of the twentieth century – not only the experience of the Soviet Union and China, but also the numerous national liberation and guerrilla movements of the 1960s and the 1970s.

If the state paradigm was the vehicle of hope for much of the century, it became more and more the assassin of hope as the century progressed. The apparent impossibility of revolution at the beginning of the twenty-first century reflects in reality the historical failure of a particular concept of revolution, the concept that identified revolution with control of the state.

Both approaches, the 'reformist' and the 'revolutionary' have failed completely to live up to the expectations of their enthusiastic supporters. 'Communist' governments in the Soviet Union, China and elsewhere may have increased levels of material security and decreased social inequalities in the territories of the states which they controlled, at least temporarily, but they did little to create a self-determining society or to promote the reign of freedom which has always been central to the communist aspiration.[3] In the case of social democratic or reformist governments, the record is no better: although increases in material security have been achieved in some cases, their record in practice has differed very little from overtly pro-capitalist governments, and most social-democratic parties have long since abandoned any pretension to be the bearers of radical social reform.

For over a hundred years, the revolutionary enthusiasm of young people has been channelled into building the party or into learning to shoot guns; for over a hundred years, the dreams of those who have wanted a world fit for humanity have been bureaucratised and militarised, all for the winning of state power by a government that could then be accused of 'betraying' the movement that put it there. 'Betrayal' has been a key word for the left over the last century, as one government after another has been accused of 'betraying' the ideals of its supporters. The notion of betrayal itself has now become so tired that there is nothing left but a shrug of 'of course'.[4] Rather than look to so many betrayals for an explanation, perhaps we need to look at the very notion that society can be changed through the winning of state power.

II

At first sight it would appear obvious that winning control of the state is the key to bringing about social change. The state claims to be sovereign, to exercise power within its frontiers. This is central to the common notion of democracy: a government is elected in order to carry out the will of the people by exerting power in the territory of the state. This notion is the basis of the social-democratic claim that radical change can be achieved through constitutional means.

The argument against this is that the constitutional view isolates the state from its social environment: it attributes to the state an autonomy of action that it just does not have. In reality, what the state does is limited and shaped by the fact that it exists as just one node in a web of social relations. Crucially, this web of social relations centres on the way in which work is organised. The fact that work is organised on a capitalist basis means that what the state does and can do is limited and shaped by the need to maintain the system of capitalist organisation of which it is a part. Concretely, this means that any government that takes significant action directed against the interests of capital will find that an economic crisis will result and that capital will flee from the state territory.

Revolutionary movements inspired by Marxism have always been aware of the capitalist nature of the state. Why then have they focused on winning state power as the means of changing society? One answer is that these movements have often had an instrumental view of the capitalist nature of the state. They have typically seen the state as being the instrument of the capitalist class. The notion of an 'instrument' implies that the relation between the state and the capitalist class is an external one: like a hammer, the state is now wielded by the capitalist class in their own interests, while after the revolution it will be wielded by the working class in *their* interests. Such a view reproduces, unconsciously perhaps, the isolation or autonomisation of the state from its social environment, the critique of which is the starting point of revolutionary politics. To borrow a concept to be developed later, this view fetishises the state: it abstracts it from the web of power relations in which it is embedded. The difficulty which revolutionary governments have experienced in wielding the state in the interests of the working class suggests that the embedding of the state in the web of capitalist social relations is far stronger and more subtle than the notion of instrumentality would suggest. The mistake of Marxist revolutionary movements has been, not to deny the capitalist nature of the state, but to misunderstand the degree of integration of the state into the network of capitalist social relations.

An important aspect of this misunderstanding is the extent to which revolutionary (and, even more so, reformist) movements have tended to assume that 'society' can be understood as a national (that is, state-bound) society. If society is understood as being British, Russian or Mexican society, this obviously gives weight to the view that the state can be the centre point of social transformation. Such an assumption, however, presupposes a prior abstraction of state and society from their spatial surroundings, a conceptual snipping of social relations at the frontiers of the state. The world, in this view, is made up of so many national societies, each with its own state, each one maintaining relations with all the others in a network of inter-national relations. Each state is then the centre of its own world and it becomes possible to conceive of a national revolution and to see the state as the motor of radical change in 'its' society.

The problem with such a view is that social relations have never coincided with national frontiers. The current discussions of 'globalisation' merely highlight what has always been true: capitalist social relations, by their nature, have always gone beyond territorial limitations. Whereas the relation between feudal lord and serf was always a territorial relation, the distinctive feature of capitalism was that it freed exploitation from such territorial limitations, by virtue of the fact that the relation between capitalist and worker was now mediated through money. The mediation of social relations through money means a complete de-territorialisation of those relations: there is no reason why employer and employee, producer and consumer, or workers who combine in the same process of production, should be within the same territory. Capitalist social relations have never been limited by state frontiers, so that it has always been a mistake to think of the capitalist world as being the sum of different national societies (see von Braunmühl 1978 and Holloway 1995b). The web of social relations in which the particular national states are embedded is (and has been since the beginning of capitalism) a global web.

The focusing of revolution on the winning of state power thus involves the abstraction of the state from the social relations of which it is part. Conceptually, the state is cut out from the clutter of social relations that surround it and made to stand up with all the appearance of being an autonomous actor. Autonomy is attributed to the state, if not in the absolute sense of reformist (or liberal) theory, then at least in the sense that the state is seen as being *potentially* autonomous from the capitalist social relations that surround it.

But, it might be objected, this is a crude misrepresentation of revolutionary strategy. Revolutionary movements inspired by Marxism have generally seen the winning of state power as just one element in a broader process of social transformation. Moreover, Lenin spoke not just of conquering state power but of smashing the old state and replacing it with a workers' state, and both he and Trotsky were more than aware that the revolution had to be international to be successful. All this is true, and it is important to avoid crude caricatures, but the fact remains that the capturing of the state has generally been seen as a particularly important element, a focal point in the process of social change,[5] one which demands a focusing of the energies devoted to social transformation. The focusing inevitably privileges the state as a site of power.

Whether the winning of state power is seen as being the exclusive path for changing society or just as a focus for action, there is inevitably a channelling of revolt. The fervour of those who fight for a different society is taken up and pointed in a particular direction: towards the winning of state power. 'If we can only conquer the state (whether by electoral or by military means), then we shall be able to change society. First, therefore, we must concentrate on the central goal – conquering state power': so the argument goes, and the young are inducted into what it means to conquer state power: they are trained either as soldiers or as bureaucrats, depending on how the conquest of state power is understood. 'First build the army, first build the party, that is how to get rid of the power that oppresses us': the party-building (or army-building) comes to eclipse all else. What was initially negative (the rejection of capitalism) is converted into something positive (institution-building, power-building). The induction into the conquest of power inevitably becomes an induction into power itself. The initiates learn the language, logic and calculations of power; they learn to wield the categories of a social science which has been entirely shaped by its obsession with power. Differences within the organisation become struggles for power. Manipulation and manoeuvring for power become a way of life.

Nationalism is an inevitable complement of the logic of power. The idea that the state is the site of power involves the abstraction of the particular state from the global context of power relations. Inevitably, no matter how much the revolutionary inspiration is guided by the notion of world revolution, the focus on a particular state as the site for bringing about radical social change implies giving priority to the part of the world encompassed by that state over other parts of the world. Even the most internationalist of revolutions oriented towards state power have rarely succeeded in avoiding the nationalist privileging of 'their' state over others, or indeed the overt manipulation of national sentiment in order to defend the revolution. The notion of changing society through the state rests on the idea that the state is, or should be, sovereign. State sovereignty is a prerequisite for changing society through the state, so the struggle for social change becomes transformed into the struggle for the defence of state sovereignty. The struggle against capital then becomes an anti-imperialist struggle against domination by foreigners, in which nationalism and anti-capitalism are blended.[6] Self-determination and state sovereignty become confused, when in fact the very existence of the state as a form of social relations is the very antithesis of self-determination. (This is an argument that will be developed in a later chapter.)

No matter how much lip service is paid to the movement and its importance, the goal of the conquest of power inevitably involves an instrumentalisation of struggle. The struggle has an aim: to conquer political power. The struggle is a means to achieve that aim. Those elements of struggle which do not contribute to the achievement of that aim are either given a secondary importance or must be suppressed altogether: a hierarchy of struggles is established. The instrumentalisation/hierarchisation is at the same time an impoverishment of struggle. So many struggles, so many ways of expressing our rejection of capitalism, so many ways of fighting for our dream of a different society are simply filtered out, simply remain unseen when the world is seen through the prism of the conquest of power. We learn to suppress them, and thus to suppress ourselves. At the top of the hierarchy we learn to place that part of our activity that contributes to 'building the revolution', at the bottom come frivolous personal things like affective relations, sensuality, playing, laughing, loving. Class struggle becomes puritanical: frivolity must be suppressed because it does not contribute to the goal. The hierarchisation of struggle is a hierarchisation of our lives and thus a hierarchisation of ourselves.

The party is the organisational form which most clearly expresses this hierarchisation. The form of the party, whether vanguardist or parliamentary, presupposes an orientation towards the state and makes little sense without it. The party is in fact a form of disciplining class struggle, of subordinating the myriad forms of class struggle to the overriding aim of gaining control of the state. The fixing of a hierarchy of struggles is usually expressed in the form of the party programme.

This instrumentalist impoverishment of struggle is not characteristic just of particular parties or currents (Stalinism, Trotskyism, and so on): it is inherent in the idea that the goal of the movement is to conquer political power. The struggle is lost from the beginning, long before the victorious party or army conquers state power and 'betrays' its promises. It is lost once power itself seeps into the struggle, once the logic of power becomes the logic of the revolutionary process, once the negative of refusal is converted into the positive of power-building. And usually those involved do not see it: the initiates in power do not even see how far they have been drawn into the reasoning and habits of power. They do not see that if we revolt against capitalism, it is not because we want a different system of power, it is because we want a society in which power relations are dissolved. You cannot build a society of non-power relations by conquering power. Once the logic of power is adopted, the struggle against power is already lost.

The idea of changing society through the conquest of power thus ends up achieving the opposite of what it sets out to achieve. Instead of the conquest of power being a step towards the abolition of power relations, the attempt to conquer power involves the extension of the field of power relations into the struggle against power. What starts as a scream of protest against power, against the dehumanisation of people, against the treatment of humans as means rather than ends, becomes converted into its opposite, into the assumption of the logic, habits and discourse of power into the very heart of the struggle against power.[7] For what is at issue in the revolutionary transformation of the world is not *whose* power but the very existence of power. What is at issue is not *who* exercises power, but how to create a world based on the mutual recognition of human dignity, on the formation of social relations which are not power relations.

It would seem that the most realistic way to change society is to focus struggle on the winning of state power and to subordinate struggle to this end. First we win power and *then* we shall create a society worthy of humanity. This is the powerfully realistic argument of Lenin, especially in *What is to be Done?*, but it is a logic shared by all the major revolutionary leaders of the twentieth century: Rosa Luxemburg, Trotsky, Gramsci, Mao, Che. Yet the experience of their struggles suggests[8] that the accepted realism of the revolutionary tradition is profoundly unrealistic. That realism is the realism of power and can do no more than reproduce power. The realism of power is focused and directed towards an end. The realism of anti-power, or, better, the anti-realism of anti-power, must be quite different if we are to change the world. And change the world we must.

3   Beyond Power?

I

The world cannot be changed through the state. Both theoretical reflection and a whole century of bad experience tell us so. 'We told you so', say the satisfied ones, 'We said so all along. We said it was absurd. We told you that you couldn't go against human nature. Give up the dream, give up!'

And millions throughout the world have given up the dream of a radically different type of society. There is no doubt that the fall of the Soviet Union and the failure of national liberation movements throughout the world have brought disillusionment to millions of people. The notion of revolution was so strongly identified with gaining control of the state that the failure of those attempts to change the world through gaining control of the state has led very many people to the conclusion that revolution is impossible.

There is a toning down of expectations. For many, hope has evaporated from their lives, giving way to a bitter, cynical reconciliation with reality. It will not be possible to create the free and just society we hoped for, but we can always vote for a centre or left-of-centre party, knowing quite well that it will not make any difference, but at least that way we will have some sort of outlet for our frustration. 'We know now that we will not be able to change the world', says one of the characters in a novel by Marcela Serrano. 'That has been the greatest blow of all for our generation. We lost our objective in the middle of the way, when we still had the age and the energy to make the changes ... The only thing that is left is to ask with humility: where is dignity?'[1]

Is the character in the book not right? If we cannot change the world through the state, then how? The state is just a node in a web of power relations. But will we not be always caught up in the web of power, no matter where we start? Is rupture really conceivable? Are we not trapped in an endless circularity of power? Is the whole world not a spider-web, which can be made a little better here and there? Or perhaps: is the whole world not a multiplicity of spider-webs, so that just when we have broken through one, we find ourselves entangled in another? Is the idea of a radical otherness not

19

best left to those who comfort themselves with religion, to those who live with a dream of heaven as the reward for living through this vale of tears?

The great problem with trying to retreat into a life of private dignity and saying 'let's make the best of what we've got' is that the world does not stand still. The existence of capitalism implies a dynamic of development which attacks us constantly, subjecting our lives more directly to money, creating more and more poverty, more and more inequality, more and more violence. Dignity is not a private matter, for our lives are so entwined with those of others that private dignity is impossible. It is precisely the pursuit of personal dignity that, far from taking us in the opposite direction, confronts us fully with the urgency of revolution.[2]

The only way in which the idea of revolution can be maintained is by raising the stakes. The problem of the traditional concept of revolution is perhaps not that it aimed too high, but that it aimed too low. The notion of capturing positions of power, whether it be governmental power or more dispersed positions of power in society, misses the point that the aim of the revolution is to dissolve relations of power, to create a society based on the mutual recognition of people's dignity. What has failed is the notion that revolution means capturing power in order to abolish power.[3] What is now on the agenda is the much more demanding notion of a direct overcoming of power relations. The only way in which revolution can now be imagined is not as the conquest of power but as the dissolution of power. The fall of the Soviet Union not only meant disillusionment for millions; it also brought the liberation of revolutionary thought, the liberation from the identification of revolution with the conquest of power.

This, then, is the revolutionary challenge at the beginning of the twenty-first century: to change the world without taking power. This is the challenge that has been formulated most clearly by the Zapatista uprising in the south-east of Mexico. The Zapatistas have said that they want to make the world anew, to create a world of dignity, a world of humanity, but without taking power.[4]

The Zapatista call to make the world anew without taking power has found a remarkable resonance. This resonance has to do with the growth in recent years of what might be called an area of anti-power. This corresponds to a weakening of the process by which discontent is focused on the state. This weakening is clear in the case of the would-be revolutionary parties, which no longer have the capacity they once had to channel discontent towards the struggle to seize state power. It is also true of social-democratic parties: whether or not people vote for them, they no longer have the same importance as focuses of political militancy. Social discontent today tends to be expressed far more diffusely, through participation in 'non-governmental organisations', through campaigning around particular issues, through the individual or collective concerns of teachers, doctors or other workers who seek to do things in a way that does not objectify people, in the development of autonomous community projects of all sorts, even in prolonged and massive rebellions such as the one taking place in Chiapas. There is a vast area of activity directed towards changing the world in a way that does not have the state as its focus, and that does not aim at gaining positions of power. This area of activity is obviously highly contra-dictory, and certainly includes many activities that might be described as 'petty bourgeois' or 'romantic' by revolutionary groups. It is rarely revolutionary in the sense of having revolution as an explicit aim, yet the projection of a radical otherness is often an important component of the activity involved. It includes what is sometimes called the area of 'autonomy', but it is far, far wider than that which is usually indicated by the term. It is sometimes, but not always, in open hostility to capitalism, but it does not find and does not seek the sort of clear focus for such activity that was formerly provided by both revolutionary and reformist parties. This is the confused area in which the Zapatista call resonates, the area in which anti-power grows.[5] It is an area in which the old distinctions between reform, revolution and anarchism no longer seem relevant, simply because the question of who controls the state is not the focus of attention. There is a loss of revolutionary focus, not because people do not long for a different type of society, but because the old focus proved to be a mirage. The challenge posed by the Zapatistas is the challenge of salvaging revolution from the collapse of the state illusion and from the collapse of the power illusion.

But how can we change the world without taking power? Merely to pose the question is to invite a snort of ridicule, a raised eyebrow, a shrug of condescension.

'How can you be so naïve?' say some, 'Do you not know that there can be no radical change in society? Have you learnt nothing in the last thirty years? Do you not know that talk of revolution is silly, or are you still trapped in your adolescent dreams of 1968? We must live with the world we have and make the best of it.'

'How can you be so naïve?' say others, 'Of course the world needs a revolution, but do you seriously think that change can be brought about without taking power, by election or otherwise? Do you not see the forces we are up against, the armies, the police, the paramilitary thugs? Do you not know that the only language they understand is power? Do you think capitalism will collapse if we all hold hands and sing "All we need is love"? Get real.'

Reality and power are so mutually encrusted that even to raise the question of dissolving power is to step off the edge of reality. All our categories of thought, all our assumptions about what is reality, or what is politics or economics or even where we live, are so permeated by power that just to say 'no!' to power precipitates us into a vertiginous world in which there are no fixed reference points to hold on to other than the force of our own 'no!'. Power and social theory exist in such symbiosis that power is the lens through which theory sees the world, the headphone through which it hears the world: to ask for a theory of anti-power is to try to see the invisible, to hear the inaudible. To try to theorise anti-power is to wander in a largely unexplored world.

How can the world be changed without taking power? The answer is obvious: we do not know. That is why it is so important to work at the answer, practically and theoretically. *Hic Rhodus, hic saltus*, but the *saltus* becomes more and more perilous, the pressures not to jump become ever greater, the danger of falling into a sea of absurdity ever more difficult to avoid.

Let us forget our 'fear of ridicule'[6] and ask then: how can we even begin to think of changing the world without taking power?

II

To think of changing the world without taking power, we need to see that the concept of power is intensely contradictory. But to make this argument we need to go back to the beginning.

In the beginning, we said, is the scream. It is a two-dimensional scream: a scream not just of rage, but of hope. And the hope is not a hope for salvation in the form of divine intervention. It is an active hope, a hope that we can change things, a scream of active refusal, a scream that points to doing. The scream that does not point to doing, the scream that turns in upon itself, that remains an eternal scream of despair or, much more common, an endless cynical grumble, is a scream which betrays itself: it loses its negative force and goes into an endless loop of self-affirmation as scream. Cynicism – I hate the world, but there is nothing that can be done – is the scream gone sour, the scream that suppresses its own self-negation.

The scream implies doing. 'In the beginning was the deed', says Goethe's Faust.[7] But before the deed comes the doing. In the beginning was the doing. But in an oppressive society, doing is not an innocent, positive doing: it is impregnated with negativity, both because it is negated, frustrated doing, and because it negates the negation of itself. Before the doing comes the scream. It is not materialism that comes first, but negativity.[8]

Doing is practical negation. Doing changes, negates an existing state of affairs. Doing goes beyond, transcends. The scream, which is our starting point in a world which negates us – the only world we know – pushes us towards doing. Our materialism, if that word is relevant at all, is a materialism rooted in doing, doing-to-negate, negative practice, projection beyond. Our foundation, if that word is relevant at all, is not an abstract preference for matter over mind, but the scream, the negation of what exists.

Doing, in other words, is central to our concern not simply because doing is a material precondition for living[9] but because our central concern is changing the world, negating that which exists. To think the world from the perspective of the scream is to think it from the perspective of doing.

Saint John is doubly wrong, then, when he says that 'in the beginning was the Word'. Doubly wrong because, to put it in traditional terms, his statement is both positive and idealist. The word does not negate, as the scream does. And the word does not imply doing, as the scream does. The world of the word is a stable world, a sitting-back-in-an-armchair-and-having-a-chat world, a sitting-at-a-desk-and-writing world, a contented world, far from the scream which would change everything, far from the doing which negates.[10] In the world of the word, doing is separated from talking and doing, practice is separated from theory. Theory in the world of the word is the thought of the Thinker, of someone in restful reflection, chin in hand, elbow on knee. 'The philosophers', as Marx says in his famous eleventh thesis on Feuerbach, 'have only *interpreted* the world in various ways; the point, however, is to change it.'

Marx's thesis does not mean that we should abandon theory for practice. It means rather that we should understand theory as part of practice, as part of the struggle to change the world. Both theory and doing are part of the practical movement of negation. This implies, then, that doing must be understood in a broad sense, certainly not just as work, and also not just as physical action, but as the whole movement of practical negativity. To emphasise the centrality of doing is not to deny the importance of thought or language but simply to see them as part of the total movement of practical negativity, of the practical projection beyond the world that exists towards a radically different world. To focus on doing is quite simply to see the world as struggle.

It might be argued, with some force, that changing society should be thought of not in terms of doing but in terms of not-doing, laziness, refusal to work, enjoyment. 'Let us be lazy in everything, except in loving and drinking, except in being lazy': Lafargue begins his classic *The Right to be Lazy* with this quotation (1999, p. 3), implying that there is nothing more incompatible with capitalist exploitation than the laziness advocated by Lessing. Laziness in capitalist society, however, implies refusal to do, an active assertion of an alternative practice. Doing, in the sense in which we understand it here, includes laziness and the pursuit of pleasure, both of which are very much negative practices in a society based on their negation. Refusal to do, in a world based on the conversion of doing into work, can be seen as an effective form of resistance.

Human doing implies projection-beyond, and hence the unity of theory and practice. Projection-beyond is seen by Marx as a distinctive characteristic of human doing:

> A spider conducts operations that resemble those of a weaver, and a bee puts to shame many an architect in the construction of her cells. But what distinguishes the worst architecture from the best of bees is this, that the architect raises his structure in imagination before he erects it in reality. At the end of every labour-process, we get a result that already existed in the imagination of the labourer at its commencement. [Marx 1965, p. 178]

The imagination of the labourer is ecstatic: at the commencement of the labour process it projects beyond what is to an otherness that might be. This otherness exists not only when it is created: it exists already, really, subjunctively, in the projection of the worker, in that which makes her human. The doing of the architect is negative, not only in its result, but in its whole process: it begins and ends with the negation of what exists. Even if she is the worst of architects, the doing is a creative doing.

Bees, to the best of our knowledge, do not scream. They do not say 'No! Enough of queens, enough of drones, we shall create a society which will be shaped by us workers, we shall emancipate ourselves!' Their doing is not a doing that negates: it simply reproduces. We, however, do scream. Our scream is a projection-beyond, the articulation of an otherness that might be. If our scream is to be more than a smug look-how-rebellious-I-am scream (which is no scream at all), then it must involve a projected doing, the project of doing something to change that which we scream against.[11] The scream and the doing-which-is-a-going-beyond distinguish humans from animals. Humans, but not animals, are ecstatic: they exist not only in, but also against-and-beyond themselves.

Why? Not because going-beyond is part of our human nature, but simply because we scream. Negation comes not from our human essence, but from the situation in which we find ourselves. We scream and push-beyond not because that is human nature, but, on the contrary, because we are torn from what we consider to be humanity. Our negativity arises not from our humanity, but from the negation of our humanity, from the feeling that humanity is not-yet, that it is something to be fought for. It is not human nature, but the scream of our starting point that compels us to focus on doing.[12]

To take doing, rather than being or talking or thinking, as the focus of our thought, has many implications. Doing implies movement. To start from doing-as-going-beyond (and not just the busy-bee doing-as-reproduction) means that everything (or at least everything human) is in movement, everything is becoming, that there is no 'being', or rather that being can only be a frustrated becoming. The perspective of the scream-doing is inevitably historical, because the human experience can only be understood as a constant moving-beyond (or possibly a frustrated moving-beyond). This is important, because if the starting point is not screaming-doing (doing-as-negation) but rather the word or discourse or a positive understanding of doing (as reproduction), then there is no possibility of understanding society historically: the movement of history becomes broken down into a series of snapshots, a diachronic series, a chronology. Becoming is broken down into a series of states of being.[13]

To put the point in other words, humans are subjects while animals are not. Subjectivity refers to the conscious projection beyond that which exists, the ability to negate that which exists and to create something that does not yet exist. Subjectivity, the movement of the scream-doing, involves a movement against limits, against containment, against closure. The doer is not. Not only that, but doing is the movement against is-ness, against that-which-is. Any definition of the subject is therefore contradictory or indeed violent: the attempt to pin down that which is a movement against being pinned down. The idea that we can start from the assertion that people are subjects has been much criticised in recent years, especially by theorists associated with postmodernism. The idea of the person as subject, we are told, is a historical construct. That may be so, but our starting point, the scream of complete refusal to accept the misery of capitalist society, takes us inevitably to the notion of subjectivity. To deny human subjectivity is to deny the scream or, which comes to the same thing, to turn the scream into a scream of despair. 'Ha! Ha!' they mock, 'you scream as though it were possible to change society radically. But there is no possibility of radical change, there is no way out.' Our starting point makes such an approach impossible. The sharpness of our No! is a sword that cuts through many a theoretical knot.

Doing is inherently social. What I do is always part of a social flow of doing, in which the precondition of my doing is the doing (or having-done) of others, in which the doing of others provides the means of my doing. Doing is inherently plural, collective, choral, communal. This does not mean that all doing is (or indeed should be) undertaken collectively. It means rather that it is difficult to conceive of a doing that does not have the doing of others as a pre-condition. I sit at the computer and write this, apparently a lonely individual act, but my writing is part of a social process, a plaiting of my writing with the writing of others (those mentioned in the footnotes and a million others), and also with the doing of those who designed the computer, assembled it, packed it, transported it, those who installed the electricity in the house, those who generated the electricity, those who produced the food that gives me the energy to write, and so on, and so on. There is a community of doing, a collective of doers, a flow of doing through time and space. Past doing (of ourselves and others) becomes the means of doing in the present. Any act, however individual it seems, is part of a chorus of doing in which all humanity is the choir (albeit an anarchic and discordant choir). Our doings are so intertwined that it is impossible to say where one ends and another begins. Clearly there are many doings that do not in turn create the conditions for the doing of others, that do not feed back into the social flow of doing as a whole: it is quite possible, for example, that no one will ever read what I am now doing. However, the doings that do not lead back into the social flow of doing do not for that reason cease to be social. My activity is social whether or not anybody reads this: it is important not to confuse sociality and functionality.

To speak of the social flow of doing is not to deny the materiality of the done. When I make a chair, the chair exists materially. When I write a book, the book exists as an object. It has an existence independent of mine, and may still exist when I no longer exist. In that sense it might be said that there is an objectification of my subjective doing, that the done acquires an existence separate from the doing, that the done abstracts itself from the flow of doing. This is true, however, only if my doing is seen as an individual act. Seen from the social flow of doing, the objectification of my subjective doing is at most a fleeting objectification. The existence of the chair as chair depends upon someone sitting upon it, reincorporating it into the flow of doing. The existence of the book as book depends upon your reading it, the braiding of your doing (reading) with my doing (writing) to reintegrate the done (the book) into the social flow of doing.[14]

It is when we understand 'we scream' as a material 'we scream', as a screaming-doing, that 'we-ness' (that question that rumbles through our book) gains force. Doing, in other words, is the material constitution of the 'we', the conscious and unconscious, planned and unplanned, braiding of our lives through time. This braiding of our lives, this collective doing, involves, if the collective flow of doing is recognised, a mutual recognition of one another as doers, as active subjects. Our individual doing receives its social validation from its recognition as part of the social flow.

III

To begin to think about power and changing the world without taking power (or indeed anything else), we need to start from doing.

Doing implies being able-to-do. The scream is of no significance without doing, and doing is inconceivable unless we are able-to-do. If we are deprived of our capacity-to-do, or rather, if we are deprived of our capacity to project-beyond-and-do, of our capacity to do negatively, ecstatically, then we are deprived of our humanity, our doing is reduced (and we are reduced) to the level of a bee. If we are deprived of our capacity-to-do, then our scream becomes a scream of despair.

Power, in the first place, is simply that: can-ness,[15] capacity-to-do, the ability to do things. Doing implies power, power-to-do. In this sense we commonly use 'power' to refer to something good: I feel powerful, I feel good. The little train in the children's story (Piper 1978) that says 'I think I can, I think I can' as it tries to reach the top of the mountain, has a growing sense of its own power. We go to a good political meeting and come away with an enhanced sense of our own power. We read a good book and feel empowered. The women's movement has given women a greater sense of their own power. Power in this sense can be referred to as 'power-to', power-to-do.

Power-to, it must be emphasised again, is always a social power, even though it may not appear to be so. The story of the little train presents power-to as a matter of individual determination, but in fact that is never the case. Our doing is *always* part of a social flow of doing, even where it appears to be an individual act. Our capacity to do is always an interlacing of our activity with the previous or present activity of others. Our capacity to do is always the result of the doing of others.

Power-to, therefore, is never individual: it is always social. It cannot be thought of as existing in some pure, unsullied state, for its existence will always be part of the way in which sociality is constituted, the way in which doing is organised. Doing (and power-to-do) is always part of a social flow, but that flow is constituted in different ways.

It is when the social flow of doing is fractured that power-to is transformed into its opposite, power-over.

The social flow is fractured when doing itself is broken.[16] Doing-as-projection-beyond is broken when some people arrogate to themselves the projection-beyond (conception) of the doing and command others to execute what they have conceived.[17] Doing is broken as the 'powerful' conceive but do not execute, while the others execute but do not conceive. Doing is broken as the 'powerful' separate the done from the doers and appropriate it to themselves. The social flow is broken as the 'powerful' present themselves as the individual doers, while the rest simply disappear from sight. If we think of 'powerful' men in history, for example, of Julius Caesar, Napoleon, Hitler, then power appears as the attribute of an individual. But of course their power to do things was not an ability to do them on their own, but an ability to command others to do what they wished them to do. The 'we' of doing appears as an 'I', or as a 'he' (more often a 'he' than a 'she'): Caesar did this, Caesar did that. The 'we' is now an antagonistic 'we', divided between the rulers (the visible subjects) and the ruled (the invisible de-subjectified subjects). Power-to now becomes 'power-over', a relation of power over others. These others are powerless (or apparently powerless), deprived of the capacity to realise our own projects, if only because we spend our days realising the projects of those who exercise power-over.

For most of us, then, power is turned into its opposite. Power means not our capacity-to-do, but our incapacity-to-do. It means not the assertion of our subjectivity but the destruction of our subjectivity. The existence of power relations means not the capacity to obtain some future good but just the contrary: the incapacity to obtain the future good,[18] the incapacity to realise our own projects, our own dreams. It is not that we cease to project, that we cease to dream, but unless the projects and dreams are cut to match the 'reality' of power relations (and this is usually achieved, if at all, through bitter experience), then they are met with frustration. Power, for those without the means of commanding others, is frustration. The existence of power-to as power-over means that the vast majority of doers are converted into the done-to, their activity transformed into passivity, their subjectivity into objectivity.[19]

Whereas power-to is a uniting, a bringing together of my doing with the doing of others, the exercise of power-over is a separation. The exercise of power-over separates conception from realisation, done from doing, one person's doing from another's, subject from object. Those who exercise power-over are Separators,[20] separating done from doing, doers from the means of doing.

Power-over is the breaking of the social flow of doing. Those who exert power over the doing of others deny the subjectivity of those others, deny their part in the flow of doing, exclude them from history. Power-over breaks mutual recognition: those over whom power is exercised are not recognised (and those who exercise power are not recognised by anyone whom they recognise as worthy of giving recognition[21]). The doing of the doers is deprived of social validation: we and our doing become invisible. History becomes the history of the powerful, of those who tell others what to do. The flow of doing becomes an antagonistic process in which the doing of most is denied, in which the doing of most is appropriated by the few. The flow of doing becomes a broken process.

The breaking of doing always involves physical force or the threat of physical force. There is always the threat: 'Work for us or you will die or suffer physical punishment.' If domination is robbery of the done from the doer, that robbery is, necessarily, armed robbery. But what makes the use or threat of physical force possible is its stabil-isation or institutionalisation in various ways, an understanding of which is crucial to understanding the dynamic and weakness of power-over.

In pre-capitalist societies, power-over is stabilised on the basis of a personal relation between ruler and ruled. In a slave society, the exercise of power-over is institutionalised around the idea that some people (whose quality as persons is denied) are the property of others. In feudal societies, it is the notion of divinely-ordained hier-archies of person-hood that gives form to the commanding of some by others. The personal nature of the relation of power-over means that the use or threat of force is always directly present in the relation of domination itself. The refusal to work is always an act of personal rebellion against one's owner or lord and punishable by that owner or lord.

In capitalist society (which is what interests us most, since that is where we live and what we scream against), the stabilisation into a 'right' of the bossing of some people by others is based not on the direct relation between ruler and doer but on the relation between the ruler and the done. The doers have now won freedom from personal dependence on the rulers, but they are still held in a position of subordination by the fracturing of the collective flow of doing. Capital is based on the freezing of the past doing of people into property. Since past doing is the precondition of present doing, the freezing and appropriation of past doing separates the precondition of present doing from that past doing, constitutes it as an identifi-able 'means of doing' (more familiarly, 'means of production'). Thus, the freed serfs and slaves are freed into a world where the only way in which they can have access to the means of doing (and therefore of living) is to sell their capacity-to-do (their power-to-do, now trans-formed into power-to-labour or labour-power) to those who 'own' the means of doing. Their freedom in no sense frees them from sub-ordination of their doing to the dictates of others.

Capital is that: the assertion of command over others on the basis of 'ownership' of the done and hence of the means of doing, the precondition for the doing of those others who are commanded. All class societies involve the separation of done (or a part of the done) from doing and doers, but in capitalism that separation becomes the sole axis of domination. There is a peculiar rigidification of the done, a peculiarly radical separation of done from doing. If, from the perspective of the social flow of doing, the objectification of the done is a fleeting objectification, immediately overcome through the incorporation of the done into the flow of doing, then capitalism depends on making that objectification a durable objectification, on converting the done into an object, a thing apart, something that can be defined as property. Capitalism thus implies a new definition of 'subject' and 'object', in which the 'object' is durably and rigidly separated from the subject's doing.[22]

This does not mean that subject and object are constituted by capitalism. Subjectivity is inherent in negativity (the scream), and negativity is inherent in any society (certainly any in which doing is subordinated to others). However, the separation between subject and object, doer and done or done-to, acquires a new meaning under capitalism, leading to a new definition and a new consciousness of subjectivity and objectivity, a new distance and antagonism between subject and object. Thus, rather than the subject being the product of modernity, it is rather that modernity expresses consciousness of the new separation of subject and object which is inherent in the focusing of social domination upon the done.[23]

Another way of formulating the same point is to say that there is a separation of the constitution of the object from its existence. The done now exists in durable autonomy from the doing which constituted it. Whereas from the perspective of the social flow of doing, the existence of an object is merely a fleeting moment in the flow of subjective constitution (or doing), capitalism depends on the conversion of that fleeting moment into a durable objectification. But of course durable autonomy is an illusion, a very real illusion. The separation of done from doing is a real illusion, a real process in which the done nevertheless never ceases to depend on the doing. Likewise, the separation of existence from constitution is a real illusion, a real process in which existence never ceases to depend on constitution. The definition of the done as private property is the negation of the sociality of doing, but this too is a real illusion, a real process in which private property never ceases to depend on the sociality of doing. The rupture of doing does not mean that doing ceases to be social, simply that it becomes *indirectly* social.

Capital is based not on the ownership of people but on the ownership of the done and, on that basis, of the repeated buying of people's power-to-do. Since people are not owned, they can quite easily refuse to work for others without suffering any immediate punishment. The punishment comes rather in being cut off from the means of doing (and of survival). The use of force comes then not as part of the direct relation between capitalist and worker. Force is focused in the first place not on the doer but on the done: its focus is the protection of property, the protection of ownership of the done. It is exercised not by the individual owner of the done, for that would be incompatible with the free nature of the relation between capitalist and worker, but by a separate instance responsible for protecting the property of the done, the state. The separation of the economic and the political (and the constitution of the 'economic' and the 'political' by this separation) is therefore central to the exercise of domination under capitalism. If domination is always a process of armed robbery, the peculiarity of capitalism is that the person with the arms stands apart from the person doing the robbery, merely supervising that the robbery conforms with the law. Without this separation, property (as opposed to mere temporary possession) of the done, and therefore capitalism itself, would be impossible. This is important for the discussion of power, because the separation of the economic and the political makes it appear that it is the political which is the realm of the exercise of power (leaving the economic as a 'natural' sphere beyond question), whereas in fact the exercise of power (the conversion of power-to into power-over) is already inherent in the separation of the done from the doing, and hence in the very constitution of the political and the economic as distinct forms of social relations (see Pashukanis 1978; Holloway and Picciotto 1977, 1978b).

The conversion of power-to into power-over always involves the fracturing of the flow of doing, but in capitalism, to a far greater extent than in any previous society, the fracturing of the social flow of doing is the principle on which society is constructed. The fact that the property of the done is the axis on which the right to command the doing of others is based puts the breaking of the flow of doing at the centre of every aspect of social relations.

The breaking of the social flow of doing is the breaking of everything.[24] Most obviously, the rupture of doing breaks the collective 'we'. The collectivity is divided into two classes of people: those who, by virtue of their ownership of the means of doing, command others to do, and those who, by virtue of the fact that they are deprived of access to the means of doing, do what the others tell them to do. That projection which distinguishes people from bees is now monopolised by the former class, the owners of the means of doing. For those who are told what to do, the unity of projection-and-doing which distinguishes the worst architect from the best bee is broken. Their humanity, in other words, is broken, denied. Subjectivity (projection-and-doing) is appropriated by the capitalists (or rather, not so much by the capitalists as by the perverse relation of capital). The doers, deprived of the unity of projection-and-doing, lose their subjectivity, become reduced to the level of bees. They become objectivised subjects. They lose too their collectivity, their 'we-ness': we are fragmented into a multitude of 'I's, or, even worse, into a multitude of 'I's, 'you's, 'he's, 'she's and 'they's. Once the social flow of doing is broken, the we-ness which it braids is broken too.

The break between projection and doing is also a break between the doers and the doing. The doing is ordained by the non-doers (the commanders of doing), so that the doing becomes an alien act (an externally imposed act) for those who do. Their doing is transformed from an active doing to a passive, suffered, alien doing. Doing becomes labour.[25] Doing which is not directly commanded by others is separated from labour and seen as less important: 'What do you do?' 'Oh, I don't do anything, I'm just a housewife.'

The separation between doer and doing, doing and done, is a growing separation. The capitalists' control of the done (and hence of the means of doing) grows and grows, accumulates and accumulates. The fact that capitalist rule is focused on the done rather than on the doers means that it is boundlessly voracious in a way in which doer-centred domination (slavery, feudalism) is not: 'Accumulate! Accumulate! That is Moses and the prophets!' (Marx 1965, p. 595). The endless drive to increase the quantitative accumulation of the done (dead labour, capital) imposes an ever faster rhythm of doing and an ever more desperate appropriation of the product of doing by the owner of the done. The done comes to dominate the doing and the doer more and more.

The crystallisation of that-which-has-been-done into a 'thing' shatters the flow of doing into a million fragments. Thing-ness denies the primacy of doing (and hence of humanity). When we use a computer, we think of it as a thing, not of the union of our writing with the flow of doing which created the computer. Thing-ness is crystallised amnesia.[26] The doing that created the thing (not just that specific doing, but the whole flow of doing of which it is a part) is forgotten. The thing now stands there on its own as a commodity to be sold, with its own value. The value of the commodity is the declaration of the commodity's autonomy from doing. The doing which created the commodity is forgotten, the collective flow of doing of which it is part is forced underground, turned into a subterranean stream. Value acquires a life of its own. The breaking of the flow of doing is carried to its ultimate consequences. Doing is pushed below the surface, and with it the doers, but it is more than that: those who exercise power-over are also pushed aside by the fragmentation on which their power-over is based. The subject in capitalist society is not the capitalist. It is not the capitalists who take the decisions, who shape what is done. It is value. It is capital, accumulated value. That which the capitalists 'own' – capital – has pushed the capitalists aside. They are capitalists only to the extent that they are loyal servants of capital. The very significance of ownership falls into the background. Capital acquires a dynamic of its own and the leading members of society are quite simply its most loyal servants, its most servile courtiers. This is true not only of capitalists themselves, but also of politicians, civil servants, professors, and so on. The rupture of the flow of doing is carried to its most absurd consequences. Power-over is separated from the powerful. Doing is denied and the crystallised negation of doing – value – rules the world.

Instead of doing being the braiding of our lives, it is now the negation of doing – value – in the form of its visible and universal equivalent – money – which braids our lives, or rather tears our lives apart and sticks the fragments back together into a cracked whole.

IV

Power-to is inherently social and is transformed into its opposite, power-over, by the form of this sociality. Our capacity to do is unavoidably part of the social flow of doing, yet the fracturing of this flow subordinates this capacity to forces we do not control.

Doing, then, exists antagonistically, as a doing turned against itself, as a doing dominated by the done, as a doing alienated from the doer. The antagonistic existence of doing can be formulated in different ways: as an antagonism between power-to and power-over, between doing and labour, between done and capital, between utility (use-value) and value, between social flow of doing and fragmentation. In each case there is a binary antagonism between the former and the latter, but it is not an external antagonism. In each case, the former exists as the latter: the latter is the mode of existence or *form* of the former. In each case, the latter denies the former, so that the former exists in the mode of being denied.[27] In each case, the content (the former) is dominated by its form but exists in antagonistic tension with this form. This domination of form over content (of labour over doing, of capital over done, and so on) is the source of those horrors against which we scream.

But what is the status of that which exists in the form of being denied? Does it exist at all? Where is power-to, where is unalienated doing, where is the social flow of doing? Do they have any sort of existence separate from the forms in which they currently exist? Are they not mere ideas, or romantic echoes of an imagined Golden Age? They are certainly not intended as a romantic harking back to a past age: whether there was ever a golden age of free doing (primitive communism) does not really matter to us now. They point not towards the past but towards a possible future: a future whose possibility depends on its real existence in the present. That which exists in the form of being denied exists, therefore and inevitably, in rebellion against this denial. There is no unalienated doing in the past, nor can it exist, hippie-like, in a present idyll: nevertheless, it exists, crucially, as present antagonism to its denial, as present projection-beyond-its-denial-to-a-different-world, as a presently existing not-yet.[28] That which exists in the form of being denied is the substance of the ecstatic, the materiality of the scream, the truth which allows us to speak of the existing world as untrue.

But it is more than that. The power-to that exists in the form of power-over, in the form, therefore, of being denied, exists not only as revolt against its denial, it exists also as material substratum of the denial. The denial cannot exist without that which is denied. The done depends on the doing.[29] The owner of the done depends on the doer. No matter how much the done denies the existence of the doing, as in the case of value, as in the case of capital, there is no way in which the done can exist without the doing. No matter how much the done dominates the doing, it depends absolutely on that doing for its existence. Rulers, in other words, always depend on those whom they rule. Capital depends absolutely upon the labour which creates it (and therefore on the prior transformation of doing into labour). That which exists depends for its existence on that which exists only in the form of its denial. That is the weakness of any system of rule and the key to understanding its dynamic. That is the basis for hope.

'Power', then, is a confusing term which conceals an antagonism (and does so in a way that reflects the power of the powerful). 'Power' is used in two quite different senses, as power-to and as power-over. The problem is sometimes addressed in English by borrowing terms from other languages and making a distinction between *potentia* (power-to) and *potestas* (power-over).[30] However, posing the distinction in these terms can be seen as pointing merely to a difference whereas what is at issue is an antagonism, or rather, an antagonistic metamorphosis. Power-to exists as power-over, but the power-to is subjected to and in rebellion against power-over, and power-over is nothing but, and therefore absolutely dependent upon, the metamorphosis of power-to.

The struggle of the scream is the struggle to liberate power-to from power-over, the struggle to liberate doing from labour, to liberate subjectivity from its objectification. In this struggle, it is crucial to see that it is not a matter of power against power, of like against like. It is not a symmetrical struggle. The struggle to liberate power-to from power-over is the struggle for the reassertion of the social flow of doing, against its fragmentation and denial. On the one side is the struggle to re-braid our lives on the basis of the mutual recognition of our participation in the collective flow of doing; on the other side is the attempt to impose and reimpose the fragmentation of that flow, the denial of our doing. From the perspective of the scream, the Leninist aphorism that power is a matter of who-whom is absolutely false, as indeed is the Maoist saying that power comes out of the barrel of a gun: power-over may come out of the barrel of a gun, but not power-to. The struggle to liberate power-to is not the struggle to construct a counter-power, but rather an anti-power, something that is radically different from power-over. Concepts of revolution that focus on the taking of power are typically centred on the notion of counter-power. The strategy is to construct a counter-power, a power that can stand against the ruling power. Often the revolutionary movement has been constructed as a mirror image of power, army against army, party against party, with the result that power reproduces itself within the revolution itself. Anti-power, then, is not counter-power, but something much more radical: it is the dissolution of power-over, the emancipation of power-to. This is the great, absurd, inevitable challenge of the communist dream: to create a society free of power relations through the dissolution of power-over. This project is far more radical than any notion of revolution based on the conquest of power and at the same time far more realistic.

Anti-power is fundamentally opposed to power-over not only in the sense of being a radically different project, but also in the fact that it exists in constant conflict with power-over. The attempt to exercise power-to in a way that does not entail the exercise of power over others, inevitably comes into conflict with power-over. *Potentia* is not an alternative to *potestas* that can simply coexist peacefully with it. It may appear that we can simply cultivate our own garden, create our own world of loving relations, refuse to get our hands dirty in the filth of power, but this is an illusion. There is no innocence, and this is true with an increasing intensity. The exercise of power-to in a way that does not focus on value creation can exist only in antagonism to power-over, as struggle. This is due not to the character of power-to (which is not inherently antagonistic) as to the voracious nature, the 'were-wolf hunger' (Marx 1965, p. 243) of power-over. Power-to, if it does not submerge itself in power-over, can exist, overtly or latently, only as power-against, as anti-power.

It is important to stress the anti-ness of power-to under capitalism, because most mainstream discussions of social theory overlook the antagonistic nature of developing one's potential. The antagonistic nature of power is overlooked and it is assumed that capitalist society provides the opportunity to develop human potential (power-to) to the full. Money, if it is seen as being relevant at all (and, amazingly, it is generally not mentioned in discussions of power, presumably on the basis that money is economics and power is sociology), is generally seen in terms of inequality (unequal access to resources, for example), rather than in terms of command. Power-to, it is assumed, is already emancipated.

The same point can be made in relation to subjectivity. The fact that power-to can exist only as antagonism to power-over (as anti-power) means of course that, under capitalism, subjectivity can only exist antagonistically, in opposition to its own objectification. To treat the subject as already emancipated, as most mainstream theory does, is to endorse the present objectification of the subject as subjectivity, as freedom. Many of the attacks on subjectivity by structuralists or postmodernists can perhaps be understood in this sense, as attacks on a false notion of an emancipated (and hence autonomous and coherent) subjectivity.[31] To argue here for the inevitability of taking subjectivity as our starting point is not to argue for a coherent or autonomous subjectivity. On the contrary, the fact that subjectivity can exist only in antagonism to its own objectification means that it is torn apart by that objectification and its struggle against it.

This book is an exploration of the absurd and shadowy world of anti-power. It is shadowy and absurd simply because the world of orthodox social science (sociology, political science, economics, and so on) is a world in which power is so completely taken for granted that nothing else is visible. In the social science that seeks to explain the world as it is, to show how the world works, power is the keystone of all categories, so that, in spite of (indeed, because of) its proclaimed neutrality, this social science participates actively in the separation of subject and object which is the substance of power. To us, power is of interest only in so far as it helps us to understand the challenge of anti-power: the study of power on its own, in abstraction from the challenge and project of anti-power, can do nothing but actively reproduce power.

V

We have presented the issue of power in terms of a binary antagonism between doing and done, in which the done, existing in the form of capital (apparently controlled by, but actually in control of, the capitalists) subordinates, ever more voraciously, all doing to the sole purpose of its self-expansion.

But is this not too simple? Surely that which we scream against is far more complex than this? What about the way that doctors treat their patients, what about the way that teachers treat their students, that parents treat their children? What of the treatment of blacks by whites? What about the subordination of women to men? Is it not too simplistic, too reductionist, to say that power is capital and capital is power? Are there not many different types of power?

Foucault in particular makes the argument that it is a mistake to think of power in terms of a binary antagonism, that we must think of it rather in terms of a 'multiplicity of force relations' (1990, p. 92). Corresponding to the multiplicity of power relations there is then a multiplicity of resistances

... present everywhere in the power network. Hence there is no single locus of great Refusal, no soul of revolt, source of all rebellions, or pure law of the revolutionary. Instead there is a plurality of resistances, each of them a special case: resistances that are possible, necessary, improbable; others that are spontaneous, savage, solitary, concerted, rampant, or violent; still others that are quick to compromise, interested, or sacrificial; by definition, they can only exist in the strategic field of power relations. [1990, pp. 95–6]

In terms of our scream, that would suggest an endless multiplicity of screams. And indeed it is so: we scream in many different ways and for many different reasons. From the beginning of our argument it was stressed that the 'we-ness' of 'we scream' is a central question in this book, not a simple assertion of identity. Why, then, insist on the binary nature of an overriding antagonism between doing and done? It cannot be a matter of an abstract defence of a Marxist approach – that would make no sense. Nor is it in any sense the intention to impose a single identity or unity upon the manifest multiplicity of resistance, to subordinate all the variety of resistances to the *a priori* unity of the Working Class. Nor can it be a matter of emphasising the empirical role of the working class and its importance in relation to 'other forms of struggle'.

In order to explain our insistence on the binary nature of the antagonism of power (or, in more traditional terms, our insistence on a class analysis), it is necessary to retrace our steps. The starting-point of the argument here is not the urge to understand society or to explain how it works. Our starting-point is much sharper: the scream, the drive to change society radically. It is from that perspective that we ask how society works. That starting-point led us to place the question of doing in the centre of our discussion, and this in turn led us to the antagonism between doing and done.

Obviously, other perspectives are possible. It is more common to start positively, with the question of how society works. Such a perspective does not necessarily lead to a focus on doing and the way in which doing is organised. In the case of Foucault, it leads rather to a focus on talking, on language. This perspective certainly allows him to elucidate the enormous richness and complexity of power relations in contemporary society and, more important from our perspective, the richness and complexity of resistance to power.

However, the richness and complexity is the richness of a still photograph, or of a painting.[32] There is no movement in the society that Foucault analyses: change from one still photograph to another, but no movement. There cannot be, unless the focus is on doing and its antagonistic existence. Thus, in Foucault's analysis, there are a whole host of resistances which are integral to power, but there is no possibility of emancipation. The only possibility is an endlessly shifting constellation of power-and-resistance.

The argument in this chapter has led to two important results, which it is worth reiterating. First, the focus on doing has led to an intimation of the vulnerability of power-over. The done depends on the doer, capital depends on labour. That is the crucial chink of light, the glimmer of hope, the turning-point in the argument. The realisation that the powerful depend on the 'powerless'[33] transforms the scream from a scream of anger to a scream of hope, a confident scream of anti-power (see Holloway 1995a). This realisation takes us beyond the merely radical-democratic perspective of an endless struggle against power to a position from which we can pose the issue of the vulnerability of capital and the real possibility of social transformation. From this perspective, then, we must ask of any theory not so much how it illuminates the present, but what light it throws on the vulnerability of rule. What we want is not a theory of domination, but a theory of the vulnerability of domination, of the crisis of domination, as an expression of our own (anti-)power. The emphasis on understanding power in terms of a 'multiplicity of relations of force' does not give us any basis for posing this question. Indeed, on the contrary, it tends to exclude the question, for, while resistance is central to Foucault's approach (at least in his later work), the notion of emancipation is ruled out as being absurd, for it presupposes, as Foucault correctly points out, the assumption of a unity in the relations of power.

To pose the question of the vulnerability of power thus requires two steps: the opening of the category of power to reveal its contradictory character, which has been described here in terms of the antagonism between power-to and power-over; and second, the understanding of this antagonistic relation as an internal relation. Power-to exists as power-over: power-over is the form of power-to, a form which denies its substance. Power-over can exist only as transformed power-to. Capital can exist only as the product of transformed doing (labour). That is the key to its weakness. The issue of form, so central to Marx's discussion of capitalism, is crucial for an understanding of the vulnerability of domination. The distinction which Negri makes (and develops so brilliantly) between constituent and constituted power takes the first of these two steps and opens up an understanding of the self-antagonistic nature of power as a precondition for talking about revolutionary transformation (see Negri 1999). However, the relation between constituent and constituted power remains an external one. Constitution (the transformation of constituent into constituted power) is seen as a *reaction* to the democratic constituent power of the multitude. This, however, tells us nothing about the vulnerability of the process of constitution. In the face of power-over (constituted power) it tells us of the ubiquity and force of the absolute struggle of the multitude, but it tells us nothing of the crucial nexus of dependence of power-over (constituted power) upon power-to (constituent power). In this sense, for all the force and brilliance of his account, Negri remains at the level of radical-democratic theory.[34]

Does this emphasis on the perspective of the scream lead us then to an impoverished view of society? The argument above seems to suggest that the perspective of the scream leads to a binary view of the antagonism between doing and done, and that in such a perspective there is no room for the 'multiplicity of forces' which Foucault sees as essential to the discussion of power. This seems to suggest a split between the revolutionary or negative perspective and the understanding of the undoubted richness and complexity of society. This would indeed be the case (and would constitute a major problem for our argument) if it were not for the second result of our previous discussion, namely that the antagonistic relation between doing and done, and specifically the radical fracturing of the flow of doing that is inherent in the fact that power-over exists as ownership of the done, means a multiple fragmentation of doing (and of social relations). In other words, the very understanding of social relations as being characterised by a binary antagonism between doing and done means that this antagonism exists in the form of a multiplicity of antagonisms, a great heterogeneity of conflict. There are indeed a million forms of resistance, an immensely complex world of antagonisms. To reduce these to an empirical unity of conflict between capital and labour, or to argue for a hegemony of working-class struggle, understood empirically, or to argue that these apparently non-class resistances must be subsumed under class struggle, would be an absurd violence. The argument here is just the contrary: the fact that capitalist society is characterised by a binary antagonism between doing and done means that this antagonism exists as a multiplicity of antagonisms. It is the binary nature of power (as antagonism between power-to and power-over) that means that power appears as a 'multiplicity of forces'. Rather than starting with the multiplicity, we need to start with the prior multiplication that gives rise to this multiplicity. Rather than starting with the multiple identities (women, blacks, gays, Basques, Irish, and so on), we need to start from the process of identification that gives rise to those identities. In this perspective, one aspect of Foucault's enormously stimulating writings is precisely that, without presenting it in those terms, he greatly enriches our understanding of the fragmentation of the flow of doing, our historical understanding of what we shall characterise in the next chapter as the process of fetishisation.

A last point needs to be dealt with before passing on to the discussion of fetishism. It is an important part of Foucault's argument that power should not be seen in purely negative terms, that we must also understand the way in which power constitutes reality and constitutes us. That is clearly so: we are conceived and born not in a power-free vacuum but in a power-traversed society: we are products of that society. Foucault, however, fails to open up the category of power, to point to the fundamental antagonism that characterises it. Thus, we can say, for example, that we are products of capital, or that everything we consume is a commodity. That is clearly so, but it is deceptive. It is only when we open up these categories, when we say, for example, that the commodity is characterised by an antagonism between value and use value (utility), that use value exists in the form of value, and in rebellion against this form, that the full development of our human potential presupposes our participation in this rebellion, and so on. It is only then that we can make sense of the statement that everything we consume is a commodity. Similarly with power: it is only when we open up the category of power and see power-over as the antagonistic form of power-to that it makes sense to say that power constitutes us. The power that constitutes us is an antagonism, an antagonism of which we are profoundly and inevitably part.

4   Fetishism:
   The Tragic Dilemma

I

In the last chapter, we argued that the transformation of power-to into power-over is centred on the rupture of the social flow of doing. In capitalism, the done is severed from and turned against the doing. This severing of the done from the doing is the core of a multiple fracturing of all aspects of life.

Without naming names, we have already entered upon a discussion of fetishism. Fetishism is the term that Marx uses to describe the rupture of doing. Fetishism is the core of Marx's discussion of power and central to any discussion of changing the world. It is the centrepiece of the argument of this book.

Fetishism is a category that does not fit easily into normal academic discourse. Partially for that reason, it has been relatively neglected by those who would force Marxism into the moulds of the different academic disciplines. Although it is a central category in Marx's *Capital*, it is almost completely ignored by those who regard themselves as Marxist economists.[1] It is similarly overlooked by Marxist sociologists and political scientists, who usually prefer to start from the category of class and adapt it to the frameworks of their disciplines. Fetishism, in so far as it is discussed at all, is often seen as falling in the realm of philosophy or cultural criticism. Relegated and classified in this way, the concept loses its explosive force.

The force of the concept lies in that it refers to an unsustainable horror: the self-negation of doing.

II

The young Marx discusses the self-negation of doing not in terms of fetishism but in terms of 'alienation' or 'estrangement'. Alienation, a term now often used to describe a general social malaise, refers in Marx's discussion to the rupturing of doing which is characteristic of the capitalist organisation of production.

43

In his discussion of 'estranged labour' in the *Economic and Philosophic Manuscripts of 1844*, Marx starts from the process of production, arguing that under capitalism production is not just production of an object, but production of an object that is alien to the producer:

> The *alienation* of the worker in his product means not only that his labour becomes an object, an *external* existence, but that it exists *outside him*, independently, as something alien to him, and that it becomes a power on its own confronting him. It means that the life which he has conferred on the object confronts him as something hostile and alien. [1975, p. 272; original emphasis]

The sundering of doer from done is inevitably the sundering of the doer himself.[2] The production of an alien object is inevitably an active process of self-estrangement:

> How could the worker come to face the product of his activity as a stranger, were it not that in the very act of production he was estranging himself from himself? ... If then the product of labour is alienation, production itself must be active alienation, the alienation of activity, the activity of alienation. [1975, p. 274]

Alienation of man from his own activity is self-estrangement: it is the worker himself who actively produces his own estrangement.

The rupture of the doer from the done is the negation of the doer's power-to. The doer is turned into a victim. Activity is turned into passivity, doing into suffering. Doing is turned against the doer:

> This relation is the relation of the worker to his own activity as an alien activity not belonging to him; it is activity as suffering, strength as weakness, begetting as emasculating, the worker's *own* physical and mental energy, his personal life – for what is life but activity? – as an activity which is turned against him, independent of him and not belonging to him. [1975, p. 275]

Alienation is the production of humans who are damaged, maimed, deprived of their humanity:

> In tearing away from man the object of his production, therefore, estranged labour tears from him his *species-life*, his real objectivity

as a member of the species, and transforms his advantage over animals into the disadvantage that his inorganic body, nature, is taken away from him. [1975, p. 277]

This 'tearing away from man the object of his production' alienates him from his collective humanity, his 'species-being': 'Estranged labour turns ... *man's species-being* ... into a being *alien* from him, into a *means* for his *individual existence'* (1975, p. 277; original emphasis). This implies the fragmentation of the collective human subject, the *'estrangement of man* from *man'* (1975, p. 277). Mutual recognition is broken, not just between ruler and ruled, but between the workers themselves:

> What applies to a man's relation to his work, to the product of his labour and to himself, also holds of a man's relation to the other man, and to the other man's labour and object of labour. In fact, the proposition that man's species-nature is estranged from him means that one man is estranged from the other, as each of them is from man's essential nature. [1975, p. 277]

The term 'species-life' or 'species-being' refers surely to nothing other than the social flow of human doing, the material braiding of a mutually recognitive 'we'.

This estrangement of man from man is not only an estrangement between workers but also the production of the non-worker, the master: 'If the product of labour does not belong to the worker, if it confronts him as an alien power, then this can only be because it belongs to some *other man than the worker'* (1975, p. 278). Estranged labour is the active producing of domination, the active conversion of power-to into power-over:

> Just as he creates his own production as the loss of his reality, as his punishment; his own product as a loss, as a product not belonging to him; so he creates the domination of the person who does not produce over the product. Just as he estranges his activity from himself, so he confers upon the stranger an activity which is not his own. [1975, p. 279][3]

The notion of alienation thus refers to the breaking of the social flow of doing, the turning of doing against itself. This is not the result of fate or divine intervention: human doing is the only subject, the sole constitutive power. We are the only gods, the sole creators. Our problem, as creators, is that we are creating our own destruction. We create the negation of our own creation. Doing negates itself. Activity becomes passivity, doing becomes non-doing, being. Alienation points both to our dehumanisation and to the fact that it is we who produce our own dehumanisation. But how can maimed, dehumanised, alienated people possibly create a liberated, human society? Alienation signals not only the urgency but also, apparently, the impossibility of revolutionary change.

III

The rupture of doing and done is introduced right at the beginning of *Capital*. Echoing the words of the 1844 Manuscripts ('The *alienation* of the worker in his product means ... that ... it exists *outside him*, independently, as something alien to him, and that it becomes a power on its own confronting him'), Marx begins the second paragraph of *Capital* saying, 'A commodity is, in the first place, an object outside us' (1965, p. 35). The commodity is an object produced by us, but standing outside us. The commodity takes on a life of its own in which its social origin in human labour is extinguished. It is a product which denies its own character as product, a done which denies its own relation to doing.

The commodity is the point of fracture of the social flow of doing. As a product produced for exchange, it stands at the unhinging or dis-articulation of social doing. It is of course the product of a social doing, but the fact that it is produced for exchange on the market breaks the flow of doing, makes the thing stand apart from the doing of which it is both product and precondition. It stands on its own to be sold on the market, the work that produced it forgotten. The labour which produces it is social (labour for others), but it is *indirectly* social – it is labour for others which exists in the form of labour for oneself. The sociality of doing is ruptured, and with it the process of mutual recognition and social validation. Mutual recognition is removed from the producers and transferred to their products: it is the product which is recognised socially, in the process of exchange. Recognition of doing is expressed as the value of the product. It is now the quantitative, monetary measure of value (price) which provides social validation for the doing of people. It is money which tells you whether what you do is socially useful.

The commodity, then, is not a thing to be taken at face value. Analysis allows us to discern the labour that has produced the commodity and to see labour as the substance of its value, but that just leads us on to a far bigger question: why is it that the doing which produced the commodity is negated?

Political Economy has indeed analysed, however incompletely, value and its magnitude, and has discovered what lies beneath these forms. But it has never once asked the question why labour is represented by the value of its product and labour-time by the magnitude of that value. [Marx 1965, p. 80]

Capital is a study of the self-negation of doing. From the commodity, Marx moves on to value, money, capital, profit, rent, interest – ever more opaque forms of the occultation of doing, ever more sophisticated forms of the suppression of power-to. Doing (human activity) disappears further and further from sight. Things rule. It is in this world where things rule, where the novum of human creativity disappears from sight, in this 'enchanted, perverted, topsy-turvy world' (Marx 1972a, p. 830), that it becomes possible to speak of the 'laws of capitalist development'. It is on the basis of the critique of this insanity that it becomes possible to criticise the categories of the political economists, the rationality and laws of their analysis of an irrational, perverted world.

The core of all this is the separation of the done from the doing. This is inherent in the commodity, and receives its fully developed form in capital, the appropriation of the done by the owners of the past done (and therefore of the means of doing), the accumulation of done upon done, the accumulation of capital: 'Accumulate! Accumulate! That is Moses and the prophets!' Accumulation is simply the voracious, relentless process of separating done from doing, of turning the done (as means of doing) against the doers in order to subject their present doing to the sole end of further accumulation. It is this ever-renewed process that gives a specific form to doing (as abstract labour, labour abstracted from any particular content, value production, surplus value production) and to the done (as value, as commodity, as money, as capital): all aspects of the ever-repeated rupture of the social flow of doing.

Marx now refers to this process of rupture not as alienation, but as 'fetishism'. In his discussion of fetishism at the end of Chapter 1 of the first volume of *Capital*, he explains:

In order ... to find an analogy, we must have recourse to the mist-
enveloped regions of the religious world. In that world the
productions of the human brain appear as independent things
endowed with life, and entering into relation both with one
another and with the human race. [1965, p. 72]

The commodity is 'a very queer thing, abounding in metaphysical
subtleties and theological niceties' (1965, p. 71). The 'mystical
character of commodities', Marx says, comes not from their use
value, but from the commodity form itself, that is, from the fact that
the product of labour assumes the form of a commodity:

> The equality of all sorts of human labour is expressed objectively
> by their products all being equally values; the measure of the
> expenditure of labour-power by the duration of that expenditure,
> takes the form of the quantity of value of the products of labour;
> and finally, the mutual relations of the producers, within which
> the social character of their labour affirms itself, take the form of
> a social relation between the products. A commodity is therefore
> a mysterious thing, simply because in it the social character of
> men's labour appears to them as an objective character stamped
> upon the product of that labour; because the relation to the sum
> total of their own labour is presented to them as a social relation,
> existing not between themselves, but between the products of
> their labour. [1965, p. 72]

Just as Marx had insisted on understanding self-estrangement as the
product of self-estranged labour, so he emphasises that the peculiar
character of commodities has its origin in the 'peculiar social
character of the labour that produces them' (1965, p. 72).
Commodity production is indirectly social labour: although the
products are produced for social use, the form of production is
private:

> Since the producers do not come into social contact with each
> other until they exchange their products, the specific social
> character of each producer's labour does not show itself except in
> the act of exchange. In other words, the labour of the individual
> asserts itself as a part of the labour of society, only by means of
> the relations the act of exchange establishes directly between the
> products, and indirectly, through them, between the producers.

To the latter, therefore, the relations connecting the labour of one individual with that of the rest appear, not as direct relations between individuals at work, but *as what they really are*, material relations between persons and social relations between things. [1965, p. 73; emphasis added]

Social relations do not merely appear to be relations between things: rather, this appearance reflects the real fracturing of doing and done, the real rupture of the sociality of doing. Relations between doers really are refracted through relations between things (between dones that deny their origin in the sociality of doing). These things are the fetishised forms of the relations between producers, and, as such, they deny their character as social relations. Commodities, value and money conceal 'instead of disclos[e], the social character of private labour, and the social relations between the individual producers' (1965, p. 76).

The fracturing of social relations is consolidated by bourgeois thought, which takes these fetishised forms as its basis rather than criticising them:

The categories of bourgeois economy consist of such like forms. They are forms of thought expressing with social validity the conditions and relations of a definite, historically determined mode of production, viz., the production of commodities. [1965, p. 76]

There is, then, no clear distinction here between thought and reality, theory and practice. Theory is an element of practice, actively contributing to the production and reproduction of the separation of doing from done.

The starting-point for our thought is the fetishised world which confronts us. We are born into a world in which the community of doing is fractured. The separation of doing and done permeates our whole relation to the world and to those around us. Our vision of the world is already pre-shaped before we begin to reflect critically. Power-over, that separation of doing and done which is inherent in the production of commodities for the market, presents itself here impersonally. Marx introduces fetishism in the context of the production and exchange of commodities. This is not, however, a pre-capitalist phase, for the generalisation of commodity production presupposes the existence of labour power as a commodity, that is, the existence of a capitalist society.[4] Commodity fetishism is, therefore, the penetration of capitalist power-over into the core of our being, into all our habits of thought, all our relations with other people.

Confronted with the fetishised world, all we can do is criticise. Value, for example,

> ... does not stalk about with a label describing what it is. It is value, rather, that converts every product into a social hieroglyphic. Later on, we try to decipher the hieroglyphic, to get behind the secret of our own social products; for to stamp an object of utility as a value, is just as much a social product as language ... Man's reflections on the forms of social life, and consequently, also his scientific analysis of those forms, take a course directly opposite to that of their actual historical development. He begins, post festum, with the results of the process of development ready to hand before him. [1965, pp. 74–5]

Bourgeois thought has, in the best of cases, managed to decipher some of the social hieroglyphics: 'Political Economy has indeed analysed, however incompletely, value and its magnitude, and has discovered what lies beneath these forms' (1965, p. 80). There is, however, a limit to bourgeois criticism. The separation of subject and object, doing and done, inevitably involves a hypostatisation of the present, a fixation of the present. As long as the separation of subject and object is not questioned, as long as the capitalist form of social organisation is not seen as transient, criticism is inevitably blind to the historicity of the phenomena criticised. The rupture of the sociality of doing is assumed to be natural, eternal. In other words, bourgeois (fetishised) thought is blind to the question of form. The question of form (value, money or capital as forms of social relations) arises only if one is alive to the historicity of bourgeois social relations, that is, to the fact that capitalism is a particular historical form of organising relations between people:

> If ... we treat this mode of production as one eternally fixed by Nature for every state of society, we necessarily overlook that which is the differentia specifica of the value-form, and consequently of the commodity-form, and of its further developments, money-form, capital-form, &c. [1965, p. 81]

Consequently, bourgeois criticism does not look to the genesis of the phenomenon criticised, does not ask why social relations exist in these forms.

The category of form is central to Marx's discussion in *Capital*. He speaks of 'money-form', 'commodity-form', 'capital-form', and so on. These are not to be understood in the sense of a species-genus distinction (money as a 'form' or 'species' of something else), but simply as a mode of existence. Money, commodity, capital are modes of existence of social relations, the forms in which social relations currently exist.[5] These are the frozen or rigidified modes of existence of relations between people. 'Form', then, is the echo of the scream, a message of hope. We scream against things as they are: yes, comes the echo, but things-as-they-are are not eternal, they are just the historically congealed forms of social relations:

> These formulae, which bear it stamped upon them in unmistakable letters that they belong to a state of society, in which the process of production has the mastery over man, instead of being controlled by him, such formulae appear to the bourgeois intellect to be as much a self-evident necessity imposed by Nature as productive labour itself. [1965, pp. 80–1]

But for us who scream, they are neither self-evident nor eternal.

It should already be clear what a central part the concept of fetishism plays in revolutionary theory. It is at once a *critique of bourgeois society*, a *critique of bourgeois theory* and an *explanation of the stability of bourgeois society*. It points at once to the dehumanisation of people, to our own complicity in the reproduction of power, and to the difficulty (or apparent impossibility) of revolution.

The concept of fetishism is central to Marx's critique of capitalist society.[6] The theme of dehumanisation is constantly present in Marx's discussion in *Capital* and elsewhere. In capitalism there is an inversion of the relation between people and things, between subject and object. There is an objectification of the subject and a subject-ification of the object: things (money, capital, machines) become the subjects of society, while people (workers) become the objects. Social relations are not just apparently but really relations between things (between money and the state, between your money and mine), while humans are deprived of their sociality, transformed into 'individuals', the necessary complement of commodity exchange. ('In order that this alienation be reciprocal, it is only necessary for men, by a tacit understanding, to treat each other as private owners, and by implication as independent individuals' (1965, p. 87).) In the long and detailed discussion of conditions in the factory and the process of exploitation, the emphasis is constantly on the inversion of subject and object:

> Every kind of capitalist production, in so far as it is not only a labour-process, but also a process of creating surplus-value, has this in common, that it is not the workman who employs the instruments of labour, but the instruments of labour that employ the workman. But it is only in the factory system that this inversion for the first time acquires technical and palpable reality. [1965, p. 423]

It is not only for the physical misery that it brings, but above all for the inversion of things and people that Marx condemns capitalism: for the fetishisation of social relations in other words.

Inextricably linked with the condemnation of the inversion of subject and object in bourgeois society is the critique of bourgeois theory which takes this inversion for granted, which bases its categories on the fetishised forms of social relations: the state, money, capital, the individual, profit, wages, rent, and so on. These categories are derived from the surface of society, the sphere of circulation, in which the subjectivity of the subject as producer is completely out of sight and all that can be seen is the interaction of things and of the individuals who are the bearers of these things. It is here, where social subjectivity is hidden from view, that liberal theory blooms. This sphere of circulation is 'a very Eden of the innate rights of man. There alone rule Freedom, Equality, Property and Bentham' (1965, p. 176). The whole three volumes of *Capital* are devoted to a critique of political economy, that is, to showing how the conceptions of political economy arise from the fetishised appearances of social relations. Political economy (and bourgeois theory in general) takes for granted the forms in which social relations exist (commodity-form, value-form, money-form, capital-form, and so on). In other words, bourgeois theory is blind to the question of form: commodities and money (and so on) are not even thought of as being forms, or modes of existence, of social relations. Bourgeois theory is blind to the transitory nature of the current forms of social relations, takes for granted the basic unchangeability (the 'is-ness') of capitalist social relations.

Bourgeois thought, however, is not just the thought of the bourgeoisie, or of capitalism's active supporters. It refers rather to the forms of thought generated by the fractured relation between doing and done (subject and object) in capitalist society. It is crucially important to see that the critique of bourgeois theory is not just a critique of 'them'. It is also, and perhaps above all, a critique of 'us', of the bourgeois nature of our own assumptions and categories, or, more concretely, a critique of our own complicity in the reproduction of capitalist power relations. The critique of bourgeois thought is the critique of the separation of subject and object in our own thought.

The fetishism which is so highly elaborated in the work of the political economists and other bourgeois theorists is equally the basis of everyday 'common-sense' conceptions in capitalist society. The assumption of the permanence of capitalism is built into the daily thought and practice of people in this society. The appearance and real existence of social relations as fragmented relations between things conceal both the basic antagonism of those relations and the possibility of changing the world. The concept of fetishism (rather than any theory of 'ideology' or 'hegemony') thus provides the basis for an answer to the age-old question, 'Why do people accept the misery, violence and exploitation of capitalism?' By pointing to the way in which people not only accept the miseries of capitalism but also actively participate in its reproduction, the concept of fetishism also underlines the difficulty or apparent impossibility of revolution against capitalism. Fetishism is the central theoretical problem confronted by any theory of revolution. Revolutionary thought and practice is necessarily anti-fetishistic. Any thought or practice which aims at the emancipation of humanity from the dehumanisation of capitalism is necessarily directed against fetishism.

IV

The tragic dilemma of revolutionary change, the fact that its urgency and its apparent impossibility are two sides of the same process, intensifies to the degree that the fetishism of social relations becomes more penetrating and more pervasive.

The separation of doing and done, of subject and object, it is clear from Marx's discussion in *Capital*, goes beyond the immediate 'tearing away from man the object of his production' by the exploiting class. It is not just that the capitalist tears away from the worker the object which she has produced. The fact that the sociality of doing is mediated (broken and stuck together cracked) through the market (the sale and purchase of commodities) means that the rupture of doing and done is by no means limited to the immediate process of exploitation, but extends to the whole society. Although Marx's focus in *Capital* is on the critique of political economy, there is no reason at all to think that fetishism extends only to the sphere conceptualised by political economy. The implication of Marx's discussion is rather that fetishism permeates the whole of society, that the whole of capitalism is 'an enchanted, perverted,[7] topsy-turvy world' (1972a, p. 830), and that the subjectification of the object and the objectification of the subject is characteristic of every aspect of life. 'Separation', says Marx, is the 'real generation process of capital' (1972b, p. 422).

The question of the all-pervasive character of fetishism is taken up by a number of authors working in the Marxist tradition. The further the argument is developed, the more intense the tragic dilemma of revolution becomes. The more urgent revolutionary change is shown to be, the more impossible it seems. In terms of reification (Lukács), instrumental rationality (Horkheimer), one-dimensionality (Marcuse), identity (Adorno), discipline (Foucault)[8], the different authors have emphasised the penetration of power into every sphere of our existence, the increasing closure of existence under capitalism. Their work raises to an excruciating pitch the intensity of the revolutionary dilemma.

Rather than try to give an account of the contributions of the different theorists, we shall try to build on their work to develop some of the points made in the previous chapter. This involves going back over the argument so far.

The starting-point is the separation of doing and done. This implies an antagonistic separation between the doers and the appro-priators of the done. The appropriators of the done (the owners of capital) use their control of the done, which is the means of doing, to get the doers to labour for them to increase the done which they appropriate. The capitalists, in other words, exploit the workers: they pay them what they need in order to survive (the value of their labour power) and appropriate the surplus that they produce (the surplus value). The separation of doing and done implies a dual class analysis, an antagonism between capital and the working class. This is fundamentally important and nothing in the argument should be taken as derogating from this position.

This class antagonism is often understood within the Marxist and socialist tradition to be an external relation. It is assumed that the antagonism between working class and capital is an external antagonism which leaves the two sides untouched in their fundamentals. The two sides of the antagonism are then a good side (working class) and a bad side (capitalist class). In such a perspective, one might expect that the question of revolution would be a relatively simple one, largely a practical question of organisation. Why, then, has there not been a successful communist revolution? The answers given are usually in terms of ideology, hegemony or false consciousness. The working class does not rise up because it is imbued with the ideology of the market; in a class society, the ideas of the ruling class are hegemonic; the working class suffers from false consciousness. In each case, the question of ideology, hegemony or false consciousness is separated from the question of the separation of doing from done: the sphere of ideology is seen as separate from the 'economic'. The emphasis on the lack of understanding of the working class is usually (inevitably?) accompanied by an assumption that the working class is a 'they'. 'They' have the wrong ideas, so our role (we who have the right ideas) is to enlighten them, to illuminate them, to bring them true consciousness.[9] The political problems inherent in such an approach should be obvious.

A second problem with such an approach is simply that it is unable to account for the complexity of the world. Lines are drawn too crudely, the complexity of social connections is short-circuited, so that Marxism loses its power of conviction. This has been particularly obvious in discussions of changing forms of social conflict in recent years – conflict around issues of gender or the environment, for example. There has been a tendency either to force such struggles into a preconceived mould of class struggle, or to speak of them as 'non-class struggles'. In the latter case, the concept of non-class struggle is accompanied either by the view that class struggle is diminishing in importance or that, in spite of everything, the fundamental conflict between capital and labour still remains the most important form of conflict. The understanding of the conflict between labour and capital as an external conflict which leaves both sides essentially untouched leads to the conception of the antagonism as an immediate one, in which both sides are immediately, empirically present. And then come the problems: where was the working class in the struggle against the Vietnam War, against nuclear weapons, where is the working class in support of the Zapatista uprising, how can we speak of working-class revolution when the working class is numerically on the decline, and so on. All of these questions can be answered, of course, but the cumulative evidence of a separation between 'the working class' as an empirically identifiable group and the most striking forms of rebellion has led to a progressive undermining of the idea that capitalism should be understood in terms of a basic class antagonism.

The argument here is that a class understanding of capitalism is fundamental, but that the class antagonism cannot be understood as an external relation, nor can class be understood in this immediate way. The separation of doing and done, as we have already begun to see in the previous chapter and in the first sections of this one, is not just a simple antagonism between doers and the appropriators of that which is done. Capitalist power-over, the separation of doing and done, is like one of those horrific modern bullets which do not simply pierce the flesh of the victim but explode inside her into a thousand different fragments. Or, less horrifically, capitalist power is like a rocket that shoots up into the sky and explodes into a multitude of coloured flares. To focus on the flares or the fragments of the bullet without seeing the trajectory of the rocket or the bullet is what much postmodern theory (or, indeed, bourgeois theory in general) does.[10] On the other hand, to focus just on the primary movement of the bullet or the rocket and to treat the flares and the fragments as something external (non-class struggle) is a crudity that is politically unhelpful and theoretically unconvincing.

The concept of fetishism is concerned with the explosion of power inside us, not as something that is distinct from the separation of doing and done (as in the concepts of 'ideology' and 'hegemony'), but as something that is integral to that separation. That separation does not just divide capitalists from workers, but explodes inside us, shaping every aspect of what we do and what we think, transforming every breath of our lives into a moment of class struggle. The problem of why revolution has not happened is not a problem of 'them', but a problem of a fragmented 'us'.

We live, then, in an 'enchanted, perverted, topsy-turvy world' in which relations between people exist in the form of relations between things. Social relations are 'thingified' or 'reified'. The term 'reification' is the one used by Lukács in his *History and Class Consciousness*, published in 1923. As the term 'reification' suggests,

Lukács insists on its relevance for every aspect of social life.[11] Reification is not just associated with the immediate labour process, nor just something that affects the 'workers': 'The fate of the worker becomes the fate of society as a whole' (1971, p. 91). And:

> The transformation of the commodity relation into a thing of 'ghostly objectivity' ... stamps its imprint upon the whole consciousness of man ... And there is no natural form in which human relations can be cast, no way in which man can bring his physical and psychic 'qualities' into play without their being subjected increasingly to this reifying process. [1971, p. 100]

V

The separation of doing from done (and its subordination to the done) establishes the reign of is-ness, or identity. Identity is perhaps the most concentrated (and most challenging) expression of fetishism or reification. The breaking of the flow of doing deprives doing of its movement. Present doing is subordinate to past done. Living labour is subordinated to dead labour. Doing is frozen in midflight, transformed into being. The beauty, transfixed by the witch's curse, losing her movement loses her beauty: sleeping beauty is a contradiction in terms. The freezing is not absolute (any more than the rupture of doing is absolute). It is not that everything stands still, but everything is locked into a perpetual continuity, everything is repeated, everything moves forward on tracks.

If the world is looked at from the point of view of doing, it is clearly impossible to say 'the world is', or 'things are', or 'I am'. From the perspective of doing, it is clear that everything is movement: the world is and is not, things are and are not, I am and am not. The contradiction that is inherent in these statements presents no problem if we think in terms of doing: in doing I go beyond myself, the world moves beyond itself, and so on. The change in me that is implied in my doing means that I am and am not. But once doing is broken, once doing is subordinated to the done, movement is halted and the statement that I am and am not seems incoherent. Once doing is ruptured, it is no longer doing and contradiction that prevail. Identity rules, contradiction is flattened. The world is, that's the way things are: if we say 'the world is and is not; that's the way things are and are not', these now seem meaningless, illogical statements.

Identity implies the homogenisation of time. When the flow of doing is broken and doing subjected to the done and its quantitative accumulation, then doing is forced onto certain tracks, contained within certain parameters. Doing is reduced to labour, limited to doing-in-the-service-of-the-expansion-of-capital. This both limits the content of doing and imposes a certain (and ever-increasing) rhythm upon doing. Labour, as doing has become, is measured quantitatively: it is labour for a certain number of hours, labour that produces something that can be sold for a price, labour that produces value, labour which is rewarded quantitatively in money by a wage. People's doing becomes converted into a train that moves faster and faster, but along pre-established tracks: 'Time sheds its qualitative, variable, flowing nature; it freezes into an exactly delimited, quantifiable continuum filled with quantifiable "things" ... : in short, it becomes space' (Lukács 1971, p. 90). Time becomes clock time, tick-tick time, in which one tick is just the same as another: a time that moves but stays still, treadmill time.[12] The varying intensity of lived time, of the time of passion and happiness and pain, is subordinated to the tick-tick of the clock.

Homogeneous time has the present as its axis. It is not that the past and the future are completely denied, but the past and especially the future are subservient to the present: the past is understood as the pre-history of the present, and the future is conceived as the pre-visible extension of the present. Time is seen as a linear movement between past and future. Radically alternative possibilities for the future are pushed aside as fiction. All that lies, lay or might lie outside the tracks of tick-tick time is suppressed. Past struggles that pointed towards something radically different from the present are forgotten: 'All reification is a forgetting', as Horkheimer and Adorno put it (1972, p. 230). The rule of identity is the rule of amnesia. Memory,[13] and with it hope, are subordinated to the relentless movement of the clock which goes nowhere: 'Only with the farewell to the closed, static concept of being does the real dimension of hope open' (Bloch 1986, p. 18).

The rule of identity implies certain linguistic hierarchies. It implies, for example, the dominance of one verb, 'is', over all the others.[14] In a world that is defined, other verbs are deactivated: their force is limited by that which is. Doing is a doing which is not just limited by, but permeated by, that which is: our everyday activity is constrained and permeated by that which is.[15] Put differently, Is-ness implies the dominance of nouns over verbs. That which is becomes crystallised, consolidated, rigidified into nouns: in nouns movement is suppressed or contained. Just as time becomes tick-tick time, movement becomes tick-tick movement, the movement of an object without subject, a movement that itself becomes a thing, a movement rather than a moving.

The separation of doing from done is the separation of constitution or genesis from existence. That which is done is separated off from the doing which did it. It acquires a separate existence distinct from the doing which constituted it. I make a chair. From the perspective of the social flow of doing, there is a fleeting objectification of the chair: it is immediately integrated through use (through doing) into the collective flow (if it is not used, it ceases to be a chair from the perspective of doing). But in capitalism, the objectification is more than fleeting. The chair which I made exists now as the property of my employer. It is a commodity which can be sold. Its existence is quite separate from its constitution. Indeed, its constitution or genesis (the doing which made it) is negated by its existence as a commodity: it is forgotten, a matter of total indifference to the existence of the chair. The purchaser uses the chair and in that sense reincorporates it into doing, but the flow is (really and apparently) broken: there is absolutely no direct relation between the doing of the user and the doing of the maker. Existence acquires a duration. The time of existence of the chair is a time of duration: the chair now is, its is-not-ness totally forgotten. Constitution and existence are sundered. The constituted denies the constituting, the done the doing, the object the subject. The object constituted acquires a durable identity. It becomes an apparently autonomous structure. This sundering (both real and apparent) is crucial to the stability of capitalism. The statement that 'that's the way things are' presupposes that separation. The separation of constitution and existence is the closure of radical alternatives.[16]

VI

The separation of doing from done and the transformation of doing into being (identity) that it implies is the core not only of the rigidification of time but also of the disintegration of every aspect of social relations. If the social flow of doing is what braids people's lives together, if it is the material formation of a 'we', then the fracturing of the collective doing which capitalism involves pulls the braid apart, tears the individual strands of the braid one from another. If the flow of doing implies community, a community across time and space, then the breaking of that flow dismembers all possibility of community.

The breaking of the collective flow of doing brings with it the individualisation of the doers. For the exchange of commodities to take place, both the commodities and their producers must be abstracted from the collectivity of doing:

> In order that this alienation [of commodities] may be reciprocal, it is only necessary for men, by a tacit understanding, to treat each other as private owners of those alienable objects, and by implication as independent individuals. But such a state of reciprocal independence has no existence in a primitive society based on property in common ... [Marx 1965, p. 87]

The starting-point for thought becomes not the person-as-part-of-the-community but the individual as a person with his[17] own distinct identity. Community can thenceforth be imagined only as the aggregation of discrete individuals, the putting together of beings rather than the flow of doings.

The individual stands apart from the collectivity. He is separated from his species-being or species-life, as the young Marx puts it. In the bourgeois notion of science, that is, in the notion of science which assumes capitalist society to be permanent, this distancing of the individual from the community is prized as a virtue. The further away the scientist of society stands from the society which he is studying the better. The ideal scientist would be an observer placed on the moon, from where he would be able to analyse society with true objectivity. The collectivity, society, becomes an object, separated from the subject by as great a distance as possible.

In this way of thinking, science and objectivity are regarded as synonymous. To study something scientifically is to study it objectively or, if it is accepted that this is not possible, then the scientist must do his best to aproximate objectivity, to maintain a distance from the object of study. Objectivity here means suppressing our own subjectivity as far as possible: a subjective statement is considered, by definition, to be unscientific. The notion of what is scientific is thus based upon an obvious falsehood, namely the idea that it is possible to express a thought that excludes the thinker. (This does not, of course, mean that a statement that is explicitly subjective is thereby necessarily correct or scientific.)

Identity thus implies a third-person discourse. To write scientifically, we write about things in the third person, as 'it' or 'they': political parties are such and such; Marxism is so and so; Britain is this or that. First-person discourse (I am bored by political parties; we want a better life; above all, we scream) is regarded as unscientific. Study or theory is therefore study *of* something or *about* something, as in: social theory is the study *of* society, that is a book *about* Marxism, today we are going to learn *about* Mexico in the nineteenth century. In each case, the preposition 'of' or 'about' marks a separation or distance between the student or theorist and the object of study.[18] 'Knowledge about' is quite simply the other side of 'power-over'. The best students or theorists of society are those who can view society as though they stood outside it. (Students who find this pretence difficult often have problems in getting their work recognised, although, again, this does not mean that first-person discourse is thereby correct.) Theory, then, is what the word 'theory' (from θεω, I view) suggests: a viewing or contemplation of an external object. The subject is present, but as a viewer, as a passive rather than an active subject, as a de-subjectified subject, in short as an objectified subject. If we write *about* 'it', then the only way in which we may appear scientifically is as viewer (*voyeur*).[19] Then, precisely because the theory is seen as existing separately from the theorist, it is seen as something that can be 'applied' to the world.

The third person of which we speak is a third-person present indicative. What is important in thought that takes identity as its basis is things as they *are*, not things as they might be or as we wish they were. There is no room for the subjunctive in the scientific discourse of identitarian thought. If *we* are excluded, then our dreams and wishes and fears are excluded too. The subjunctive mood, the mood of uncertainties, anxieties, longings, possibilities, the mood of the not yet, has no place in the world of objectivity. The language of the world of 'that's-the-way-things-are' is firmly in the indicative mood.

The breaking of the social flow of doing implies, then, that I (no longer the vague 'we') as a social scientist abstract from my feelings and my position in society and try to understand society as it is. Society presents itself to me as a mass of particulars, a multitude of discrete phenomena. I proceed by trying to *define* the particular phenomena that I want to study and then seeking the connection between those defined phenomena.

Identity implies definition. Once the flow of doing is fractured, once social relations are fragmented into relations between discrete things, then a knowledge which takes that fragmentation for granted can only proceed through defining, delimiting each thing, each phenomenon, each person or group of people. Knowledge proceeds through definition: something is known if it can be defined. What is politics? What is sociology? What is economics? What is a political party? What is Marxism? The introductory questions to study in schools or universities are typically *definitional* questions. Postgraduate theses typically begin with a definition or delimitation of the object of study. Definition is the description of an identity which is distinct from other identities. Definition aims to delimit identities in a non-contradictory manner: if I define x, it does not make any sense, from a definitional perspective, to say that x is both x and non-x. Definition fixes social relations in their static, fragmented, reified is-ness. A definitional world is a clean world, a world of clear divisions, a world of exclusion, a world in which the other is clearly separated as other. Definition constitutes otherness. The definition of x constitutes non-x as other. If I define myself as English, then I am not Irish; if I define myself as white, then I am not black; if I define myself as Aryan, then I am not Jewish. The Irish, the blacks, the Jews are Others, not-Us. A whole world of horror is contained in the process of definition.

Definition excludes *us* as active subjects. The 'we' who started this book, the still unexplored 'we' who want to change the world, are excluded from a definitional view of the world. When we define something, we normally define it as separate from us. Definition constitutes that which is defined as an object, as an object which, by its definition, is separated from the subject. It is no different when 'we' are defined, as in 'we are women' or 'we are the working class': the definition delimits us, denies our active subjectivity (at least in relation to that which is defined), objectifies us. The we-who-want-to-change-the-world cannot be defined.[20]

The world of identity is a world of particulars, individualised and atomised. The table is a table, the chair is a chair, Britain is Britain, Mexico is Mexico. Fragmentation is fundamental to identitarian thought. The world is a fragmented world. A world of absolute identity is thereby also a world of absolute difference. Knowledge of the world is equally fragmented, into the distinct disciplines. Study *of* society takes place through sociology, political science, economics, history, anthropology, and so on, with all their distinct sub-disciplines and endless specialisations, which rest in turn on fragmented concepts of space (Britain, Mexico, Spain), time (the nineteenth century, the 1990s) and social activity (the economy, the political system).

VII

But what is beyond this fragmentation? A world composed purely of particulars would be impossible to conceptualise and impossible to inhabit. The fracturing of doing is the fracturing of sociality, but some sort of sociality is necessary, both conceptually and practically. The sociality is no longer a communal braiding of doing, more a lumping together of particulars into the same bag, much as potatoes in a sack might be said to form a collectivity, to adapt Marx's famous description of the peasants as a class.[21] Collectivities are formed on the basis of identity, on the basis of being, rather than on the movement of doing. This is the process of classification. Doing may well be part of the process of classification, but it is a dead doing, doing that is contained within an identity, within a role or character-mask: classification of doctors as a group, say, is based not on the weaving together of their doing, but on their definition as a certain type of doer, on the imposition of a character-mask as doctor. Classes in this sense are always more or less arbitrary: any collection of identities can be thrown into a sack together, sub-divided into smaller bags, put together into larger containers, and so on.

It is the fracturing of doing that, through definition and classification, constitutes collective identities. It is the fracturing of doing that creates the idea that people *are* something – whatever, doctors, professors, Jews, blacks, women – as though that identity excluded its simultaneous negation. From the perspective of doing, people simultaneously are and are not doctors, Jews, women, and so on, simply because doing implies a constant movement against-and-beyond whatever we are. From the perspective of doing, definition can be no more than an evanescent positing of identity which is immediately transcended.[22] The barrier between what one is and what one is not, between collective self and collective other cannot therefore be seen as fixed or absolute. It is only if one takes identity as one's standpoint, only if one starts from the acceptance of the rupture of doing, that labels such as 'black', 'Jewish', 'Irish', and so on, take on the character of something fixed. The idea of an 'identity' politics which takes such labels as given inevitably contributes to the fixation of identities. The appeal to being, to identity, to what one *is*, always involves the consolidation of identity, the strengthening, therefore, of the fracturing of doing, in short, the reinforcement of capital.[23]

As long as one remains within the concept of identity, then, it makes little difference whether one thinks of that identity as woman or man, black or white, gay or heterosexual, Irish or English. This does not mean, however, that these categories are symmetrical, that the struggles of blacks can simply be treated as equivalent to the struggles of whites, or that the women's movement is the same as a men's movement. The distinction cannot be made on the basis of identity: it would be nonsensical to say there are good identities and bad identities. The distinction lies rather in the fact that there are many situations in which an apparently affirmative, identitarian statement carries a negative, anti-identitarian charge. To say 'I am black' in a society characterised by discrimination against blacks is to challenge the society in a way in which to say 'I am white' in those same societies clearly does not: despite its affirmative, identitarian form, it is a negative, anti-identitarian statement. To say 'we are indigenous' in a society that systematically denies the dignity of the indigenous is a way of asserting dignity, of negating the negation of dignity, of saying 'we are indigenous and more than that'. The negative charge of such statements, however, cannot be understood in a fixed manner: it depends on the particular situation and is always fragile. To say 'I am Jewish' in Nazi Germany is not the same as saying 'I am Jewish' in contemporary Israel; to say 'I am black' in apartheid South Africa is not the same as saying it in post-apartheid South Africa. There is a tension in such positive-negative statements, a tension in which the positive constantly threatens to engulf the negative. Thus, for example, the nationalism of the oppressed (anti-imperialist nationalism), although it may aim at radical social transformation, is easily diverted from its broader aims into simply replacing 'their' capitalists with 'ours', as the history of anti-colonial movements makes clear. Alternatively, of course, the positive-negative tension may also explode in the opposite direction, into an explicitly anti-identitarian movement, as is currently the case of the Zapatista movement in Mexico.

Classification, the formation of collective identities on the basis of definition, is, of course, not just of immediately political relevance. It is fundamental to the scientific procedure as it is conceived in capitalist society.[24] It is the core of formal abstraction – the attempt to conceptualise the world on the basis of static and non-contradictory categories, rather than on the basis of movement and contradiction (substantive or determinate abstraction) (see Gunn, 1987b, 1992; Bonefeld, 1987, 1992). Formal abstraction, abstraction on the basis of identity in other words, is the basis of all the methods and procedures which are recognised as scientific in our institutions of teaching and learning.

Through classification, conceptual hierarchies are formed. Particulars are ordered under universals, universals under higher universals, and so on. This is a desk chair; the desk chair is an upright chair; the upright chair is a chair; the chair is a piece of furniture. A hierarchy of species and genera is established: a desk chair is a species, or type, or form, or class, of upright chair. The hierarchical ordering of concepts is at the same time a process of formalisation: the concept of chair (or furniture) becomes increasingly separated from any particular content. Lips touch in a kiss; a bullet flies towards the victim. Both the touching of the lips and the flying of the bullet are forms of motion. We can speak of the motion of both in a way that abstracts completely from the different contents of kissing and killing.

Formalisation, the abstraction from content, makes possible the quantification and mathematisation of the object of study.[25] Once lip-touching and bullet-flying are classified as forms of motion, it becomes possible to compare them quantitatively by comparing the speed with which the different objects move. In quantification all content is left behind: lips and bullet are brought together on the unassailable assumption that $1=1$, $2=2$, $3=3$, and so on.

Quantification, however, is just one aspect of the way in which mathematics develops the formal abstraction which is inherent in identification. If x is x and y is y, then the only way in which we can bring them into relation with each other is formally, by abstracting from their particular content. If we classify John and Jane as people, we do so not by denying their particular identities (John remains John, Jane remains Jane), but by abstracting from them, by leaving aside their particular contents as John or Jane and focusing on their formal equivalence as people. Formal abstraction is at the same time homogenisation: in identitarian thought one person is equal to another in the same homogeneous way that one tick of time is equal to another, one square metre of space is equal to another. Once particularities are left behind, it is possible to develop a formal reasoning which aims at making the whole structure of identification and classification as rigorous, orderly and non-contradictory as possible. Formal logic[26] and mathematics start from the simple identity $x=x$ and develop its implications to the highest degree possible. If x is not x, if x is both x and not-x, then the basis of mathematics is undermined. The mutual exclusion of x and non-x is expressed most clearly in binary logic (Boolean algebra), in which everything is expressed as 1 or 0, True or False, Yes or No. There is no room here for the yes-and-no or maybe of common experience.[27]

The separation of doing from done which is the basis of fetishism or reification thus involves an increasing formalisation of social relations and a corresponding formalisation of thought. In the course of the Enlightenment, the philosophical accompaniment to the establishment of capitalist social relations, reason becomes increasingly formalised. Where previously the notion of reason had been related to the pursuit of the good or the true, it now becomes progressively limited to the establishment of the formally correct. Truth is reduced to 'formally correct': beyond that, truth is seen as a matter of subjective judgement. What is formally correct can be seen as a mathematical problem which abstracts entirely from the content of the matter. The tendency of theory is 'towards a purely mathematical system of symbols' (Horkheimer 1972, p. 190). In this

... increasingly formalistic universality of reason ... value judgement has nothing to do with reason and science. It is regarded as a matter of subjective preference whether one decides for liberty or obedience, democracy or fascism, enlightenment or authority, mass culture or truth. [Horkheimer 1978b, p. 31]

Reason is separated from understanding, thought from being. Reason becomes a matter of efficiency, 'the optimum adaptation of means to ends' (Horkheimer 1978b, p. 28). Reason, in other words, becomes instrumental reason, a means to achieve an end rather than a scrutiny or critique of the end itself. Reification involves the loss of meaning, or rather meaning becomes the purely formal process of measuring means to an end. Nuclear destruction is the outcome of rational thought. It is when judged by such rationality that our scream appears irrational.

The formalisation of reason is at the same time the separation of what is from what ought to be. Rational thought is now concerned with what is and its rational (efficient) ordering. This means not the elimination of 'ought' but its separation from 'is': what is is one thing and what ought to be another. Most people would agree that there ought to be no children forced to live on the streets, but (so the argument goes) the reality is different. The study of society, whether it be sociology, politics, economics or whatever 'discipline' of social science, is the study of what *is*. The question of what ought to be may be interesting too, but we must not blur the distinction between the two, we must not confuse reality with dreams. As long as they are kept separate, there is no problem. Moralistic reasoning about what ought to be, far from undermining what is, actually reinforces it:

> the 'ought' presupposes an existing reality to which the category of 'ought' remains *inapplicable* in principle. Whenever the refusal of the subject simply to accept his empirically given existence takes the form of an 'ought', this means that the immediately given empirical reality receives affirmation and consecration at the hands of philosophy: it is philosophically immortalised. [Lukács 1971, p. 160]

To the extent that there really is a formal abstraction of social relations, those relations can be understood as being governed by laws, and it becomes possible to speak of the 'laws of capitalist development'. The owners of capital do not control capitalist society. Rather, they too are subject to the laws of capitalist development, laws which reflect the separation of the doer from the doing, the autonomy of the doing. The most that people can do is adapt themselves to these 'laws' which they do not control:

> man in capitalist society confronts a reality 'made' by himself (as a class) which appears to him to be a natural phenomenon alien to himself; he is wholly at the mercy of its 'laws', his activity is confined to the exploitation of the inexorable fulfilment of certain individual laws for his own (egoistic) interests. But even while 'acting' he remains, in the nature of the case, the object and not the subject of events. [Lukács 1971, p. 135]

Freedom, in this context, becomes simply knowledge of and subordination to the laws, the acceptance of necessity.[28] The law-bound
nature of capitalist society, then, and the possibility of the scientific
study of these laws is nothing other than an expression of the fact
that doers do not control their doing and that 'all human relations
... assume increasingly the objective forms of the abstract elements
of the conceptual systems of natural science and of the abstract
substrata of the laws of nature' (Lukács, 1971, p. 131).

VIII

The argument could go on and on. The point is that at the basis of
an immensely complex social structure lies a simple principle –
identity. The principle of identity is so basic to capitalist social organisation that to underline its importance seems absolutely
meaningless, simply because it seems so obvious. And yet it is not so
obvious. The idea that someone *is* x without the simultaneous realisation that she *is not* x is rooted in something that is very far from
obvious: namely, the daily repeated separation of done from doing,
the daily repeated seizure from the doers of the product of their
doing and its definition as the property of someone else. This very
real, very material identification (this thing is mine, not yours)
spreads like a crack into every aspect of our social organisation and
every aspect of our consciousness.

Identity is the antithesis of mutual recognition, of community,
friendship and love.[29] If I say that 'I am *x*', it implies that my being
x does not depend on anyone else, that it does not depend on
anyone else's recognition. I stand alone, my relations with other
people are quite peripheral to my being. Social recognition is
something that stands outside me, something that comes through
the market when I can sell my product or sell my own capacity to do
things at a higher price (promotion, for example). Other people are
just that, other. Seen through the prism of identity, relations between
people are external. As Bublitz (1998, pp. 34ff) points out in her
discussion of Aristotle, friendship and love are impossible to conceptualise on the basis of a formal logic of identity. There can be no
mutual recognition, no recognition of ourselves in others, of others
in ourselves. From an identitarian perspective, the 'we' with which
we started can be no more than an arbitrary sack of potatoes, or else
a false (and threatening) chumminess with no real basis. There is no

room there for the mutual inter-penetration of existence which we experience as friendship or love. Enmity, on the other hand, is easy to understand: the other is the other. The other is not part of us and we are not part of the other.[30]

It is clear that the process of identification is not external to us. We are active in the process of identifying or reifying social relations, just as we are active in producing the done which is turned against our doing. There is no innocent subject. Power-over reaches into us and transforms us, forcing us to participate actively in its reproduction. The rigidification of social relations, the that's-the-way-things-are-ness that confronts our scream is not just outside us (in society), but reaches into us as well, into the way that we think, the way we act, the way we are, the fact that we are. In the process of being separated from our done and from our doing, we ourselves are damaged. Our activity is transformed into passivity, our will to do things is transformed into greed for money, our cooperation with fellow-doers is transformed into an instrumental relation mediated by money or competition. The innocence of our doing, of our power-to, becomes a guilty participation in the exercise of power-over. Our estrangement from doing is a self-estrangement. Here is no pure, eager revolutionary subject, but damaged humanity. We are all deeply involved in the construction of identitarian reality, and this process is the construction of ourselves.

The reality that confronts us reaches into us. What we scream against is not just out there, it is also inside us. It seems to invade all of us, to become us. That is what makes our scream so anguished, so desperate. That too is what makes our scream seem so hopeless. At times it seems that our scream itself is the only fissure of hope. Reality, the reality of capital, seems completely inescapable. As Marcuse puts it:

> ... the unfree individual introjects his masters and their commands into his own mental apparatus. The struggle against freedom reproduces itself in the psyche of man, as the self-repression of the repressed individual, and his self-repression in turn sustains his masters and their institutions. [1998, p. 16]

This introjection of our masters is the introjection of an identitarian, alienated reality (theorised by Freud as an absolute, biologically determined reality rather than a historically specific form of reality), to which we subordinate our pursuit of pleasure.[31]

Reification, therefore, refers not just to the rule of the object but to the creation of a peculiarly dislocated subject. The separation of doer from doing and done creates a doer who is cut adrift from doing, who is subordinate to the done, but appears to be completely independent of it. The separation of people from the social tapestry of doing constitutes them as free individuals, free not only in the double sense indicated by Marx, namely free from personal bondage and free of access to the means of survival, but free also from responsibility to the community and free from a sense of meaningful participation in the collective doing. While our discussion has shown that the fracture of doing means that the subject too is fractured (alienated, anguished, damaged), the subject of bourgeois theory is an innocent, healthy, freely self-determining individual: admittedly, certain individuals have psychological problems, but they are just personal problems, nothing to do with the social schizophrenia that cuts through every aspect of our existence. The more subordination to the done is taken for granted, the more free the individual subject appears. The more thoroughly identification is established as something that is simply beyond question, beyond thought, the freer the society appears. The more profoundly unfree we are, the more liberated we appear to be. The illusory freedom of the citizen is the counterpart of the illusory community of the state. We live in a free society, don't we? No wonder our scream is so violent.

We have, then, two concepts of the subject. The subject of bourgeois theory is the free individual, whereas the subjectivity that has been central to our account is a collective subjectivity rent asunder by the tearing of doing from done, an atomised subject damaged to our depths. The subject of bourgeois theory does not scream, while our subject screams to high heaven, not because of any particularity, just because of our sundered subjectivity. For bourgeois theory, subjectivity is identity, whereas in our argument, subjectivity is the negation of identity.

There is no doubt that the first concept, that of the innocent, wholesome, subject, has often been transferred by some currents in Marxist theory to the notion of the working class. Soviet images of the heroic working class come to mind, but the image of the heroic revolutionary goes far beyond the Soviet experience. It is in this context that it becomes possible to understand the concern of some theorists (structuralists, post-structuralists, postmodernists) to attack the notion of the subject. Much of what is seen as an attack on subjectivity is simply an attack on identity, on the bourgeois identification of subjectivity with identity. Thus, for example, when Foucault speaks of (and analyses in detail) the 'immense work to which the West has set generations to produce ... the subjection of men; I mean their constitution as "subjects" in both senses of the word' (1990, p. 60), then this is surely correct in relation to the constitution of the 'free' subject of capitalist society, who is indeed subject in both senses of the word. To identify the bourgeois subject with subjectivity as a whole, however, is a most murderous throwing of the baby out with the bathwater. To confound subjectivity with identity and criticise subjectivity in an attempt to attack identity leads only to a total impasse, since subjectivity, as movement, as negation of is-ness, is the only possible basis for going beyond identity, and therefore beyond the bourgeois subject.[32]

IX

The fetish is a real illusion. Marx, as we saw, insists that in a commodity-producing society, 'the relations connecting the labour of one individual with that of the rest appear, not as direct social relations between individuals at work, but as what they really are, material relations between persons and social relations between things' (1965, p. 73). The fetishised categories of thought express a really fetishised reality. If we see theory as a moment of practice and thinking as a moment of doing, then there is a continuity between the fetishisation of thought and the fetishisation of practice. Fetishisation (and hence alienation, reification, identification, and so on) refer not just to processes of thinking but to the material separation of done from doing of which those conceptual processes are part. It follows that fetishisation cannot be overcome in thought alone: the overcoming of fetishisation means the overcoming of the separation of doing and done.

This is important because the concept of fetishism (alienation, and so on) loses its force if it is separated from the material separation of doing and done in which it is founded. Fetishisation is central to the material process by which the done is torn from the doer. If a separation is made between the material process of exploitation and the fetishisation of thought, then alienation or fetishisation becomes reduced to a tool of cultural critique, a sophisticated moan. This is indeed, as Adorno points out (1990, p. 190), to make 'critical theory idealistically acceptable to the reigning consciousness and to the collective unconscious'.[33] It is to reproduce in the concept of fetishisation itself precisely that separation of 'economic' and 'cultural' which the concept of fetishism criticises.

The violence of identification, then, is by no means merely conceptual. The scientific method of identitarian thought is the exercise of power-over. Power is exercised over people through their effective identification.[34] Thus, capitalist production is based on identification: this is mine. Law too is based on identity: the person subjected to legal process is identified, separated off from all those others who might be considered as co-responsible in some way. The identification is expressed very physically: in the handcuffs that identify the person as accused of a crime, in the treatment of the person as an identified individual, in the physical enclosure in a prison or a cell, possibly in execution, that supreme act of identification which says 'you are and have been, and shall not become'. Is-ness, identity, the denial of becoming, is death.

Identification, definition, classification is a physical as well as a mental process. The Jews who were identified, classified and numbered in the concentration camps were the objects of more than a mental exercise. Identification, definition, classification is the basis of the physical, spatial and temporal organisation of armies, hospitals, schools and other institutions, the core of what Foucault refers to as discipline, the micro-physics of power, the political economy of detail (see especially Foucault 1990). Bureaucratic power is based on the same process of identification and classification, as indeed is the whole operation of the state. The state identifies people, defines them, classifies them. A state is inconceivable without the definition of citizens and the simultaneous exclusion of non-citizens: 856,000 Mexicans were detained on the frontier with the United States in the last six months.[35] That is identification, definition, classification on a grand scale.

X

The argument of this chapter has taken us forward in our understanding of power, but we are left with a depressing dilemma.

It should be clear now that power cannot be taken, for the simple reason that power is not possessed by any particular person or institution. Power lies rather in the fragmentation of social relations. This is a material fragmentation which has its core in the constantly repeated separation of the done from the doing, which involves the real mediation of social relations through things, the real transformation of relations between people into relations between things. Our practical intercourse is fragmented and, with it and as part of it, our patterns of thought, the way we think and talk about social relations. In thought and in practice, the warm interweaving of doing, the loves and hates and longings which constitute us, become shattered into so many identities, so many cold atoms of existence, standing each one on its own. Power-over, that which makes our scream echo hollowly, that which makes radical change difficult even to conceive, lies in this shattering, in identification.

The state, then, is not the locus of power that it appears to be. It is just one element in the shattering of social relations. The state, or rather the states, define us as 'citizens' and 'non-citizens', giving us national identities in what is one of the most directly murderous aspects of the process of identification. How many millions of people were killed in the twentieth century for no other reason than that they were defined as being nationals of a particular state? How many millions of people did the killing for the same reason? How many times has the scream against oppression been diverted into the assertion of national identity in national liberation movements which have done little more than reproduce the oppression against which the scream was directed? The state is exactly what the word suggests, a bulwark against change, against the flow of doing, the embodiment of identity.[36]

The understanding of power as the fragmenting of social relations takes us back again to Foucault's attack on the binary concept of power and his insistence that power must be understood in terms of a multiplicity of forces. It should now be clear that the dichotomy between a binary and a multiple view of power is a false one. The multiplicity of power relations derives precisely from the binary antagonism between doing and done. To reduce this complexity to a simple binary antagonism between capitalist class and proletariat, as has often been done, leads to both theoretical and political problems. Similarly, to focus on the multiplicity and forget the underlying unity of power relations leads to a loss of political perspective: emancipation becomes impossible to conceive, as Foucault is at pains to point out. Moreover to focus on a multiplicity of identities without asking as to the process of identification which gives rise to those identities is inevitably to reproduce those identities, that is, to participate actively in the process of identification. It is essential, then, to insist on the unity-in-separation, separation-in-unity of the binary and the multiple.

We are left with a dilemma. The power of capital is all-penetrating. It shapes the way in which we perceive the world, our sexuality, our very constitution as individual subjects, our ability to say 'I'. There seems to be no way out. 'Absolute reification ... is now preparing to absorb the mind entirely', as Adorno (1967, p. 34) puts it.[37] And absolute reification is absolute death. Identity negates possibility, denies openness to other life. Identity kills, both metaphorically and very, very literally. Over all our reflections on identity stands the terrible warning of Adorno: 'Auschwitz confirmed the philosopheme of pure identity as death' (1990, p. 362).

The more we think about power in capitalist society, the more anguished our scream becomes. But the more anguished it becomes, the more desperate, the more helpless. The penetration of power-over into the core of those who are subject to that power-over is the central problem that any revolutionary theory has to deal with. The reaching of the separation of doing and done into the doer herself is both the reason why revolution is desperately urgent and the reason why it is increasingly difficult to conceive. The maiming of the subject through the penetration of power-over into the depths of her existence stirs both indignation and resignation: how can we live in a society based on dehumanisation? But how can we possibly change a society in which people are so dehumanised? This is the dilemma of the urgent impossibility of revolution.

There are three possible ways out of the dilemma.

The first is to give up hope. Instead of thinking that it might be possible to create a society free of exploitation, free of war, free of violence, an emancipated society based on mutual recognition, this approach accepts that the world cannot be changed radically and focuses instead on living as well as can be and making whatever small changes may be possible. Alienation is recognised, perhaps, but regarded as being permanent.[38] The concepts of revolution and emancipation are abandoned and replaced with the idea of 'micro-politics'. The multiplicity of power comes to be seen as the underpinning of a multiplicity of struggles focused on particular issues or particular identities: struggles which aim at a rearrangement but not an overcoming of power relations.

Disillusionment is associated most commonly with postmodern theory and politics,[39] but it spreads much further than that. In other cases, the notion of revolution may be retained as a point of reference, but left-wing discourse becomes more melancholic, more and more focused on denouncing the horrors of capitalism and more and more removed from considering the possibility of a solution. Left-wing intellectuals adopt the position of Cassandra, prophesying the doom that is to come, but with little hope of being heard.

The melancholic Cassandras and the postmodernists may, of course, be quite right. Perhaps there is no hope, perhaps there is no possibility of creating a society that is not based on exploitation and dehumanisation. It may well be that when humanity finally destroys itself in a nuclear blast or otherwise, the last postmodernist will be able to say with glee to the last hopeful Marxist, 'You see, I told you so, now you can see that my approach was scientifically correct.' It may well be so, but it does not help us very much. The scream with which we started announced an obstinate refusal to give up hope, a refusal to accept that the miseries and inhumanities of capitalism are inevitable. From the perspective of the scream, then, giving up hope is simply not an option.

The second possible option is to forget the subtleties and focus exclusively on the binary nature of the antagonism between proletariat and capitalist class. Power, then, is quite simply a matter of 'who-whom', as the Leninist phrase has it.

In the mainstream Marxist tradition, fetishism has always been a rather suspect category, a mark of heterodoxy. It has always arisen as a critique of the 'scientificity' which defined Marxist orthodoxy, and which was upheld by the Communist Parties during the first two thirds of the twentieth century and continues to dominate much of Marxist discussion today. Especially during the reign of the Communist Parties, emphasis on the question of fetishism always had something of the character of 'anti-Marxist Marxism', with all the dangers of political or physical exclusion that that implied. Lukács's book, *History and Class Consciousness*, caused him serious political problems within the Communist Party when it was published in 1923. The tensions that exist already in his work between the consistency of his criticism and his loyalty to the Party led him in practice to give priority to the Party and to denounce his own work. Other authors who suffered even more seriously for their attempt to return to Marx's concern with fetishism and form were I.I. Rubin and Evgeny Pashukanis, both of them working in Russia just after the revolution. Rubin, in his *Essays on Marx's Theory of Value*, first published in 1924, insisted on the centrality of commodity fetishism and the concept of form for Marx's critique of political economy. One of the implications of this insistence on the question of form was to underline the specifically capitalist character of value relations, and as a result Rubin disappeared during the purges of the 1930s. A similar fate was shared by Pashukanis who, in his *General Theory of Law and Marxism*, argued that Marx's critique of political economy should be extended to the critique of law and the state, that law and the state should be understood as fetishised forms of social relations in the same way as value, capital and the other categories of political economy. This meant that law and the state, like value, were specifically capitalist forms of social relations. At a time when the Soviet state was consolidating itself, this argument did not find favour with the Party authorities.

Orthodox Marxism has generally preferred a simpler picture of power, in which the taking of state power has been central to the concept of revolutionary change. In a later chapter we shall examine in more detail this tradition and some of the problems associated with it.

The third possible approach to solving the dilemma of the urgent impossibility of revolution is to accept that there can be absolutely no certainty of a happy ending, but nevertheless to look for hope in the nature of capitalist power itself. Ubiquitous power implies ubiquitous resistance. Ubiquitous yes implies ubiquitous no. Power-over, we have seen, is the negation of power-to, the denial of the social flow of doing. Power-to exists in the form of its negation, power-over. The social flow of doing exists in the form of its negation, individual performance. Doing exists in the form of labour, community in the form of a mass of individuals, non-identity in the form of identity, human relations in the form of relations between things, lived time in the form of clock time, the subjunctive in the form of the indicative, humanity in the form of inhumanity. All of those different expressions of human emancipation, all those images of a society based on the mutual recognition of human dignity, all exist only in the form of their negation. But they exist. It is to the force of that which exists in the form of being denied that we must look for hope. That is the stuff of dialectical thought: dialectics is the 'consistent sense of non-identity', the sense of the explosive force of that which is denied.

What is the status, then, of all of these categories that exist only in the form of being denied? Certainly they are not recognised by mainstream social science: for mainstream social science, there is absolutely no room for that which exists in the form of being denied.

Are they then a mere chimera, mere fancies of discontented intellectuals, a romantic harking back to a mythical golden age? No, they are none of those. They are hopes, aspirations, prefigurations of a human society. But for these hopes to have force, we must understand them also as substratum, as that without which their denial could not exist, as that upon which their negating forms depend.

The third approach is to try to understand and thereby to participate in the force of all that which exists in antagonism, in the form of being denied.

5   Fetishism and Fetishisation

The focus on fetishism does not in itself resolve all theoretical and political problems. As we saw in the previous chapter, fetishism leaves us with the dilemma of the urgent impossibility of revolution.

Fetishism is a theory of the negation of our power-to-do. It draws attention both to the process of negation and to that which is negated. In most cases, however, discussions of fetishism have focused on the negation rather than on the presence of that which is negated. In order to find a way beyond our theoretical impasse, we have to open up the concept of fetishism, to try and discover in the concepts themselves that which the concepts deny.

The emphasis on one or other moment of the antagonism between negation and negated is connected with differences in the understanding of fetishism. There are, in other words, two different ways of understanding fetishism, which we can refer to as 'hard fetishism' on the one hand, and 'fetishisation-as-process', on the other. The former understands fetishism as an established fact, a stable or intensifying feature of capitalist society. The latter understands fetishisation as a continuous struggle, always at issue. The theoretical and political implications of the two approaches are very different.

The more common approach among those who have emphasised the concept of fetishism is the 'hard fetishism' approach. Fetishism is assumed to be an accomplished fact. In a capitalist society, social relations really do exist as relations between things. Relations between subjects really do exist as relations between objects. Although people are, in their species-characteristic, practical creative beings, they exist under capitalism as objects, as dehumanised, as deprived of their subjectivity.

The constitution or genesis of capitalist social relations is here understood as a historical constitution, something that took place in the past. Implicitly, a distinction is made between the origins of capitalism, when capitalist social relations were established through struggle (what Marx refers to as primitive or original accumulation), and the established capitalist mode of production, when capitalist social relations are in place. In the latter phase, fetishism is assumed to be stably established. In this view, the importance of Marx's insistence on form is simply to show the historicity of capitalist social relations. Within this historicity, within the capitalist mode of production, fetishised social relations can be regarded as basically stable. Thus, for example, the transition from feudalism to capitalism involved a struggle to impose value relations, but it is assumed that, once the transition has been accomplished, value is a stable form of social relations. Value is seen as struggle only in relation to the transitional period; after that it is regarded as simply domination, or as part of the laws which determine the reproduction of capitalist society.[1]

Similarly with all other categories: if the reification of social relations is understood as stable, then all the forms of existence of those social relations (and their interrelation) will also be understood as stable, and their development will be understood as the unfolding of a closed logic. Thus, money, capital, the state and so on may be understood as reified forms of social relations, but they are not seen as forms of active reification. These categories are understood as 'closed' categories, in the sense of developing according to a self-contained logic.

What happens here is that identity creeps in again through the back door just when we thought we had finally got rid of it. The whole point of talking of fetishism is to undermine the apparently insuperable rigidity of social relations under capitalism by showing that these rigidities (money, state, and so on) are merely historically specific forms of social relations, the products of social doing and changeable by social doing. However, if one assumes that these forms were established at the dawn of capitalism and shall remain until capitalism is overcome, rigidity is reintroduced. The 'capitalist mode of production' becomes an overriding arch, a circle that defines. We know that the capitalist mode of production is historically transient, but within its confines relations are sufficiently reified for us to understand their development in terms of law-bound interactions between the fetishised phenomena. Instability is implicitly banished to the outer reaches of capitalism, to the temporal, spatial and social margins: to the period of primitive accumulation, the few areas of the world where capitalism is not yet fully established, and those who are marginalised from the social process of production. The core of capitalism is an increasingly reified world: away from the margins, capitalism *is*.

The hard fetishism approach involves a fetishisation of fetishism: fetishism itself becomes a rigidified and rigidifying concept. The idea that the fetishisation of social relations took place at the origins of capitalism, the idea that value, capital, and so on, are forms of social relations which were established on a stable basis a few hundred years ago, is inevitably based on the separation of constitution and existence: capital was constituted hundreds of years ago, now it exists, one day it will be destroyed. The time between constitution and destruction is a time of duration, a time of identity, a homogenised time. The understanding of fetishism as accomplished fact involves an identification of the fetishised forms.[2] It is as though those who criticise the homogenisation of time have themselves fallen into that homogenisation, simply by assuming fetishism as accomplished fact.

There is a central problem for those who understand fetishism as accomplished fact. If social relations are fetishised, how do we criticise them? Who are we who criticise? Are we on the margins, privileged perhaps by our insights as marginalised intellectuals? The hard understanding of fetishism implies that there is something special about *us*, something that gives us a vantage point above the rest of society. *They* are alienated, fetishised, reified, suffering from false consciousness; *we* are able to see the world from the point of view of the totality, or true consciousness, or superior understanding. Our criticism derives from our special position or experience or intellectual abilities, which allow us to understand how *they* (the masses) are dominated. We are implicitly an intellectual elite, a vanguard of some sort. The only possible way of changing society is through *our* leadership of *them*, through *our* enlightening *them*. If fetishism is something stable and fixed within capitalism, then we are back with the Leninist problematic of how we lead the fetishised masses to revolution. The hard concept of fetishism leads to the obvious dilemma: if people exist as objects under capitalism, then how is revolution conceivable? How is criticism possible?

III

The author who has grappled most resolutely with the problem of the critical-revolutionary subject is undoubtedly Lukács, in his *History and Class Consciousness*.

Lukács's attempt to solve the question is based, first, on a distinction of class, between the bourgeoisie and the proletariat. Both bourgeoisie and proletariat exist in a reified world, but for the bourgeoisie, there is no way out. There is nothing in their class position which would drive them beyond the world of reification, for the perspective of totality, which is inevitably a historical perspective, would be suicidal, since it would reveal to them the transitory nature of their own class.

In relation to reification, the position of the working class is, in the first place, no different from that of the bourgeoisie:

> For the proletariat makes its appearance as the product of the capitalist social order. The forms in which it exists are ... the repositories of reification in its acutest and direst form and they issue in the most extreme dehumanisation. Thus the proletariat shares with the bourgeoisie the reification of every aspect of its life. [1971, p. 149]

The difference between the bourgeoisie and the proletariat is that while the class interests of the bourgeoisie keep it entrapped in reification, the proletariat is driven beyond it:

> This same reality employs the motor of class interests to keep the bourgeoisie imprisoned within this immediacy while forcing the proletariat to go beyond it ... For the proletariat to become aware of the dialectical nature of its existence is a matter of life and death ... [p. 167]

It is the experience of having to sell his labour power as a commodity that makes it possible for the proletarian to breach the fetishised appearances of social relations:

> ... it is true that the worker is objectively transformed into a mere object of the process of production by the methods of capitalist production ... i.e. by the fact that the worker is forced to objectify his labour power over against his total personality and to sell it as a commodity. But because of the split between subjectivity and objectivity induced in man by the compulsion to objectify himself as a commodity, the situation becomes one that can be made conscious. [pp. 167–8]

Or, in other words:

> ... while the process by which the worker is reified and becomes a
> commodity dehumanises him and cripples and atrophies his 'soul'
> – as long as he does not consciously rebel against it – it remains
> true that precisely his humanity and his soul are not changed into
> commodities. [p. 172]

The worker, then, becomes 'aware of himself as a commodity' and,
with that, 'the fetishistic forms of the commodity system begin to
dissolve: in the commodity the worker recognises himself and his
relations with capital' (p. 168).

Lukács's argument here points to the incomplete or, better, self-
contradictory nature of fetishism. The process of objectification
induces a split between the subjectivity and the objectivity of the
worker, between the worker's humanity and his dehumanisation.
The experience of the worker is at once fetishising and de-fetishising.
At this point, Lukács seems to be laying the basis for a theory of
revolution as the self-emancipation of the workers.

Lukács insists, however, that this incipient de-fetishisation is not
sufficient. The consciousness of the worker of himself as a
commodity does not resolve the problem:

> It could easily appear at this point that the whole process is
> nothing more than the 'inevitable' consequence of concentrating
> masses of workers in large factories, of mechanising and standard-
> ising the processes of work and levelling down the standard of
> living. It is therefore of vital importance to see the truth concealed
> behind this one-sided picture ... the fact that this commodity is
> able to become aware of its existence as a commodity does not
> suffice to eliminate the problem. For the unmediated conscious-
> ness of the commodity is, in conformity with the simple form in
> which it manifests itself, precisely an awareness of abstract
> isolation and of the merely abstract relationship – external to con-
> sciousness – to those factors that create it socially. [p. 173]

To solve the problem of the proletarians who need to go beyond
fetishism but are unable to do so, Lukács introduces a distinction
between the empirical or psychological consciousness of the proletariat and the 'imputed' consciousness of the proletariat. The
empirical or psychological consciousness refers to the consciousness

of individual proletarians or of the proletariat as a whole at any given moment. This consciousness, being reified, does not express a true consciousness of the class position of the proletariat. It is characteristic of opportunism that it '*mistakes the actual, psychological state of consciousness of proletarians for the class consciousness of the proletariat*' (p. 74; original emphasis). True class consciousness is 'neither the sum nor the average of what is thought or felt by the single individuals who make up the class' (p. 51). Class consciousness consists rather of the 'appropriate and rational reactions' which can be 'imputed' to the class:

> By relating consciousness to the whole of society it becomes possible to infer the thoughts and feelings which men would have in a particular situation if they were *able* to assess both it and the interests arising from it in their impact on immediate action and on the whole structure of society. That is to say, it would be possible to infer the thoughts and feelings appropriate to their objective situation. [p. 51]

This notion of de-reified class consciousness or the perspective of totality obviously returns us to our original question: who is the critical-revolutionary subject? Who can have this 'imputed' consciousness that is distinct from the psychological consciousness of the proletariat? Lukács resolves this problem by sleight of hand, by bringing in a *deus ex machina*: the bearer of the 'correct class consciousness of the proletariat' is its organised form, the Communist Party (p. 75). And elsewhere: 'The form taken by the class consciousness of the proletariat is the *Party* ... the Party is assigned the sublime role of *bearer of the class consciousness of the proletariat and the consciousness of its historical vocation*' (p. 41; original emphasis).

The Party is drawn out of a hat. Unlike the tight and rigorous argument that characterises the essays as a whole, there is never any explanation of *how* the Party is able to go beyond reification and adopt the perspective of totality. In contrast to the long and detailed argument on the consciousness of the bourgeoisie and of the proletariat, the 'sublime role' of the Party as the 'bearer of class consciousness' is just asserted. It is as though Lukács's reasoning has hit precisely that 'dark and void' space which he saw as the limit to bourgeois rationality.

If the Party is simply drawn out of the hat, however, it is because it is in the hat from the beginning. The answer of the Party is already implicit in the way in which the theoretical problem is set up. From the beginning the whole question of dialectics, of overcoming reification, of class consciousness and of revolution is posed in terms of the category of totality: '... only the dialectical conception of totality can enable us to understand reality as a social process. For only this conception dissolves the fetishistic forms necessarily produced by the capitalist mode of production ...' (p. 13). However, the emphasis on totality immediately poses the question of the Know-All: who is it that can know the totality? Clearly, in a reified world, it cannot be the proletariat itself, so it can only be some Knower who knows *on behalf of* the proletariat. The category of totality already implies the problematic (if not necessarily the answer) of the Party. The whole theoretical construction already sets up the problem in such a way that it can be resolved only by introducing some Hero-figure, some *deus ex machina*. The attempt to combat fetishism leads, because of the way in which fetishism is understood, to the creation (or consolidation) of a new fetish: the idea of a Hero (the Party) which somehow stands above the reified social relations of which, however, it is inevitably a part.

Despite the radical character of his essays, Lukács is operating in a theoretical and political context which is already pre-constituted. His approach is far from the crude 'scientific Marxism' of the Engelsian-Leninist tradition,[3] yet his theoretical-political world is the same. In that tradition, the claim that scientific Marxism (or historical materialism) provides knowledge of reality grows together politically with the notion of the Party as Knower. To operate politically within the Party, as Lukács did for the whole of his life, poses, in its turn, the idea of Marxism as knowledge of reality. The political context and the conception of theory as the 'self-knowledge of reality' are mutually reinforcing (the legitimation of the Party depends on its proclaimed 'knowledge of reality', while the notion of theory as knowledge of reality suggests there has to be a Knower, the Party). It is within this context that Lukács pitches his argument. Curiously, despite its radical emphasis on 'totality', the whole argument takes place within certain parameters, within the framework of certain categories that are not questioned, such as Party, proletariat, economics, Marxism, seizure of power. Thus, although he insists that everything must be understood as process, and that 'the nature of history is precisely that every definition degenerates into an illusion' (p. 186), he nevertheless starts with a definitional question, the first essay being entitled 'What is

Orthodox Marxism?'. Although he sets out in this essay by criticising the Engelsian conception of the dialectic (and, by implication, that of the Engelsian tradition), it remains true that he stays within the realist problematic of Engels, the idea that Marxist theory gives us knowledge of *reality*. With that, the idea that there is a distinction between correctness and falseness is given, and with it the idea of the Party as guardian of that correctness.

That solution, but also that problematic, is historically closed to us now. Whether or not it ever made sense to think of revolutionary change in terms of the 'Party', it is no longer open to us to even pose the questions in those terms. To say now that the Party is the bearer of the class consciousness of the proletariat no longer makes any sense at all. What Party? There no longer exists even the social basis for creating such a 'Party'.

What makes Lukács's work so fascinating, however, are the tensions within it. The very focus on reification places us in an unavoidable field of tension from the beginning simply because talk of reification implicitly poses the question of the coexistence of reification with its antithesis (de- or anti-reification) and the nature of the antagonism and tension between them. This tension creeps into the category of totality itself on several occasions, in the form of the 'aspiration towards totality'. As though to modify the absolutist claims of the perspective of totality, he writes:

> The category of totality begins to have an effect long before the whole multiplicity of objects can be illuminated by it. It operates by ensuring that actions which seem to confine themselves to particular objects, in both content and consciousness, yet preserve an aspiration towards the totality, that is to say: action is directed objectively towards a transformation of totality. [p. 175]

And again:

> ... the relation to totality does not need to become explicit, the plenitude of the totality does not need to be consciously integrated into the motives and objects of action. What is crucial is that there should be an aspiration towards totality, that action should serve the purpose, described above, in the totality of the process. [p. 198]

The notion of the 'aspiration towards totality' potentially dissolves the problem of the Know-All Party: we presumably do not have to be the bearers of true consciousness in order to aspire towards totality.[4] However, the argument is not developed.

The introduction of the 'aspiration towards totality' and the emphasis on the contradictory nature of the reification of the consciousness of the proletariat suggests a rather different politics, in which the proletariat is assigned a more active role in its own emancipation. It is clear that Lukács, although he remained within the Party framework, strained towards a more radical, self-emancipatory conception of politics. Thus, he criticises Engels's notion of revolution as 'the leap from the realm of necessity into the realm of freedom' as undialectical:

> If we separate the 'realm of freedom' sharply from the process which is destined to call it into being, if we thus preclude all dialectical transitions, do we not thereby lapse into a utopian outlook similar to that which has already been analysed in the case of the separation of final goal and the movement towards it? [p. 313]

He defends the Party as a form of organisation on the ground that it involves the active engagement of the total personality:

> ... every human relationship which breaks with this pattern, with this abstraction from the total personality of man and with his subsumption beneath an abstract point of view, is a step in the direction of putting an end to the reification of human consciousness. Such a step, however, presupposes the *active engagement of the total personality*. [p. 319]

Without this, party 'discipline must degenerate into a reified and abstract system of rights and duties and the party will relapse into a state typical of a party on the bourgeois pattern' (p. 320). It is little wonder, then, that the book was condemned by the Soviet authorities in 1924 at the Fifth World Congress of the Comintern; and little wonder too that Lukács repudiated his own argument in the interests of party discipline.

Lukács's discussion of reification has the enormous merit of treating it not only as a theoretical but a political problem, not only as a question of understanding domination but as a matter of thinking about revolution. He failed in his attempt to provide a theoretical and political answer to the revolutionary dilemma, to the 'urgent impossibility of revolution', but at least he focused on the problem. After Lukács, there is a historical falling apart. It becomes clear that there is no place within the Party for the development of critical Marxism, with the result that critical Marxism becomes, on the whole, more and more divorced from the issue of revolution, more and more concerned simply with criticising the all-pervasive character of capitalist domination.

In the writings of those theorists associated with the Frankfurt School, there is the same critical distance from the empirical consciousness or present psychological state of the proletariat, which the concept of fetishism implies. As Horkheimer puts it:

> ... the situation of the proletariat is, in this society, no guarantee of correct knowledge. The proletariat may indeed have experience of meaninglessness in the form of continuing and increasing wretchedness and injustice in its own life. Yet this awareness is prevented from becoming a social force by the differentiation of social structure which is still imposed on the proletariat from above and by the opposition between personal [and] class interests which is transcended only at very special moments. Even to the proletariat the world superficially seems quite different than it really is. [1972, pp. 213–14]

The Party, however, is no longer a significant figure and cannot fulfil the role that it did in Lukács's discussion. Consequently: 'under the conditions of later capitalism and the impotence of the workers before the authoritarian state's apparatus of oppression, truth has sought refuge among small groups of admirable men' (1972, p. 237). Or, as Adorno puts it, in modern society 'criticising privilege becomes a privilege' (1990, p. 41). A privilege and a responsibility:

> ... if a stroke of undeserved luck has kept the mental composition of some individuals not quite adjusted to the prevailing norms – a stroke of luck they have often enough to pay for in their relations with their environment – it is up to these individuals to make the moral and, as it were, representative effort to say what most of those for whom they say it cannot see, or, to do justice to reality, will not allow themselves to see. [1990, p. 41]

In the work of Marcuse, the triumph of fetishism is captured by the title of his most famous work, *One Dimensional Man*. Positive thinking and instrumental rationality have permeated society so absolutely that society has become one-dimensional. Meaningful resistance can only come from the margins, 'the substratum of the outcasts and outsiders, the exploited and persecuted of other races and other colours, the unemployed and unemployable' (1968, p. 200). It is not that this 'substratum' has revolutionary consciousness, but 'their opposition is revolutionary even if their consciousness is not. Their opposition hits the system from without and is therefore not deflected by the system' (p. 200). It is to be understood that the unconscious political practice of the marginalised corresponds in some way to the conscious theoretical practice of the academically marginalised critical theorists.

For all the differences between these authors, the important point for our argument is that the understanding of fetishism as established fact (the emphasis on the all-pervasive character of fetishism in modern capitalism) leads to the conclusion that the only possible source of anti-fetishism lies outside the ordinary – whether it be the Party (Lukács), the privileged intellectuals (Horkheimer and Adorno), or the 'substratum of the outcasts and the outsiders' (Marcuse). Fetishism implies anti-fetishism, but the two are separated: fetishism rules normal, everyday life, while anti-fetishism resides elsewhere, on the margins. If one discounts Lukács's faith in the Party as being now historically irrelevant at best, the result is that the emphasis on fetishism (or the depth of capitalist power) tends to lead to a deep pessimism, to intensify the sense of the urgent impossibility of revolution. To break with this pessimism, we need a concept in which fetishism and anti-fetishism are not separated. To develop the concept of fetishism today inevitably means trying to go beyond the classic authors on fetishism, in this respect at least.

IV

The second approach, what we called the 'fetishisation-as-process' approach, maintains that there is nothing special about our criticism of capitalism, that our scream and our criticism are perfectly ordinary, that the most we can do as intellectuals is to give voice to that which is voiceless.[5] If that is the starting-point, however, then there is no way that fetishism can be understood as hard fetishism.

If fetishism were an accomplished fact, if capitalism were characterised by the total objectification of the subject, then there is no way that we, as ordinary people, could criticise fetishism.

The fact that we criticise points to the contradictory nature of fetishism (and therefore also to the contradictory nature of our selves), and gives evidence of the present existence of anti-fetishism (in the sense that criticism is directed against fetishism). The point is made by Ernst Bloch:

> ... alienation could not even be seen, and condemned of robbing people of their freedom and depriving the world of its soul, if there did not exist some measure of its opposite, of that possible coming-to-oneself, being-with-oneself, against which alienation can be measured. [1964 (2), p. 113][6]

The concept of alienation, or fetishism, in other words, implies its opposite: not as essential non-alienated 'home' deep in our hearts, but as resistance, refusal, rejection of alienation in our daily practice. It is only on the basis of a concept of non- (or better anti-) alienation or non- (that is, anti-) fetishism that we can conceive of alienation or fetishism. If fetishism and anti-fetishism coexist, then it can only be as antagonistic processes. Fetishism is a process of fetishisation, a process of separating subject and object, doing and done, always in antagonism to the opposing movement of anti-fetishisation, the struggle to reunite subject and object, to recompose doing and done.

If we start, then, from the idea that our scream is not the scream of a vanguard but the scream of an antagonism that is inseparable from living in capitalist society, a universal (or almost universal) scream, then the hardness of fetishism dissolves and fetishism is revealed as process of fetishisation. With that, the hardness of all categories dissolves and phenomena which appear as things or established facts (such as commodity, value, money, the state) are also revealed as processes. The forms come to life. The categories are opened[7] to reveal that their content is struggle.

Once fetishism is understood as fetishisation, then the genesis of the capitalist forms of social relations is not of purely historical interest. The value-form, money-form, capital-form, state-form, and so on, are not established once and for all at the origins of capitalism. Rather, they are constantly at issue, constantly questioned as forms of social relations, constantly being established and re-established (or not) through struggle. The forms of social relations are processes of form-ing social relations. Every time a small child takes sweets from a shop without realising that money has to be given in exchange for them, every time workers refuse to accept that the market dictates that their place of work should be closed or jobs lost, every time that the shopkeepers of São Paulo promote the killing of street children to protect their property, every time that we lock our bicycles, cars or houses – value as a form of relating to one another is at issue, constantly the object of struggle, constantly in process of being disrupted, reconstituted and disrupted again.[8] We are not a sleeping beauty, a humanity frozen in our alienation until our prince-party comes to kiss us, we live rather in constant struggle to free ourselves from the witch's curse.

Our existence, then, is not simply an existence within fetishised forms of social relations. We do not exist simply as the objectified victims of capitalism. Nor can we exist outside the capitalist forms: there is no area of capitalism-free existence, no privileged sphere of unfetishised life, for we are always constituting and constituted by our relations with others. Rather, as the starting-point of this discussion – the scream – suggests, we exist against-and-in capital. Our existence against capitalism is not a question of conscious choice, it is the inevitable expression of our life in an oppressive, alienating society. Gunn puts the point nicely when he says that 'unfreedom subsists solely as the (self-contradictory) revolt of the oppressed' (1992, p. 29). Our existence-against-capital is the inevitable constant negation of our existence-in-capital. Conversely, our existence-in-capital (or, more clearly, our containment within capital) is the constant negation of our revolt against capital. Our containment within capital is a constant process of fetishising, or form-ing, our social relations, a constant struggle.

All of those apparently fixed phenomena which we often take for granted (money, state, power: they are there, always have been, always will, that's human nature, isn't it?) are now revealed to be raging, bloody battlefields. It is rather like taking a harmless speck of dust and looking at it through a microscope to discover that the 'harmlessness' of the speck of dust conceals a whole micro-world in which millions of microscopic organisms live and die in the daily battle for existence. But in the case of money the invisibility of the battle it conceals has nothing to do with physical size, it is the result rather of the concepts through which we look at it. The banknote we hold in our hand seems a harmless thing, but look at it more closely and we see a whole world of people fighting for survival, some dedicating their lives to the pursuit of money, some (many) desperately trying to get hold of money as a means of surviving another day, some trying to evade money by taking what they want without paying for it or setting up forms of production that do not go through the market and the money form, some killing for money, many each day dying for lack of money. A bloody battlefield in which the fact that the power-to do exists in the form of money brings untold misery, disease and death and is always at issue, always contested, always imposed, often with violence. Money is a raging battle of monetisation and anti-monetisation.

Seen from this perspective, money becomes monetisation, value valorisation, commodity commodification, capital capitalisation, power power-isation, state statification, and so on (with ever uglier neologisms). Each process implies its opposite. The monetisation of social relations makes little sense unless it is seen as a constant movement against its opposite, the creation of social relations on a non-monetary basis. Neoliberalism, for example, can be seen as a drive to extend and intensify the monetisation of social relations, a reaction in part to the loosening of that monetisation in the post-war period and its crisis in the 1960s and 1970s. These forms of social relations (commodity, value, money, capital, and so on) are interconnected, of course, all forms of the capitalist separation of subject and object, but they are interconnected not as static, accomplished, sleeping-beauty forms, but as forms of living struggle. The existence of forms of social relations, in other words, cannot be separated from their constitution. Their existence is their constitution, a constantly renewed struggle against the forces that subvert them.

V

Take the state, for example. What does criticism of the state as a form of social relations mean when the forms are understood as form-processes, processes of forming?

The state is part of the fixed firmament of Is-ness. It is an institution, apparently necessary for the ordering of human affairs, a phenomenon the existence of which is taken completely for granted by political science, the discipline dedicated to its study. Criticism in the Marxist tradition has often focused on showing the capitalist character of the state, on showing that, despite appearances, the state acts in the interests of the capitalist class. This leads easily to the conception that it is necessary to conquer the state in some way so that it can be made to function in the interests of the working class.

If we start from the centrality of fetishism and the understanding of the state as an aspect of the fetishisation of social relations, then the matter presents itself differently. To criticise the state means in the first place to attack the apparent autonomy of the state, to understand the state not as a thing in itself, but as a social form, a form of social relations. Just as in physics we have come to accept that, despite appearances, there are no absolute separations, that energy can be transformed into mass and mass into energy, so, in society too there are no absolute separations, no hard categories. To think scientifically is to dissolve the categories of thought, to understand all social phenomena as precisely that, as forms of social relations. Social relations, relations between people, are fluid, unpredictable, unstable, often passionate, but they rigidify into certain forms, forms which appear to acquire their own autonomy, their own dynamic, forms which are crucial for the stability of society. The different academic disciplines take these forms (the state, money, the family) as given and so contribute to their apparent solidity, and hence to the stability of capitalist society. To think scientifically is to criticise the disciplines, to dissolve these forms, to understand them as forms; to act freely is to destroy these forms.

The state, then, is a rigidified or fetishised form of social relations. It is a relation between people which does not appear to be a relation between people, a social relation which exists in the form of something external to social relations.

But why do social relations rigidify in this way and how does that help us to understand the development of the state? This was the question posed by the so-called 'state derivation debate', a slightly peculiar but very important discussion which spread from West Germany to other countries during the 1970s (see Holloway and Picciotto 1978a; Clarke 1991). The debate was peculiar in being conducted in extremely abstract language, and often without making explicit the political and theoretical implications of the argument. The obscurity of the language used and the fact that the participants often did not develop (or were not aware of) the implications of the debate left the discussion open to being misunderstood, and the approach has often been dismissed as an 'economic' theory of the state, or as a 'capital-logic' approach which seeks to understand political development as a functionalist expression of the logic of capital. While these criticisms can fairly be made of some of the contributions, the importance of the debate as a whole lay in the fact that it provided a basis for breaking away from the economic determinism and the functionalism which has marred so many of the discussions of the relation between the state and capitalist society, and for discussing the state as an element or, better, moment of the totality of the social relations of capitalist society.

The focus of the debate on the state as a particular *form* of social relations is the crucial break with the economic determinism implied for example by the base-superstructure model (and its structuralist variants). In the base-superstructure model, the economic base determines (in the last instance, of course) what the state *does*, the functions of the state. The focus on the functions of the state takes the existence of the state for granted: there is no room in the base-superstructure model to ask about the form of the state, to ask why, in the first place, social relations should rigidify into the apparently autonomous form of the state. To ask about the form of the state is to raise the question of its historical specificity: the existence of the state as a thing separated from society is peculiar to capitalist society, as is the existence of the 'economic' as something distinct from overtly coercive class relations (Gerstenberger 1990). The question then is not: how does the economic determine the political superstructure? Rather, it is: what is peculiar about the social relations of capitalism that gives rise to the rigidification (or particularisation) of social relations in the form of the state? The corollary of this is the question: what is it that gives rise to the constitution of the economic and the political as distinct moments of the same social relations? The answer is surely that there is something distinctive about the social antagonism on which capitalism (like any class society) is based. Under capitalism, social antagonism (the relation between classes) is based on a form of exploitation which takes place not openly but through the 'free' sale and purchase of labour power as a commodity on the market. This form of class relation presupposes a separation between the immediate process of exploitation, which is based on the 'freedom' of labour, and the process of maintaining order in an exploitative society, which implies the necessity of coercion (cf. Hirsch 1978).

Seeing the state as a form of social relations obviously means that the development of the state can only be understood as a moment of the development of the totality of social relations: it is a part of the antagonistic and crisis-ridden development of capitalist society. As a form of capitalist social relations, its existence depends on the reproduction of those relations: it is therefore not just a state in a capitalist society, but a capitalist state, since its own continued existence is tied to the promotion of the reproduction of capitalist social relations as a whole. The fact that it exists as a particular or rigidified form of social relations means, however, that the relation between the state and the reproduction of capitalism is a complex one: it cannot be assumed, in functionalist fashion, either that everything that the state does will necessarily be in the best interests of capital, nor that the state can achieve what is necessary to secure the reproduction of capitalist society. The relation between the state and the reproduction of capitalist social relations is one of trial and error.

Criticism of the state as a form of social relations points both to the interrelation of the state with the general reproduction of capital and to the historical specificity of the state as a form of organising human affairs. Although it certainly suggests the possibility of organising life in a different way in the future, such an approach does not question the present existence of the state: the present existence of the state is simply taken for granted. Criticism stands back from the object of criticism.

If, however, the state is understood not just as a form of social relations but as a process of forming social relations, then all that has been said above about the relation between the state and the reproduction of capital still stands, but both that reproduction and the existence of the state are opened up as being constantly at issue.[9] The existence of the state implies a constant process of separating off certain aspects of social relations and defining them as 'political', and hence as separate from 'the economic'. The antagonism on which society is based is thus fragmented: struggles are channelled into political and economic forms, neither of which leaves room for raising questions about the structure of society as a whole. This process of imposing definitions on social struggles is at the same time a process of self-definition by the state: as a rigidified form of social relations, the state is at the same time a process of rigidifying social relations, and it is through this process that the state is constantly reconstituted as an instance separate from society.

The state is a process of statification of social conflict. Conflict, once defined as 'political', is separated off from anything that might question the 'economic' realm of private property, that is to say the fundamental structures of power-over. Conflict is defined and sub-defined, so that it can go through the proper channels and be dealt with (administratively or through overt repression) in such a way that the existence of capital as a form of organising social relations is not called into question. Incipient expressions of power-to, of the demand by people to control their own lives, are metamorphosed through the state into the imposition of power-over: sometimes through outright repression, sometimes by 'providing' changes that respond to the demands, sometimes by developing new administrative structures that integrate (and subordinate) the incipient forms of self-organisation into the structure of state administration and finance. The channelling, however, is never complete, for the state is constantly reacting to new conflicts, new outbreaks of the human revolt against definition.

Central to understanding the state as a process of statification is an aspect generally overlooked by the state derivation debate, namely the existence of the state as a multiplicity of states. Often it is assumed in discussions (both Marxist and non-Marxist) of the relation between the state and society that state and society are co-terminous, that the state relates to *its* society, the society to *its* state. The notions of national state, national economy and national society are just taken for granted. Only on this basis can it possibly be imagined that the gaining of control of the state apparatus represents the seizure of power. Notions of revolution through the conquest of power tend to take at face value the state's assertion that it is sovereign, autonomous within its boundaries.

The assumption that state and society are coterminous overlooks completely that which distinguishes capital as a form of domination from previous forms of class domination, namely its essential mobility. Capital, unlike the feudal lord, is not tied to any particular group of workers or any particular place. The transition from feudalism to capitalism liberated the exercise of power-over from territorial ties. Whereas the feudal lord could command workers only within his territory, the capitalist in London can command workers in Buenos Aires or Seoul just as easily as in Swindon. The capitalist constitution of social relations is essentially global. Its non-territoriality is of the essence of capital and not just the product of the current phase of 'globalisation'.

The very existence of the state as one of a multiplicity of states thus conceals the global constitution of social relations and hence the nature of the capitalist exercise of power-over. Even before it does anything, even before the police, the bureaucrats or the politicians make a move, the state fragments, classifies, defines, fetishises. The very existence of the state is a territorial definition of 'its' territory, 'its' society, 'its' citizens. The very existence of the state is a discrimination against non-citizens as 'foreigners'. The existence of the state, however, is not simply given. It is a constant process of self-constitution, of self-definition, not something that is accomplished once national boundaries are set. On the contrary, all national states are engaged in a constantly repeated process of fragmenting global social relations: through assertions of national sovereignty, through exhortations to 'the nation', through flag ceremonies, through the playing of national anthems, through administrative discrimination against 'foreigners', through passport controls, through the maintenance of armies, through war. The more feeble the social basis of this national fragmentation of society – as in Latin America, for example – the more obvious its forms of expression. This form of fragmentation, this form of classification or identification, is surely one of the most brutal and savage manifestations of capital's rule, as the mountains of corpses accumulated over the last century testify.

And yet so much 'left' discourse is blind to the violence that the existence of the state entails. The notion of taking power, for example, understanding by that the winning of control over the state apparatus, inevitably endorses the notion of the national (statebound) constitution of social relations and so partakes in the fragmentation of society into national units. It is difficult to imagine a state-oriented politics that does not actively participate in the discrimination between 'citizens' and 'foreigners', that does not in some way become nationalistic. Stalin's strategy of 'socialism in one country', so often portrayed as a betrayal of the Bolshevik cause, was in reality the logical outcome of a state-centred concept of social change.

The existence of the state is a movement of definition and exclusion. 'Citizens' are defined, 'foreigners' are excluded. In mainstream discussions, the focus is usually on the relation between 'the state' and 'its citizens', but in fact the notion of citizenship implies the definition and exclusion of non-citizens or foreigners. In a world in which more and more people travel or migrate, to sell their labour power or for other reasons, the exclusion of foreigners means that more and more people live in fear or in inhibition of their potential, their power-to do things. For the included, the defined, the citizens, the notion of citizenship is an element of the fiction upon which the existence of states, and particularly democratic states, is based. The idea of democracy assumes that social relations are, or should be, constituted on a national (state-bound) basis, that power is located in the state. When this fiction comes into conflict with the fact that social relations (that is, relations of power) are constituted at a global level, then the rupture between the democratically expressed wishes of the people ('people' meaning 'citizens') and the actions of the state can only be explained in terms of outside forces (the world economy, the financial markets) or the intervention of foreigners (American imperialism, the gnomes of Zurich). Thus, the notion of citizenship both contributes to the reproduction of the democratic mirage (wait till the next election) and to the daily violence against foreigners which extends from racist attacks on the street to the forcible separation of millions of families by immigration officials.

It might be objected that this argument attributes too much to the state, that racism and nationalism are far more deeply ingrained in society. This is true. Clearly the process by which one comes to say 'I am Irish', 'I am English', and so on, is very complex, part of the general identification of society. The existence of the state is just one form of fetishisation, identification-through-the-state blends with other forms of identification that are indissociable from the basic separation of subject and object in the process of production and creation. The state does not stand on its own: it is one of the forms of capitalist social relations, that is, one of the inter-linking, inter-blending processes of form-ing social relations, of reproducing power-to in the form of power-over.

The movement of the state (as of all the other forms of social relations) as a form-process is a movement to impose patterns on a refractory reality. The movement of fetishisation can be understood only in terms of an anti-movement, a movement of anti-fetishisa-tion. Most obviously, the imposition of state definitions of nationality is confronted by experiences and overt movements against such definitions, as expressed in the slogan 'nobody is illegal' or the movement of the *sans papiers* in France or the cry of the French students of 1968, *'Nous sommes tous des juifs allemands.'* More subtly, citizenisation is a process of redefinition of the movement of power-to. The claim to exert control over our own lives is redefined as democracy, democracy being understood as a state-defined process of electorally influenced decision making. The movement of asserting power-to shape our own lives, expressed in so many forms of social activity and organisations, is contained by redefining the movement as a movement for democracy, a movement of citizens, with all that this means in terms of depriving the movement of any possibility of controlling the shaping of social relations. Yet the movement of power-to is contained and not contained, for it constantly re-arises in new shapes. The movement of the state, like the movement of society as a whole, is the movement of the antagonism between fetishisation and anti-fetishisation. To find anti-power, we do not need to look outside the movement of domination: anti-power, anti-fetishisation is present against-in-and-beyond the movement of domination itself, not as economic forces or objective contradictions or future, but as now, as us.

VI

This understanding of fetishism as fetishisation, and hence of our existence in capitalist society as an existence against-and-in capital, affects our understanding of all the categories of thought. If the forms of social relations (expressed in the categories of the political economists) are understood as processes of forming social relations, and hence as struggle, it is clear that the categories must be understood as being open categories. If value, for example, is understood not as an economic category, nor as a form of domination, but as a form of struggle, then the actual meaning of the category will depend on the course of the struggle. Once the categories of thought are understood as expressions not of objecti-fied social relations but of the struggle to objectify them, then a whole storm of unpredictability blows through them. Once it is understood that money, capital, the state are nothing but the struggle to form, to discipline, then it is clear that their development can be understood only as practice, as un-predetermined struggle (cf. Bonefeld et al. 1992a). Marxism, as a theory of struggle, is inevitably a theory of uncertainty. Fetishism is (false) certainty, anti-fetishism is uncertainty. The notion of struggle is inconsistent with any idea of a guaranteed negation-of-the-negation happy ending: the only way that dialectics can be understood is as negative dialectics (cf. Adorno 1990), as the open-ended negation of the untrue, as revolt against unfreedom.

Criticism, then, is not the voice of those-who-stand-outside, but part of the daily struggle against fetishism, just part of the daily struggle to establish social relations on a human basis. Criticism does not come riding up on a white horse with the hope of kissing the world into life: it *is* the life of the world. Criticism can only be a moving outwards from ourselves. Like a fly trapped in a spider's web, we hack at the reified strands that hold us imprisoned. There is no way that we can stand outside the web and view things dispassionately. Trapped in the web, there is no way that we can be all-knowing. There is no way we can know reality, no way that we can know the totality. We cannot adopt the point of view of totality, as Lukács would have us do:[10] at most we can only aspire to totality. Totality cannot be a standpoint, for the simple reason that there is no one who can stand there: it can only be a critical category – the social flow of doing. This is not yet dusk: the owl of Minerva can do no more than flap her wings and struggle to get off the ground.[11] The only truth we can proclaim is the negation of untruth. There is nothing fixed to which we can cling for reassurance: not class, not Marx, not revolution, nothing but the moving negation of untruth. Criticism is the restlessness of Prometheus bound, the desperation of the 'sheer unrest of life' (Hegel 1977, p. 27), of 'the absolute movement of becoming' (Marx 1973, p. 488). Our criticism is vertiginous, the vertiginous theory of a vertiginous world.[12]

Vertiginous indeed. To insist on seeing fetishism as a process of fetishisation is directly to attack identity. Identity, we saw, is the separation of constitution and existence, the separation of doing and done. Identity is a space of is-ness, a time of duration, an area in which the done exists independently of the doing which constituted it, an apparent haven of security. To say that fetishism must be understood as process is to reject any separation between constitution and existence. Money is a process of monetisation because it is impossible to separate the constitution of money as a form of social relations from its existence: the existence of money is the process of its constitution, a raging struggle. There is no respite, there is no moment in which money can rest on its laurels and say to itself 'Now that monetary relations have been established, I exist and shall continue to exist until capitalism is abolished.' That is the way it appears to be, but the appearance is the negation of present doing and present struggle. The capitalist whom we see sitting back comfortably over a big meal is a capitalist only because he is at that very moment involved in violent struggle to exploit.

There is no identity, then. Or rather: there is no identity other than the continual struggle to identify, to impose a layer of stability on the seething violence that the separation of done from doing inevitably involves. Capital presents itself as stable: class struggle, they say, *and we accept*, comes from us. Class struggle from below, it appears, disrupts the stability of capitalism. What nonsense! To understand class struggle as coming primarily from below, as most Marxist discussions do, is really to turn the world on its head. The very existence of capital is a violent struggle to separate done from doing. Yet the very violence of this struggle, the tearing away of done from doing, of existence from constitution, is what creates the apparent stability, identity, of capitalism. The appearance of stability is given in the nature of the struggle itself. The separation of done from doing is the product of the unceasing struggle to separate done from doing, which, in so far as it succeeds, obliterates itself from view. Identity is an illusion really generated by the struggle to identify the non-identical. We, the non-identical, fight against this identification. The struggle against capital is the struggle against identification. It is not the struggle for an alternative identity.

To understand fetishism as fetishisation is to insist on the fragility of existence. To say that the forms of social relations are processes of formation means not only that they are forms of struggle but also that their existence as forms depends on their constant reconstitution. The existence of capital depends on the process of its continual reconstitution through the separation of the done from the doing. Its existence, therefore, is always at issue, always a matter of struggle. If one day capital fails to convert doing into labour or to exploit labour, then capital ceases to exist. Its existence is always insecure: hence the ferocity of its struggle.

Capitalism is two-faced. The very nature of its instability (the separating of done from doing) generates the appearance of stability (the separation of done from doing). The identity (is-ness) of capitalism is a real illusion: an effective illusion generated by the process of production (the process of separating done from doing). The separation of constitution from existence is a real illusion: an effective illusion generated by the process of production (the process of separating existence from constitution). The illusion is effective because it belies the fragility of capitalism. It appears that capitalism 'is': but capitalism never 'is', it is always a struggle to constitute itself. To treat capitalism as a mode of production that 'is' or, which is the same thing, to think of class struggle as struggle from below against the stability of capitalism, is to fall head-first into the filthiest mire of fetishism. Capital, by its nature, appears to 'be', but it never 'is'. That is important, both to understand the violence of capital (the continued presence of what Marx called 'primitive accumulation') and to understand its fragility. The urgent impossibility of revolution begins to open towards an urgent possibility.

But, it may be objected, it is necessary to distinguish constitution from reconstitution. Even accepting that the existence of capital is a struggle constantly renewed, is there not a difference between the original constitution and the reconstitution which is required to maintain the existence of the capitalist forms of social relations? Even if we say that a relation of love depends upon its constant reconstitution, upon falling in love each day, is there not a difference between the initial falling in love and its daily repetition? Even if money must be daily reconstituted in order to exist, is there not a difference between the original imposition of money as a social relation and its daily repetition? It may be that every time we go to a shop and pay with money, we are conscious of the violence of money, but surely the fact that we have gone through the same monetisation of social relations hundreds of times before means that the struggle (from capital's side) to monetise our behaviour is less intense than before? If we deny the distinction between constitution and reconstitution, do we not risk falling into a world of amnesia, in which there is no possible accumulation of experience?

This is so. The conditions in which the struggle to constitute capital (to separate done from doing) takes place change all the time. The repetition of the process of exploitation changes the conditions in which the struggle to exploit takes place, in much the same way as a wave of factory occupations to prevent exploitation (or indeed the speeding up of the labour process to intensify exploitation) also changes the conditions in which the struggle to exploit takes place. There is indeed an accumulation of experience (albeit not a linear accumulation) on both sides of the struggle. But that does nothing to affect the basic argument: capital never 'is', its existence is never one of duration, it always depends on the struggle to reconstitute itself. Reconstitution can never be assumed.[13]

But, it may be objected again, this was not Marx's understanding of fetishism: Marx treats the capitalist forms of social relations in *Capital* as being stable forms. This is indeed the traditional reading of *Capital*, but, first, what Marx thought cannot by itself stand as a refutation of the argument (what matters is not what Marx thought but what we think), and, second, the traditional reading of *Capital* overlooks its character as a critique. Marx's work is a critique of political economy, a critique of the political economists' hypostatisation of their categories. In *Capital*, Marx speaks of the forms of social relations as constituted forms because he is criticising those forms as real illusions. Marx criticises by showing not just the historical but the continual genesis of these forms in the process of production, in the antagonistic existence of the labour process as concrete labour and abstract labour. By showing the continual generation of these forms, Marx implicitly shows that the forms of social relations cannot be understood as being stable, that fetishism cannot be understood as accomplished fact. The forms of social relations are form-processes, processes of forming social relations (see Holloway 1991b, p. 239; Sohn-Rethel 1978, p. 17).

But, it may be objected yet again, to think of the struggle against capital as being anti-identitarian is to place us in an impossible position, theoretically and practically. All conceptualisation involves identification: if we cannot identify, we cannot think. All struggle too, it is argued, involves identification. Or are we simply to forget the struggles of blacks against discrimination, the women's movement, the indigenous movements?

The difference is between an identification that stops there and an identification that negates itself in the process of identifying. The difference is between conceptualising on the basis of being and conceptualising on the basis of doing. Doing, it was argued above, is the antagonistic movement of identity and non-identity. The doer is and is not, just as the done is and is not, fleetingly objectified and then reintegrated into the social flow of doing. To think on the basis of being is simply to identify. To think on the basis of doing is to identify and, in the same breath, to negate that identification. This is to recognise the inadequacy of the concept to that which is conceptualised: 'The name of dialectics says no more, to begin with, than that objects do not go into their concepts without leaving a remainder, that they come to contradict the traditional norm of adequacy' (Adorno 1990, p. 5). Thinking on the basis of doing means, then, thinking against-and-beyond our own thought: 'We can think against our own thought, and if it were possible to define dialectics, this would be a definition worth suggesting' (Adorno 1990, p. 141).

The same is true of struggle. There is a world of difference between a struggle that simply identifies (that says 'we are black', 'we are Irish', 'we are Basque', as though these were fixed identities rather than moments of struggle) and a struggle that identifies and, in the very moment of identification, negates that identification: we are indigenous-but-more-than-that, we are women-but-more-than-that.

Whereas the latter moves against identification in the very process of asserting identity, the former is easily absorbed into a fragmented world of identities. What matters to the stability of capitalism is not the particular composition of identities (black is the same as white, Basque the same as Spanish, women the same as men), but identity as such. A struggle that does not move against identification as such blends easily with the shifting patterns of capitalist domination. The strength and resonance of the Zapatista movement, for example, comes not from the fact that it is an indigenous movement, but from the fact that it goes beyond that to present itself as a movement fighting for humanity, for a world of many worlds.[14]

Yet again, it may be objected that to argue that our struggle is anti-identical in thought and practice, that it is directed against the separation of constitution and existence, is to raise life to an unbearable pitch of intensity. That is so. Identity makes life bearable.[15] Identity kills pain. Identity dulls feelings. It is only the identification of a Them that makes it possible for us to live with the epidemic of Aids in Africa or the death of thousands of children each day from curable diseases. The existence of capitalism is conceivable only on the basis of the dulling of our feelings: this is not just a question of drugs (very important), but above all of identity, that fragmentation that enables us to erect private morality into a wall to keep out the pain of the world. The scream is the recognition and confrontation of social pain. Communism is the movement of intensity against the dulling of feeling that makes the horrors of capitalism possible.

If possible objections keep arising, it is not because the argument is flawed but because we are walking on the edge of possibility. (To pose the question of changing the world without taking power is already to teeter on the edge of an abyss of insane impossibility.) And yet there is no alternative. The understanding of fetishisation as process is the key to thinking about changing the world without taking power. If we abandon fetishisation-as-process, we abandon revolution as self-emancipation. The understanding of fetishism as hard fetishism can lead only to an understanding of revolution as changing the world *on behalf of* the oppressed, and this inevitably means a focus on taking power. Taking power is the political goal that makes sense of the idea of a revolution 'on behalf of': a revolution that is not 'on behalf of' but self-moving has no need even to think of 'taking power'.

If, on the other hand, we overlook fetishism completely, we are back with the subject as hero. If power does not penetrate into us and tear us apart, if, on the contrary, it is possible for a healthy subject to exist in a sick society, then we can treat the subject as wholesome, healthy and sane: the good hero battling against the bad society. This view appears in different versions, perhaps not so far removed from one another as they first appear to be. In orthodox Marxist theory (not only the theory of Communist Parties, but far beyond that), the hero appears, not as the working class, but as the Party. In autonomist theory, which, although it criticises orthodox theory, does not take that criticism to all its conclusions,[16] the wholesome hero appears as the working-class militant. The good hero battling against the bad society is also the leading character of liberal theory, of Hollywood-theory, with the sole difference that the hero is not now the class or the Party but the individual. The problem, however, is not just the individualism: it is the hero-subject as such.

There is no hero. Above all, the theorist is no hero. She is not a Knower. Theory does not stand above the fray but is simply part of the articulation of our daily existence of struggle. It does not look down at society from above, but is part of the daily struggle for emancipation, striking out at the forms that negate our subjectivity. Theory is practical because it is part of the practice of living: it does not have to jump across a gulf to become practice. If fetishism is understood not as a state which permeates the whole of society, but as the antagonistic movement of fetishisation against anti-fetishisation, and if critical theory is understood as part of the movement of anti-fetishisation against fetishisation, part of the struggle to defend, restore and create the collective flow of doing, then it is clear that we are all, in different ways, the subjects of critical theory in so far as we are part of that movement. The subject of criticism is not the innocent, individual, apparently unfetishised subject of liberal and democratic theory, or of party-Marxism. I am not the subject: we are the subject. Not a we who are a simple coming together of innocent 'I's, but a we who are maimed, broken, perverted 'I's struggling towards our we-ness. Criticism is part of this struggle towards we-ness, part of the aspiration towards the we-ness that would make our I-ness whole.

There is a world of difference, therefore, between saying that fetishism is not absolute but rather a continuous struggle between fetishisation and anti-fetishisation, and saying that fetishism leaves certain areas or people (the party, the intellectuals, the marginalised) unfetishised. We are not unfetishised, we are part of an antagonistic movement against fetishisation. The struggle against fetishism implies a struggle to overcome our fragmentation, a struggle to find adequate forms of articulating our we-ness, to find ways of uniting in mutual respect our distinct dignities, whose dignity lies precisely in the recognition and negation of its own negation as dignity. This is not a democratic struggle, if by democratic struggle is understood (as it usually is) the coming together of whole individuals. On the contrary, the struggle against fetishisation is the struggle of people who respect each other mutually not because we are whole individuals, but because we are all part of the movement against the process by which we are maimed and perverted. That is why struggles continuously give rise to forms of social relations and ways of articulating I-and-we-ness that have little in common with the lumping together of individuals that is typical of bourgeois democracy. The Paris Commune discussed by Marx, the workers' councils theorised by Pannekoek, the village councils of the Zapatistas, and so on and so on: all are experiments in the movement of anti-fetishism, the struggle for the collective flow of doing, for self-determination.

6   Anti-Fetishism and Criticism

I

Theory is simply part of the daily struggle to live with dignity. Dignity means the struggle to emancipate doing and liberate that which exists in the form of being denied. Theoretically, this means fighting through criticism for the recovery of doing. This is what Marx means by science.

II

Criticism is an assault on identity. The scream against the way things are becomes a why? Why is there so much inequality in the world? Why are there so many people unemployed when there are so many others who are overworked? Why is there so much hunger in a world where there is such abundance? Why are there so many children living on the streets?

We attack the world with all the stubborn curiosity of a three-year-old, with the difference perhaps that our 'why's are informed by rage. Our why asks for a reason. Our why holds that which exists up to the judgement of reason. Why do so many children die of curable illnesses? Why is there so much violence? Our why moves against that which is and asks it to justify itself. Initially, at least, our why attacks identity and asks why that which is has come to be. 'Initially, at least', because soon our 'why's come up against the same problem that confronts anyone who tries to satisfy the curiosity of a three-year-old: the problem of infinite regress.

The problem of infinite regress lies at the heart of identitarian thought. The problem is inherent in identity. In a world composed of particular identities, what is it that allows us to conceptualise those identities? The answer lies, we saw, in classification, the grouping of particular identities into classes.[1] The problem is that the classificatory concepts remain arbitrary unless they in turn can be validated by a third-order discourse and that in turn by a fourth-order discourse, and so on, so that there is a potentially infinite regress of theoretical foundation (cf. Gunn, 1991).

It is ironic that identitarian thought, founded as it is on the common-sense view that of course x is x (as sure as eggs is eggs), is unable to provide itself with a firm foundation. Time and time again, attempts to show that a system of classification can have a rational basis have come up against the impossibility of providing such firm foundations. The search for a rational foundation for identitarian thought leads inevitably to an irrational Given, a thing-in-itself (Kant) that cannot be explained, a 'hidden hand' (Smith) behind the functioning of the economy, a space that is 'dark and void' (Fichte). The attempt, promoted by Hilbert at the beginning of the twentieth century, to prove that mathematics is a coherent non-contradictory system, was shown by Gödel to be incapable of fulfilment. The result, of course, is that identitarian thought has preferred, on the whole, not to worry about the rationality of its own foundation, devoting itself instead to improving the 'exactness' of its own fragmented disciplines:

> And the fact that these sciences are 'exact' is due precisely to this circumstance. Their underlying material base is permitted to dwell inviolate and undisturbed in its irrationality ('non-createdness', 'givenness') so that it becomes possible to operate with unproblematic, rational categories in the resulting methodically purified world. These categories are then applied not to the real material substratum (even that of the particular science) but to an 'intelligible' subject matter. [Lukács 1971, p. 120]

This is the problem uncovered by our 'why'. In the face of our why, identity always tries to limit the damage, to recuperate, to turn the interrogation to its advantage, to enclose the attack within an identitarian framework. We are all familiar with this. A persistent 'Why are there so many children living on the streets?' is likely to come up eventually against the answer of 'private property', given with the understanding that private property is immutable; or possibly, against the answer that 'God made it that way', with the understanding that God is who is; or possibly against the simplest, most direct answer: 'That's the way things are', or 'What is, is necessary'.

Often we accept those limits. We accept that the struggle implicit in our 'why' has limits. We struggle for better conditions within the university, but we do not question the existence of the institution. We struggle for better housing but do not necessarily question the existence of private property which is so fundamental in shaping housing conditions. Our struggle takes place within an accepted framework of that's-the-way-things-are. We know that this framework limits or partially invalidates anything we might achieve, but we accept it in the interests of obtaining concrete results. We accept the bounds of identity and, contradictorily, reinforce them in so doing.

But supposing we do not accept the limits? Supposing we persist with our why in the true manner of the stubborn three-year-old? A solution to infinite regress can come only when being is reconverted into doing. To say that God made it so is not a true transition from being to doing because God is confined immutably and eternally within being: 'I am who am.' The only answer that can take us out of the circle of identity is one that points to a creator who is not unchangeable, a creator that creates herself in the process of creation. That answer is a horrific one, but the only basis for hope: there are so many children living in the street, because we humans have made it so. We are the only creators, the only gods. Guilty gods, negated gods, damaged, schizophrenic gods, but above all self-changing gods. And that answer turns the whole world upside down. Our doing becomes the pivot of all comprehension.

Marx deals very quickly with this initial movement of why, the movement of critical analysis, of trying to go behind appearances, in the opening pages of *Capital*. Starting from the commodity and its contradictory character as useful article (use value) and object produced for exchange (exchange value), he discovers that behind this contradiction lies the two-fold character of labour as useful or concrete labour (which creates use value) and abstract labour (which produces value, which appears as exchange value in exchange): 'This two-fold nature of the labour contained in commodities ... is the pivot on which a clear comprehension of Political Economy turns' (1965, p. 41). The being of the commodity is quickly brought back to doing and its existence as concrete and abstract labour. The commodity is so because we have made it so. The pivot is human doing and the way in which it is organised.

But then our why takes a turn. If we are the only creators, why are we so powerless? If we are so powerful, why do these things that are our products take on an independent life and dominate us? Why do we produce our own enslavement? Why ('for God's sake', we are tempted to say, only there is no god, just ourselves) did we make society in such a way that millions of children are forced to live on the streets?

The why, which initially tries to go behind the appearance of things and discover their origin, now tries to recompose those appearances and see how their origin (human doing) gives rise to its own negation. Criticism acquires a double movement: an analytical movement and a genetic movement, a movement of going behind appearances and a movement of tracing the origin or genesis of the phenomenon criticised.

The idea that understanding involves genetic criticism does not begin with Marx. Philosophers from the time of Hobbes have argued that understanding involves tracing the process of construction of a phenomenon, and it is basic to the development of mathematics that a proof is 'constructed'. The eighteenth-century philosopher Giambattista Vico formulated the link between understanding and making with particular force when he made his central principle the idea that *verum et factum convertuntur*: the true and the made are interchangeable, so that we can only know for certain that which we have created. An object of knowledge can only be fully known to the extent that it is the creation of the knowing subject. The link between knowledge and creation is central for Hegel, for whom the subject-object of knowledge-creation is the movement of absolute spirit, but it is with Marx that the *verum–factum* principle acquires full critical force.

Knowledge, in this view, is the reappropriation of the object by the subject, the recuperation of power-to. The object confronts us as something separate from us, something out there. The process of knowing is, therefore, critical: we deny the out-there-ness of the object and seek to show how we, the subject, have created it. We see money, for example, and it confronts us as an external force: in order to understand it, we criticise its externality and try to show how money is in reality our own product. This type of criticism does not necessarily involve denunciation, but it goes much deeper. It questions the very existence of the object as object. It shakes objectivity to its foundations. Criticism in this sense is the stirring of anti-power, the beginnings of the reunification of subject and object.[2]

For Marx, criticism in this sense is central to his whole approach. In his early Introduction to the *Contribution to the Critique of Hegel's Philosophy of Law*, he makes the point clearly: 'The basis of irreligious criticism is this: *Man makes religion*, religion does not make man' (1975, p. 175; original emphasis). Criticism of religion is not criticism of its ill-doings or evil effects, but of its very existence as

religion. It is a criticism that emanates from the exclusive subjectivity of humanity. The point of criticism is to recuperate the lost
subjectivity, to recover that which is denied. In religion, God
presents himself not as our creation but as an independent subject
who has created us (as object). The aim of criticism is to reverse the
subjectivity, to restore subjectivity to where it should be, saying 'We
are the subject, it is we who created God.' The subjectivity of God is
then revealed as the self-estrangement of human subjectivity.
Criticism is an act of bringing subject and object together, the
assertion of the centrality of human creativity:

> The criticism of religion disillusions man to make him think and
> act and shape his reality like a man who has been disillusioned
> and has come to reason, so that he will revolve round himself and
> therefore round his true sun. Religion is only the illusory sun
> which revolves round man as long as he does not revolve round
> himself. [1975, p. 176]

The purpose of criticism is to restore humans to our proper place as
our own true sun. For the young Marx, it is essential to move on
from the 'holy form' of self-estrangement 'to unmask self-estrangement in its *unholy forms*. Thus the criticism of heaven turns into the
criticism of the earth, the *criticism of religion* into the *criticism of law*
and the *criticism of theology* into the the *criticism of politics*' (1975, p.
176; original emphasis).

Marx remained true to the project he set himself. For him,
'science' is not correct, objective knowledge, but rather the
movement of criticism, and hence the movement of anti-power.
Criticism tries not just to get behind a phenomenon and analyse it,
but above all to see how it has been constructed:

> It seems to be correct to begin with the real and the concrete, with
> the real precondition, thus to begin, in economics, with e.g. the
> population, which is the foundation and the subject of the entire
> social act of production. However, on closer examination this
> proves false. The population is an abstraction if I leave out, for
> example, the classes of which it is composed. These classes, in
> turn, are an empty phrase if I am not familiar with the elements
> on which they rest. E.g. wage labour, capital, etc. These latter in
> turn presuppose exchange, division of labour, prices, etc. For
> example, capital is nothing without wage labour, without value,

money, price, etc. Thus, if I were to begin with the population, this would be a chaotic conception [*Vorstellung*] of the whole, and I would then, by means of further determination, move analytically towards ever more simple concepts [*Begriff*], from the imagined concrete towards ever thinner abstractions until I had arrived at the *simplest determinations*. From there the journey would have to be retraced until I had finally arrived at the population again, but this time not as the chaotic conception of a whole, but as a rich totality of many determinations and relations ... The latter is obviously the scientifically correct method. The concrete is concrete because it is the unity of many determinations, hence unity of the diverse. It appears in the process of thinking, therefore, as a process of concentration, as a result, not as a point of departure, even though it is the point of departure in reality and hence also the point of departure for observation [*Anschauung*] and conception. Along the first path the full conception was evaporated to yield an abstract determination; along the second, the abstract determinations lead towards a reproduction of the concrete by way of thought ... But this is by no means the process by which the concrete itself comes into being. [Marx 1973, pp. 100–1; emphasis added]

The '*simplest determinations*' can only be understood as doing (or the two-fold existence of labour): this is surely the pivot, the turning-point which gives meaning to the retracing of the journey.

The same point is made repeatedly in *Capital*, as, for example, in a concise remark in a footnote in which Marx starts from the critique of technology and moves on to the critique of religion:

It is, in reality, much easier to discover by analysis the earthly core of the misty creations of religion, than, conversely, it is, to develop from the actual relations of life the corresponding celestialised forms of those relations. The latter method is the only materialistic, and therefore the only scientific one. [Marx 1965, pp. 372–3]

Why does Marx insist that this is the only scientific method? That it is theoretically more demanding is clear, but why does this matter? And how are we to understand the genetic connection? The remark on the critique of religion suggests an answer. The reference to discovering 'by analysis the earthly core of the misty creations of religion' is a reference to Feuerbach and his argument that belief in the existence of a god is an expression of human self-alienation, that human self-alienation, in other words, is the 'earthly core' of religion. The second part of Marx's sentence, on developing 'from the actual relations of life the corresponding celestialised forms of those relations', refers to Marx's own criticism of Feuerbach, to the effect that self-alienation must be understood not in an abstract, but in a practical (and therefore historical) sense. Feuerbach is correct in pointing out that god is a human creation (and not vice versa), but the process of creation must be understood practically, sensually. The concept of 'god' must be understood as the product of human thought, and this thought, in turn, is not an individual ahistorical act, but an aspect of social practice in certain historical conditions.

The criticism of Feuerbach has important political implications. Religion presents humans as objects, as beings created by God, the sole creator, the genesis of all things, the source of all power, the only Subject. Feuerbach's criticism of religion puts humans in the centre of the world, but Feuerbach's human is trapped in a timeless self-alienation. Humans are at once deified and rendered powerless. Once the production of god is understood as a social, historical human practice, however, then humans are no longer trapped in a timeless vacuum of powerlessness: it becomes possible to think of a time of non-alienation, of different sociohistorical conditions in which humans would no longer produce god, would no longer produce their own objectification.

Marx's critique of the political economists follows the same pattern as his critique of Feuerbach. In *Capital*, his attention has moved to a much more powerful god than the god of religion, namely Money (value). Money, in everyday thought, proclaims itself as ruler of the world, as the sole source of power. Ricardo (taking the place of Feuerbach) has shown that that is not so: he has discovered 'by analysis' that the 'earthly core of the misty creations' of economics (the religion of money) is human labour, as the substance of value. However, Ricardo treats value in the same way as Feuerbach treats god: as a timeless, ahistorical feature of the human condition:

Political economy has indeed analysed, however incompletely, value and its magnitude, and has discovered what lies beneath these forms. But it has never once asked the question why labour is represented by the value of its product and labour-time by the magnitude of that value. These formulae, which bear it stamped upon them in unmistakable letters that they belong to a state of society, in which the process of production has the mastery over man, instead of being controlled by him, such formulae appear to the bourgeois intellect to be as much a self-evident necessity imposed by Nature as productive labour itself. [1965, pp. 80–1]

The result is that Ricardo, like Feuerbach, puts humans at the centre of the world, but leaves humanity entrapped in a timeless, unchanging vacuum of powerlessness. It is only by tracing the production of value and money by social, historical human practice that the critique of the Power of Money (and powerlessness of humans) becomes a theory of human anti-power, of the anti-power of human practice.

Genetic criticism is crucial, therefore, to the understanding of existing phenomena as historically specific, and therefore changeable, forms of social relations. In a footnote to the passage on political economy just quoted, Marx says:

Even Adam Smith and Ricardo, the best representatives of the school, treat the form of value as a thing of no importance, as having no connexion with the inherent nature of commodities. The reason for this is not solely because their attention is entirely absorbed in the analysis of the magnitude of value. It lies deeper. The value-form of the product is not only the most abstract, but is also the most universal form, taken by the product in bourgeois production, and stamps the production as a particular species of social production, and thereby gives it its special historical character. If then we treat this mode of production as one eternally fixed by Nature for every state of society, we necessarily overlook that which is the diferentia specifica of the value-form, and consequently of the commodity-form, and of its further developments, money-form, capital-form, &c. [1965, p. 81]

It is genetic criticism that opens up the question of form, that helps us to understand that our power-to exists in the form of being denied, that points us towards the all-important question of the force and reality of that which exists in the form of being denied.

These examples make it clear that the genetic method is not just a question of applying a superior logic.[3] Marx's method is sometimes described as based on the logical 'derivation' of categories (money from value, capital from money, and so on). This is correct, but in so far as the derivation, or the genetic link, is understood in purely logical terms, then the core of Marx's approach is misunderstood. The claim that Marx's method is scientific is not a claim that its logic is superior, or that it is more rigorous, but that it follows in thought (and therefore consciously takes part in) the movement of the process of doing. Genesis can only be understood as human genesis, as human power-to. Marx's method is above all politically important.

III

Criticism, understood as an analytical and genetic movement, is the movement of defetishisation, the theoretical voice of the scream. Criticism is both destructive and regenerative. It is destructive because it is directed relentlessly against everything that *is*. It destroys *is*-ness itself. No identitarian statement, no claim (whether 'left', 'right' or 'centre') that something *is* something, can be immune from the destructive force of criticism. However, criticism is not solely destructive: the destruction of being is at the same time the recuperation of doing, the restoration of human power-to. In so far as criticism destroys that which denies, it is also the emancipation of that which is denied. Criticism is emancipatory to the extent to which it is destructive.

The recuperation of doing is, of course, just a theoretical recuperation. The being which we criticise, the objectivity which we criticise, is not a mere illusion, it is a real illusion. There is a real separation of doing and done, of subject and object. The objects which we create really do stand over against us as something alien, as things that are. Genetic criticism involves the recuperation of our lost subjectivity, the understanding that those alien objects are the product of our own self-alienated subjectivity, but the objects do not cease to be alienated objects just because of our criticism. Their objectivity is not the result of our lack of understanding but of the self-alienated process of work which produced them. To say this is not at all to minimise the importance of theory, but to make the obvious point that theory makes sense only if it is understood as part of the more general struggle for the real recuperation of doing.

In the context of this struggle, it is important to emphasise that the doing that is recovered is not an individual but a social doing. In order to understand the genesis of phenomena, in order to understand the origin of fetishised appearances, we are always brought back to social doing and the form in which it exists. Understanding the origin of money, for example, is not a question of saying 'x made it', but seeing that money is generated by the organisation of human doing as labour to produce commodities for a market. Money, like value, like the state, like capital, are, as Marx points out, forms of social relations, but it is crucial to understand that social relations are relations between doers, between active subjects. The doing that is recovered through genetic criticism is social doing, what we have called the 'social flow of doing'.

This social doing is not just something in the past, it is present substratum. That is all-important in understanding the force of our scream. That which is denied, social doing, is not just the historical origin of the being which denies that doing, it is its present inescapable substratum. The genetic critique of money (in Chapter 1 of *Capital*) does not just point to the historical origin of money: it reveals rather the continuous regeneration of money through the existence of social doing as commodity producing labour. Money could not exist if doing did not exist as abstract labour.

The understanding of fetishism as fetishisation makes it clear that genesis must be understood not just as historical genesis but above all as present genesis. We do not ask simply 'How did value, money, state arise as forms of social relations?' but rather 'How *do* value, money, state arise as forms of social relations? How are these forms disrupted and re-created each day? How do *we* disrupt and recreate these forms each day?' Moving out from our scream, we are confronted by a world that is fixed, a world of Is-ness. Criticism breaches that fixedness, first by showing all phenomena to be *forms*, historical modes of existence of social relations, and now by showing that these forms are highly volatile, highly unstable, constantly challenged, disrupted, re-formed, challenged again.

The doing that is revealed by genetic criticism, is not Pure Subjectivity. It is damaged subjectivity, the only kind we know. Criticism seeks to understand social phenomena in terms of human creativity and the forms in which that creativity exists. The man[4] who makes religion is not a whole man. He is a sick, damaged, self-estranged man:

> Religion is the self-consciousness and self-esteem of man who has either not yet found himself or has already lost himself again ... Religion is the sigh of the oppressed creature, the heart of a heartless world, just as it is the spirit of spiritless conditions. [1973, p. 175]

Similarly, in *Capital*, Marx does not derive all the categories of political economy from human creativity but rather from the self-divided, self-antagonistic dual existence of human creativity as abstract and concrete labour.

Genetic criticism points to the exclusive subjectivity of humanity. In that sense, it is a great chest-thumping cry of power-to: 'It is *we* who create society, not God, not capital, not chance: therefore *we* can change it.' Our initial scream of frustration here begins to become a scream of anti-power. On the other hand, if we create society in such a way that it stands over against us as something alien, if we subjects create an objectivity that we do not recognise as the expression of our own subjectivity, then it is because we ourselves are self-estranged, self-alienated, turned against ourselves.

There is a tendency, perhaps, for left-wing critics of capitalism to adopt a moral high ground, to place ourselves above society. Society is sick, but we are healthy. We know what is wrong with society, but society is so sick that others do not see it. We are right, we have true consciousness: those who do not see that we are right are duped by the sick society, enveloped in false consciousness. The scream of anger from which we started becomes so easily a self-righteous denunciation of society, a moralistic elitism.

Perhaps we should listen to the upholders of reality when they turn our scream against us and tell us that we are sick, unreasonable, immature, schizophrenic. How can we possibly say that society is sick and that we are not? What arrogance! And what nonsense! If society is sick, then of course we too are sick, since we cannot stand outside society. Our cry is a cry against our own sickness which is the sickness of society, a cry against the sickness of society which is our own sickness. Our cry is not just a cry against a society that is 'out there': it is equally a cry against ourselves, for we are shaped by the out-there-ness of society, by the standing-over-against-us-ness of reality. It makes no sense for the subject to criticise the object in a holier-than-thou fashion when the subject is (and is not) part of the object criticised and is in any case constituted by her separation (and non-separation) from the object. Such holier-than-thou criticism assumes and therefore reinforces the separation of subject and object which is the source of the sickness of both subject and object in the first place. It is better therefore to assume from the beginning that criticism of society must also be criticism of ourselves, that struggle against capitalism must also be struggle against the 'we' who are not only against but also in capitalism. To criticise is to recognise that we are a divided self. To criticise society is to criticise our own complicity in the reproduction of that society.

That realisation does not weaken our scream in any way. On the contrary, it intensifies it, makes it more urgent.

7   The Tradition of Scientific Marxism

The concept of fetishism implies a negative concept of science. If relations between people exist as relations between things, then the attempt to understand social relations can proceed only negatively, by going against and beyond the form in which social relations appear (and really exist). Science is critical.

The concept of fetishism implies, therefore, that there is a radical distinction between 'bourgeois' science and critical or revolutionary science. The former assumes the permanence of capitalist social relations and takes identity for granted, treating contradiction as a mark of logical inconsistency. Science, in this view, is the attempt to understand reality. In the latter case, science can only be negative, a critique of the untruth of existing reality. The aim is not to understand reality, but to understand (and, by understanding, to intensify) its contradictions as part of the struggle to change the world. The more all-pervasive we understand reification to be, the more absolutely negative science becomes. If *everything* is permeated by reification, then absolutely everything is a site of struggle between the imposition of the rupture of doing and the critical-practical struggle for the recuperation of doing. No category is neutral.

For Marx, science is negative. The truth of science is the negation of the untruth of false appearances. In the post-Marx Marxist tradition, however, the concept of science is turned from a negative into a positive concept. The category of fetishism, so central for Marx, is almost entirely forgotten by the mainstream Marxist tradition. From being the struggle against the untruth of fetishism, science comes to be understood as knowledge of reality. With the positivisation of science, power-over penetrates into revolutionary theory and undermines it far more effectively than any government undercover agents infiltrating a revolutionary organisation.

II

It is convenient to see the positivisation of science as being Engels's contribution to the Marxist tradition, although there are certainly dangers in over-emphasising the difference between Marx and Engels: the attempt to put all the blame on to Engels diverts attention from the contradictions that were undoubtedly present in Marx's own work.[1]

The classic claim for the scientific character of Marxism in the mainstream tradition is Engels's pamphlet, *Socialism: Utopian and Scientific*, which probably did more than any other work to define 'Marxism'. Criticism of scientificism in the Marxist tradition often takes the form of a critique of Engels, but, in fact, the 'scientific' tradition is far more deep-rooted than that would suggest. It certainly finds expression in some of Marx's own writings (most famously in the '1859 Preface' to his *Contribution to the Critique of Political Economy*), and is developed in the 'classical' era of Marxism by writers as diverse as Kautsky, Lenin, Luxemburg and Pannekoek. Although Engels's writings possibly have relatively few explicit defenders today, the tradition which Engels represents continues to provide the unspoken and unquestioned assumptions upon which a great deal of Marxist discussion is based. In what follows, our principal concern is not who said what, but to draw out the main constituents of the scientific tradition.

In speaking of Marxism as 'scientific', Engels means that it is based on an understanding of social development that is just as exact as the scientific understanding of natural development. The course of both natural and human development is characterised by the same constant movement:

> When we consider and reflect upon Nature at large or the history of mankind or our own intellectual activity, at first we see the picture of an endless entanglement of relations and reactions, permutations and combinations, in which nothing remains what, where and as it was, but everything moves, changes, comes into being and passes away ... This primitive, naïve but intrinsically correct conception of the world is that of ancient Greek philosophy, and was first clearly formulated by Heraclitus: everything is and is not, for everything is fluid, is constantly changing, constantly coming into being and passing away. [1968, p. 43]

Dialectics is the conceptualisation of nature and society as being in constant movement: it

> ... comprehends things and their representations, ideas, in their essential connection, concatenation, motion, origin, and ending ... Nature is the proof of dialectics, and it must be said for modern science that it has furnished this proof with very rich materials increasing daily, and thus has shown that, in the last resort, Nature works dialectically and not metaphysically. [1968, p. 45]

Through dialectics we can reach an exact understanding of natural and social development:

> An exact representation of the universe, of its evolution, of the development of mankind, and of the reflection of this evolution in the minds of men, can therefore only be obtained by the methods of dialectics with its constant regard to the innumerable actions and reactions of life and death, of progressive and retrogressive changes. [1968, p. 46]

For Engels, dialectics comprehends the objective movement of nature and society, a movement independent of the subject.

The task of science, then, is to understand the laws of motion of both nature and society. Modern materialism, unlike the mechanical materialism of the eighteenth century, is dialectical:

> ... modern materialism sees in [history] the process of evolution of humanity and aims at discovering the laws thereof ... Modern materialism embraces the more recent discoveries of natural science, according to which Nature also has its history in time, the celestial bodies, like the organic species that, under favourable conditions, people them, being born and perishing ... In both aspects, modern materialism is essentially dialectic ... [1968, pp. 47–8]

It need hardly be underlined that Engels's understanding of the dialectic method is an extremely diluted one. Lukács brought upon himself the wrath of the Party by pointing this out in *History and Class Consciousness*:

> Dialectics, he [Engels] argues, is a continuous process of transition from one definition into the other. In consequence a one-sided

and rigid causality must be replaced by interaction. But he does not even mention the most vital interaction, namely the *dialectical relation between subject and object in the historical process*, let alone give it the prominence it deserves. Yet without this factor dialectics ceases to be revolutionary, despite attempts (illusory in the last analysis) to retain 'fluid' concepts. For it implies a failure to recognise that in all metaphysics the object remains untouched and unaltered so that thought remains contemplative and fails to become practical; while for the dialectical method the central problem is *to change reality*. [Lukács 1971, p. 3; original emphasis]

Dialectics, for Engels, becomes a natural law, not the reason of revolt, not the 'consistent sense of non-identity', the sense of the explosive force of the denied. It is no doubt for this reason that some authors, in their criticism of the orthodox Marxist tradition, have been concerned to criticise the whole idea of a dialectical method.[2]

For Engels, the claim that Marxism is scientific is a claim that it has understood the laws of motion of society. This understanding is based on two key elements:

These two great discoveries, the materialistic conception of history and the revelation of the secret of capitalistic production through surplus-value, we owe to Marx. With these two discoveries Socialism becomes a science. The next thing was to work out all its details and relations. [1968, p. 50]

Science, in the Engelsian tradition which became known as 'Marxism', is understood as the exclusion of subjectivity: 'scientific' is identified with 'objective'. The claim that Marxism is scientific is taken to mean that subjective struggle (the struggle of socialists today) finds support in the objective movement of history. The analogy with natural science is important not because of the conception of nature that underlies it but because of what it says about the movement of human history. Both nature and history are seen as being governed by forces 'independent of men's will', forces that can therefore be studied objectively.

The notion of Marxism as scientific socialism has two aspects. In Engels's account there is a double objectivity. Marxism is objective, certain, 'scientific' knowledge of an objective, inevitable process. Marxism is understood as scientific in the sense that it has understood correctly the laws of motion of a historical process taking place independently of men's will. All that is left for Marxists to do is to fill in the details, to apply the scientific understanding of history.

The attraction of the conception of Marxism as a scientifically objective theory of revolution for those who were dedicating their lives to struggle against capitalism is obvious. It provided not just a coherent conception of historical movement, but also enormous moral support: whatever reverses might be suffered, history was on our side. The enormous force of the Engelsian conception and the importance of its role in the struggles of that time should not be overlooked. At the same time, however, both aspects of the concept of scientific socialism (objective knowledge, objective process) pose enormous problems for the development of Marxism as a theory of struggle.

If Marxism is understood as the correct, objective, scientific knowledge of history, then this begs the question, 'Who says so?' Who holds the correct knowledge and how did they gain that knowledge? Who is the subject of the knowledge? The notion of Marxism as 'science' implies a distinction between those who know and those who do not know, a distinction between those who have true consciousness and those who have false consciousness.

This distinction immediately poses both epistemological and organisational problems. Political debate becomes focused on the question of 'correctness' and the 'correct line'. But how do we know (and how do they know) that the knowledge of 'those who know' is correct? How can the knowers (party, intellectuals or whatever) be said to have transcended the conditions of their social time and place in such a way as to have gained a privileged knowledge of historical movement? Perhaps even more important politically: if a distinction is to be made between those who know and those who do not, and if understanding or knowledge is seen as important in guiding the political struggle, then what is to be the organisational relation between the knowers and the others (the masses)? Are those in the know to lead and educate the masses (as in the concept of the vanguard party) or is a communist revolution necessarily the work of the masses themselves (as 'left communists' such as Pannekoek maintained)?

The other wing of the concept of scientific Marxism, the notion that society develops according to objective laws, also poses obvious problems for a theory of struggle. If there is an objective movement of history which is independent of human volition, then what is the role of struggle? Are those who struggle simply carrying out a human destiny which they do not control? Or is struggle important simply in the interstices of the objective movements, filling in the smaller or larger gaps left open by the clash of forces and relations of production? The notion of objective laws opens up a separation between structure and struggle. Whereas the notion of fetishism suggests that *everything* is struggle, that nothing exists separately from the antagonism of social relations, the notion of 'objective laws' suggests a duality between an objective structural movement of history independent of people's will, on the one hand, and the subjective struggles for a better world, on the other. Engels's conception tells us that the two movements coincide, that the former gives support to the latter, but they do not cease to be separate. This duality is the source of endless theoretical and political problems in the Marxist tradition.

Engels's notion of the objective movement of history towards an end gives a secondary role to struggle. Whether struggle is simply seen as supporting the movement of history or whether it is attributed a more active role, its significance in any case derives from its relation to the working out of the objective laws. Whatever the differences in emphasis, struggle in this perspective cannot be seen as self-emancipatory: it acquires significance only in relation to the realisation of the goal. The whole concept of struggle is then instrumental: it is a struggle to achieve an end, to arrive somewhere. The positivisation of the concept of science implies a positivisation of the concept of struggle. Struggle, from being struggle-against, is metamorphosed into being struggle-for. Struggle-for is struggle to create a communist society, but in the instrumentalist perspective which the positive-scientific approach implies, struggle comes to be conceived in a step-by-step manner, with the 'conquest of power' being seen as the decisive step, the fulcrum of revolution. The notion of the 'conquest of power', then, far from being a particular aim that stands on its own, is at the centre of a whole approach to theory and struggle.

III

The implication of Engels's analysis, namely that the transition to communism would come about inevitably as a result of the conflict between the development of the forces of production and the relations of production, did not satisfy the revolutionary theorists-activists of the early part of the century. They insisted on the importance of active struggle for communism, yet they retained much of the dualism of Engels's presentation of 'Marxism'.[3]

The problems posed by the dualistic separation of subject and object came to the fore in the revolutionary turbulence of the beginning of the century. Virtually all the debates of the 'classical' period of Marxism (roughly the first quarter of the twentieth century) took place on the assumed foundation of the 'scientific' interpretation of Marxism. Despite their very important political and theoretical differences, all the major theorists of the period shared certain common assumptions about the meaning of Marxism – assumptions associated with key words such as 'historical material-ism', 'scientific socialism', 'objective laws', 'Marxist economics'.

This is not to say that there was no theoretical development. Perhaps most important, attention in this period of upheaval came to focus on the importance of subjective action. Against the quietistic, wait-and-see interpretations of historic necessity favoured by the main body of the Second International, all the revolutionary theorists of the period (Luxemburg, Lenin, Trotsky, Pannekoek, and so on) stressed the need for active revolutionary intervention. But this emphasis on the subjective was seen in all cases as complemen-tary to (if not subordinate to) the objective movement of capitalism. Now that the theoretical criticism of Engels as the 'distorter' of Marx has gained such wide diffusion, it should be emphasised that the assumptions of scientific Marxism were accepted not only by the reformists of the Second International but by most if not all the major revolutionary theorists.

The dualist concept of Marxism as science has, it was seen, two axes: the notion of an objective historical process and the notion of objective knowledge. The theoretical-political problems connected with both of these axes provided the stuff of theoretical debate in this period.

The first of these axes, the concept of history as an objective process independent of human will, was the main issue in Rosa Luxemburg's classic defence of Marxism against the revisionism of Bernstein, in her pamphlet, *Reform or Revolution*, first published in 1900. Luxemburg's pamphlet is above all a defence of scientific socialism. For her, the understanding of socialism as objective historic necessity was of central importance to the revolutionary movement:

The greatest conquest of the developing proletarian movement has been the discovery of grounds of support for the realisation of socialism in the economic condition of capitalist society. As a result of this discovery, socialism was changed from an 'ideal' dream by humanity for thousands of years to a thing of historic necessity. [1973, p. 35]

Echoing the distinction made by Engels between scientific and utopian socialism, Luxemburg sees the notion of economic or historic necessity as essential if the emptiness of endless calls for justice is to be avoided. Criticising Bernstein, she writes:

'Why represent socialism as the consequence of economic compulsion?' he complains. 'Why degrade man's understanding, his feeling for justice, his will?' (*Vorwärts*, 26 March 1899) Bernstein's superlatively just distribution is to be attained thanks to man's free will, man's will acting not because of economic necessity, since this will itself is only an instrument, but because of man's comprehension of justice, because of man's *idea of justice*. We thus quite happily return to the principle of justice, to the old war horse on which the reformers of the earth have rocked for ages, for the lack of surer means of historic transportation. We return to that lamentable Rosinante on which the Don Quixotes of history have galloped towards the great reform of the earth, always to come home with their eyes blackened. [1973, pp. 44–5]

The scientific character of Marxism is thus seen as its defining feature. The scientific basis of socialism is said to rest

... on three principal results of capitalist development. First, on the growing anarchy of capitalist economy, leading inevitably to its ruin. Second, on the progressive socialisation of the process of production, which creates the germs of the future social order. And third, on the increased organisation and consciousness of the proletarian class, which constitutes the active factor in the coming revolution. [1973, p. 11]

The third element, the 'active factor', is important for Luxemburg:

It is not true that socialism will arise automatically from the daily struggle of the working class. Socialism will be the consequence of (1) the growing contradictions of capitalist economy and (2) the comprehension by the working class of the unavoidability of the suppression of these contradictions through a social transformation. [1973, p. 31]

Thus, although Luxemburg, in common with all the revolutionary theorists, rejects the quietistic interpretation of the inevitability of socialism favoured by many in the German Social Democratic Party, the emphasis on the importance of subjective action is located against the background of the objective, historic necessity of socialism. Socialism will be the consequence of (1) objective trends, and (2) subjective comprehension and practice. The focus on the subjective is added to the understanding of Marxism as a theory of the historic necessity of socialism; or, perhaps more precisely, Marxism, as a theory of objective necessity complements and fortifies subjective class struggle. Whichever way around it is put, there is the same dualist separation between the objective and the subjective – 'the classic dualism of economic law and subjective factor' (Marramao 1978, p. 29).

The central issue arising from this dualism was the question of the relation between the two poles of the dualism – between historic necessity and the 'active factor'. The terms of the question posed by scientific socialism already suggest an endless debate between determinism and voluntarism, between those who attribute little importance to subjective intervention and those who see it as crucial. The argument, however, is about the space to be granted to the subject within an objectively determined framework. The space is essentially intersticial, the argument being over the nature of the interstices.

Whatever the weight attached to the 'active factor', the argument is about how to reach the objectively determined 'final goal'. Luxemburg opens her argument against Bernstein in *Reform or Revolution* by accusing him of abandoning the 'final goal' of the socialist movement. She quotes him as saying 'The final goal, no matter what it is, is nothing; the movement is everything' (1973, p. 8). To this Luxemburg objects:

... the final goal of socialism constitutes the only decisive factor distinguishing the social democratic movement from bourgeois democracy and from bourgeois radicalism, the only factor transforming the entire labour movement from a vain effort to repair the capitalist order into a class struggle against this order, for the suppression of this order ... [1973, p. 8]

And what is this final goal, according to Luxemburg? 'The conquest of political power and the suppression of wage labour' (1973, p. 8).

The goal, then, according to Luxemburg, is to bring about social revolution through the conquest of political power: 'From the first appearance of class societies having the class struggle as the essential content of their history, the conquest of political power has been the aim of all rising classes' (1973, p. 49). 'It is necessary to extract the kernel of socialist society from its capitalist shell. Exactly for this reason must the proletariat seize political power and suppress completely the capitalist system' (1973, p. 52). Class struggle is instrumental, the aim being 'to extract the kernel of socialist society from its capitalist shell'. Struggle is not a process of self-emancipation which would create a socialist society (whatever that might turn out to be) but just the opposite: struggle is an instrument to achieve a preconceived end which would then provide freedom for all.

In the classical debates of Marxism, the issue of the relation between the 'active factor' and 'historic necessity' was focused most clearly in the discussions surrounding the collapse of capitalism. These discussions had important political implications since they centred on the transition from capitalism to socialism, and therefore on revolution and revolutionary organisation (although the different positions did not follow any simple left–right split (cf. Marramao 1978)).

At one extreme was the position usually identified with the Second International, and formulated most clearly by Cunow at the end of the 1890s (Cunow 1898–99): since the collapse of capitalism was the inevitable result of the working out of its own contradictions, there was no need for revolutionary organisation. Those who argued that the collapse of capitalism was inevitable did not all draw the same conclusions, however. For Luxemburg, as we have seen, the inevitable collapse of capitalism (which she attributed to the exhaustion of the possibilities of capitalist expansion into a non-capitalist world) was seen as giving support to anti-capitalist struggle rather than detracting from the need for revolutionary organisation.

The opposite view, the view that collapse was not inevitable, also led to diverse political conclusions. For some (Bernstein, for example) it led to the abandonment of a revolutionary perspective and the acceptance of capitalism as a framework within which social improvements could be sought. For others, such as Pannekoek, the rejection of the idea of the inevitability of capitalist collapse was part of an emphasis on the importance of revolutionary organisation: he argued that the objective movement of capitalist contradictions would lead not to collapse, but to ever more intense crises, which must be understood as opportunities for subjective action to overthrow capitalism (1977). It is interesting that Pannekoek, the leading theorist of left or council communism, denounced by Lenin in his *Left-Wing Communism – An Infantile Disorder*, accepted, in spite of all his emphasis on the importance of developing the 'active side', the framework of Marx's 'economic materialism' as the analysis of the objective movement of capitalism. His emphasis on activism did not take the form of challenging the objectivist interpretation of Marx, but of arguing that it was necessary to complement the objective development by subjective action.

The second axis of scientific Marxism, the question of scientific knowledge and its organisational implications, formed the core of the discussion between Lenin and his critics.

In Lenin's theory of the vanguard party, the organisational implications of the positive notion of scientific knowledge are developed to the point of creating a sharp organisational distinction between the knowers (those who have true consciousness) and the non-knowers (the masses who have false consciousness). In the pamphlet which spelt out the theory of the vanguard party, *What is to be Done?*, Lenin argues the point very explicitly. After discussing the limitations of the strike movement of the 1890s, he makes his central point about class consciousness and socialism:

We said that *there could not yet* be Social-Democratic consciousness among the workers. This consciousness could only be brought to them from without. The history of all countries shows that the working class, exclusively by its own effort, is able to develop only trade union consciousness, i.e., it may itself realise the necessity for combining in unions, for fighting against the employers and for striving to compel the government to pass necessary labour legislation, etc. The theory of socialism, however, grew out of the philosophic, historical and economic theories that were elaborated by the educated representatives of the propertied classes, the intellectuals. According to their social status, the founders of modern scientific socialism, Marx and Engels, themselves belonged to the bourgeois intelligentsia. Similarly, in Russia, the theoretical doctrine of Social-Democracy arose quite independently of the spontaneous growth of the labour movement; it arose as a natural and inevitable outcome of the development of ideas among the revolutionary socialist intelligentsia. [1966, pp. 74–5, original emphasis]

It has been suggested (by del Barco 1980) that the clear separation of theory (developed by bourgeois intellectuals) and experience (that of the workers) was a reflection of the particular history of the Russian revolutionary movement. Lenin's own references, however, suggest that his ideas have a wider basis within the Marxist tradition. He quotes both Engels and Kautsky at length. Particularly significant is the passage quoted with evident approval from an article by Kautsky, in which Kautsky writes:

Of course, socialism, as a theory, has its roots in modern economic relationships just as the class struggle of the proletariat has, and just as the latter emerges from the struggle against the capitalist-created poverty and misery of the masses. But socialism and the class struggle arise side by side and not one out of the other; each arises under different conditions. Modern socialist consciousness can arise only on the basis of profound scientific knowledge. Indeed, modern economic science is as much a condition for socialist production as, say, modern technology, and the proletariat can create neither one nor the other, no matter how much it may desire to do so; both arise out of the modern social process. The vehicles of science are not the proletariat, but the *bourgeois intelligentsia* [Kautsky's italics]: it was in the minds of some members of this stratum that modern socialism originated, and it was they who communicated it to the more intellectually developed proletarians who, in their turn, introduced it into the proletarian class struggle where conditions allow that to be done. Thus, socialist consciousness is something introduced into the proletarian class struggle from without (*von aussen Hineingetragenes*), and not something that arose within it spontaneously (*urwüchsig*). Accordingly, the old Hainfeld programme quite rightly stated that the task of Social-Democracy is to imbue the proletariat with the *consciousness* of its position and the consciousness of its tasks. There would be no need for this if consciousness emerged itself from the class struggle. [1966, pp. 81–2]

The quotation from Kautsky makes clear that the central issue is not the peculiarities of the Russian revolutionary tradition: however important those peculiarities might have been, ascribing the problems of Leninism to them lets mainstream Marxism off the hook. The central issue is rather the concept of science or theory which was accepted by the mainstream of the Marxist movement. If science is understood as an objectively 'correct' understanding of society, then it follows that those most likely to attain such an understanding will be those with greatest access to education (understood, presumably, as being at least potentially scientific). Given the organisation of education in capitalist society, these will be members of the bourgeoisie. Science, consequently, can come to the proletariat only from outside. If the movement to socialism is based on the scientific understanding of society, then it must be led by bourgeois intellectuals and those 'proletarians distinguished by their intellectual development' to whom they have transmitted their scientific understanding. Scientific socialism, understood in this way, is the theory of the emancipation of the proletariat, but certainly not of its self-emancipation. Class struggle is understood instrumentally, not as a process of self-emancipation but as the struggle to create a society in which the proletariat would be emancipated: hence the pivotal role of 'conquering power'. The whole point of conquering power is that it is a means of liberating others. It is the means by which class-conscious revolutionaries, organised in the party, can liberate the proletariat. In a theory in which the working class is a 'they', distinguished from a 'we' who are conscious of the need for revolution, the notion of 'taking power' is simply the articulation that joins the 'they' and the 'we'.

The genius of Lenin's theory of the vanguard party, then, was that it developed to their logical conclusion the organisational consequences of Engels's notion of scientific socialism. From being a negative concept in Marx (science as the negation of fetishised appearances), science in Engels becomes something positive (objective knowledge of an objective process), so that 'unscientific' then denotes the absence of something: absence of knowledge, absence of class consciousness. The question that Marx leaves us with ('How can we, who live against and in fetishised social relations, negate this fetishism?') becomes turned around to become 'How can the workers acquire class consciousness?' 'Simple,' replies Lenin, 'since their consciousness is limited to trade union consciousness, true consciousness can only come from outside, from (us) bourgeois intellectuals.' The inconvenient question of the material source of the bourgeois intellectual consciousness is lost, since it is seen as just the acquisition of scientific knowledge.

Marxist practice then becomes a practice of bringing conscious-ness to the workers, of explaining to them, of telling them where their interests lie, of enlightening and educating them. This practice, so widely established in revolutionary movements in all the world, has its roots not just in the authoritarian tradition of Leninism but in the positive concept of science which Engels established. Knowledge-about is power-over. If science is understood as knowledge-about, then there is inevitably a hierarchical relation between those who have this knowledge (and hence access to the 'correct line') and those (the masses) who do not. It is the task of those-in-the-know to lead and educate the masses.[4]

It is not that scientific Marxism simply reproduces bourgeois theory: clearly the perspective is revolutionary change, the point of reference is a communist society. It introduces new categories of thought, but those categories are understood positively. The revolu-tionary character of the theory is understood in terms of content, not in terms of method, in terms of the what, not the how. Thus, for example, 'working class' is a central category, but it is taken to refer, in the manner of bourgeois sociology, to a definable group of people, rather than to the pole of an antagonistic relation. Similarly, the state is seen as the instrument of the ruling class rather than as one moment in the general fetishisation of social relations, and categories such as 'Russia', 'Britain', and so on, go entirely unques-tioned. The concept of revolutionary theory is much too timid. Revolutionary science is understood as a prolongation of bourgeois science rather than a radical break with it.

The Engelsian concept of science implies a monological political practice. The movement of thought is a monologue, the unidirec-tional transmission of consciousness from the party to the masses. A concept that understands science as the critique of fetishism, on the other hand, leads (or should lead) to a more dialogical concept of politics, simply because we are *all* subject to fetishism and because science is just part of the struggle against the rupture of doing and done, a struggle in which we are all involved in different ways. Understanding science as critique leads more easily to a politics of dialogue, a politics of talking-listening, rather than just of talking.[5]

The great attraction of Leninism is of course that he cut through what we have called the tragic dilemma of revolution. He solved the problem of how those who lacked class consciousness could make a revolution: through the leadership of the Party. The only problem is that it was not the revolution that we (or they) wanted. The second part of the sentence 'We shall take power and liberate the proletariat' was not, and could not be, realised.

IV

The concept of scientific socialism has left an imprint that stretches far beyond those who identify with Engels, Kautsky or Lenin. The separation of subject and object implied by the idea of scientific socialism continues to shape the way that capitalism is understood in much modern Marxist debate. In its modern form, scientific socialism is sometimes referred to as 'structuralism', but the impact of the 'scientific' position is not limited to those who would recognise themselves as structuralists. Rather, the 'scientific' separation of subject and object is expressed in a whole series of categories and specialised fields of study developed by people who do not feel themselves addressed in any sense by criticisms of Engels or of modern structuralism. It is important, therefore, to get some sense of just how much modern Marxism has been marked by the assumptions of scientific socialism.

The basic feature of scientific socialism is its assumption that science can be identified with objectivity, with the exclusion of subjectivity. This scientific objectivity, it was seen, has two axes or points of reference. Objectivity is understood to refer to the course of social development: there is a historical movement which is independent of people's will. It is also taken to refer to the knowledge which we (Marxists) have of this historical movement: Marxism is the correct 'discovery' of the objective laws of motion that govern social development. In each of these two axes, the objectivity shapes the understanding of both object and subject.

Although the notion of scientific Marxism has implications for the understanding of both subject and object, in so far as science is identified with objectivity, it is the object which is privileged. Marxism, in this conception, becomes the study of the objective laws of motion of history in general, and of capitalism in particular. Marxism's role in relation to working-class struggle is to provide an understanding of the framework within which struggle takes place. Marxists typically take as the point of departure, certainly not a denial of the importance of class struggle, but an assumption of it which amounts to virtually the same thing: class struggle becomes an 'of course',[6] an element so obvious that it can simply be taken for granted and attention turned towards the analysis of capitalism.

A special role falls to 'Marxist economics' in the analysis of history and especially of capitalism. Since the driving force of historical development is seen as lying in the economic structure of society, since (as Engels puts it) the key to social change is to be found in economics and not in philosophy, the Marxist study of economics is central to the understanding of capitalism and its development.

Marx's *Capital* is the key text of Marxist economics, in this view. It is understood as the analysis of the laws of motion of capitalism, based on the development of the central categories of value, surplus value, capital, profit, the tendency for the rate of profit to fall, and so on. Thus, recent discussions in Marxist economics have focused on the validity of the category of value, the 'transformation problem' (concerning Marx's transformation of value into price), the validity of the tendency for the rate of profit to fall and the various theories of economic crisis. As in mainstream economic discussion, much attention is devoted to defining the terms, to establishing precise definitions for 'constant capital', 'variable capital', and so on.

The understanding of *Capital* as a book on economics is certainly supported by some of Marx's own comments, but it owes much to the influence of Engels. Engels, who was responsible for the editing and publication of Volumes II and III of *Capital* after Marx's death, fostered through his editing and his comments a certain interpretation of Marx's work as economics. In the ten years which separated the publication of Volume II (1884) and Volume III (1894), for example, he promoted the so-called 'prize essay competition' to see if other authors could anticipate Marx's solution to the 'transformation problem', the problem of the quantitative relation between value and price, thus focusing attention on the quantitative understanding of value (cf. Howard and King 1989, pp. 21ff; Engels's Preface to Vol. III of *Capital*). In a supplement which he wrote to Volume III on the 'Law of Value and Rate of Profit', he presents value not as a form of social relations specific to capitalist society but as an economic law valid 'for the whole period of simple commodity-production ... a period of from five to seven thousand years' (Marx 1972a, pp. 899–900). It was through Engels's interpretation that the later volumes of *Capital* were presented to the world. As Howard and King put it: 'he conditioned the way in which successive generations of socialists viewed Marx's economics, both in his editions of Marx's writings and in what he left unpublished' (1989, p. 17).

For the Marxists of the early part of this century, Marxist economics was the keystone of the whole structure of scientific Marxism, that which provided the certainty which was the crucial moral support for their struggles. In more recent times, Marxist economics has continued to play a central role in Marxist debate, but it has acquired the newly important dimension of also dovetailing with the structure of university disciplines: for many academics Marxist economics has come to be seen as a particular (albeit deviant) school within the broader discipline of economics.

The defining feature of Marxist economics is the idea that capitalism can be understood in terms of certain regularities (the so-called laws of motion of capitalist development). These regularities refer to the regular (but contradictory) pattern of the reproduction of capital, and Marxist economics focuses on the study of capital and its contradictory reproduction. The contradictory nature of this reproduction (understood variously in terms of the tendency for the rate of profit to fall, underconsumption or disproportionality between the different departments of production) is expressed in periodic crisis and in a long-term tendency towards the intensification of these crises (or towards the collapse of capitalism). Class struggle does not play any direct part in this analysis of capitalism. It is generally assumed that the role of Marxist economics is to explain the framework within which struggle takes place. Class struggle is intersticial: it fills in the gaps left by economic analysis, does not determine the reproduction or crisis of capitalism, but affects the conditions under which the reproduction and crisis take place.[7] Thus, for example, the left Marxists of the early part of the century, it was seen, argued that class struggle was essential to convert the crisis of capitalism into revolution: class struggle was seen as an ingredient to be added to the understanding of the objective movement of capital.

The understanding of Marxist economics as an alternative approach to a particular discipline (economics) suggests the possibility of complementing it with other disciplinary branches of Marxism, such as Marxist sociology and Marxist political science.[8] Marxist sociology focuses principally on the question of class and the analysis of class structures, while Marxist political science has the state as its principal focus. Neither of these disciplinary approaches is as well developed as Marxist economics, but they start from the same basic understanding of Marx's work and of the Marxist tradition, according to which *Capital* is a study of economics, which needs now to be complemented (since Marx did not live to do it) by similar studies of politics, society, and so on.

What all these modern disciplinary strands of Marxism have in common, and what unites them with the underlying concept of scientific Marxism, is the assumption that Marxism is a theory *of* society. In a theory *of* society, the theorist seeks to looks at society objectively and to understand its functioning. The idea of a 'theory *of*' suggests a distance between the theorist and the object of the theory. The notion of a theory *of* society is based on the suppression of the subject, or (and this amounts to the same thing) based on the idea that the knowing subject can stand outside the object of study, can look at human society from a vantage point on the moon, as it were (Gunn 1992). It is only on the basis of this positing of the knowing subject as *external* to the society being studied that the understanding of science as objectivity can be posed.

Once it is understood as a theory of society, Marxism can be ranged alongside other theories of society, compared with other theoretical approaches which seek to understand society. Through this comparison, emphasis falls on the continuity rather than the discontinuity between Marxism and the mainstream theories of social science. Thus, Marx the economist is seen as a critical disciple of Ricardo, Marx the philosopher as a critical disciple of Hegel and Feuerbach; in Marxist sociology, there has been discussion of enriching Marxism with the insights of Weber; in Marxist political science, especially in the writings of many who claim to derive their inspiration from Gramsci, it is assumed that the purpose of a theory of the state is to understand the reproduction of capitalist society.

The understanding of Marxism in disciplinary terms, or as a theory of society, leads almost inevitably to the adoption of the questions posed by the mainstream disciplines or by other theories of society. The central question posed by mainstream social science is: how do we understand the functioning of society and the way in which social structures reproduce themselves? Marxism, in so far as it is understood as a theory *of* society, seeks to provide alternative answers to these questions. Those authors who look to Gramsci to provide a way of moving away from the cruder orthodoxies of the

Leninist tradition, have been particularly active in trying to develop Marxism as a theory of capitalist reproduction, with their emphasis on the category of 'hegemony' as an explanation of how capitalist order is maintained.

The attempts to use Marx's own categories to develop a theory of capitalist reproduction are, however, always problematic, in so far as the categories of Marxism derive from a quite different question, based not on the reproduction but on the destruction of capitalism, not on positivity but on negativity. The use of Marxist categories to answer the questions of social science inevitably involves a reinterpretation of those categories – for example, a reinterpretation of value as an economic category, or class as a sociological category. The attempt to use Marxist categories to construct an alternative economics or an alternative sociology is always problematic, not because it involves a deviation from the 'true meaning' of 'true Marxism', but because the categories do not always stand up to such reinterpretation. Thus, these reinterpretations have often given rise to considerable debate and to a questioning of the validity of the categories themselves. For example, once value is reinterpreted as the basis for a theory of price, then doubts can be (and have been) raised about its relevance; once 'working class' is understood as a sociological category describing an identifiable group of people, then doubts can fairly be raised about the significance of 'class struggle' for understanding the dynamic of contemporary social development. The integration of Marxism into social science, far from giving it a secure home, actually undermines the basis of the categories which Marxists use.[9]

The understanding of Marxism as a theory *of* society gives rise to a particular type of social theory which can be described as functionalist. In so far as Marxism emphasises the regularities of social development, and the interconnections between phenomena as part of a social totality, it lends itself very easily to a view of capitalism as a relatively smoothly self-reproducing society, in which whatever is necessary for capitalist reproduction automatically happens. By a strange twist, Marxism, from being a theory of the destruction of capitalist society, becomes a theory of its reproduction.[10] The separation of class struggle from the laws of motion of capitalism leads to a separation between revolution and the reproduction of capitalist society. This does not necessarily mean that the idea of revolution is abandoned: it may indeed be given up (in the name of realism), but often it is simply taken for granted (in the way that class struggle is taken for granted in so much Marxist analysis), or relegated to the future. Thus, in the future there will be revolution, but in the meantime, the laws of capitalist reproduction operate. In the future, there will be a radical break, but in the meantime we can treat capitalism as a self-reproducing society. In the future, the working class will be the subject of social development, but in the meantime capital rules. In the future, things will be different, but in the meantime we can treat Marxism as a functionalist theory, in which the 'requirements of capital', a phrase which recurs frequently in Marxist discussions, can be taken as an adequate explanation of what does or does not happen. The emphasis on reproduction, combined with an analysis of reproduction as class domination, leads to a view of society in which capital rules and capital's will (or requirements) prevails. Rupture, then, if the idea is maintained at all, can only be seen as something external, something that is brought in from outside.

Functionalism, or the assumption that society should be understood in terms of its reproduction, inevitably imposes a closure upon thought. It imposes bounds upon the horizons within which society can be conceptualised. In Marxist functionalism, the possibility of a different type of society is not excluded, but it is relegated to a different sphere, to a future. Capitalism is a closed system *until* – until the great moment of revolutionary change comes. Consequently, social activity is interpreted within the bounds imposed by this closure. The relegation of revolution to a distinct sphere shapes the way in which all aspects of social existence are understood. Categories are understood as closed categories rather than as categories bursting with the explosive force of their own contradictions, as categories containing the uncontainable. That which might be (the subjunctive, the denied) is subordinated to that which is (the indicative, the positive which denies) ... at least until.

Twist and turn the issue as one may, the notion of scientific Marxism, based on the idea of an objective understanding of an objective course of history, comes up against insuperable theoretical and political objections. Theoretically, the exclusion of the subjectivity of the theorist is an impossibility: the theorist, whether Marx, Engels, Lenin or Mao, cannot look at society from outside, cannot stand on the moon. Even more damaging, the theoretical subordination of subjectivity leads to the political subordination of the subject to the objective course of history and to those who claim to have a privileged understanding of that course.

V

The tradition of 'scientific Marxism' is blind to the issue of fetishism. If fetishism is taken as a starting-point, then the concept of science can only be negative, critical and self-critical. If social relations exist in the form of relations between things, it is impossible to say 'I have knowledge of reality', simply because the categories through which one apprehends reality are historically specific categories which are part of that reality. We can proceed only by criticising, by criticising the reality and the categories through which we apprehend that reality. Criticism inevitably means self-criticism.

In the tradition of scientific Marxism, criticism does not play a central role. Certainly there is criticism in the sense of denunciation of the evils of capitalism; but there is no criticism in the sense of the genetic criticism of identity. To be blind to fetishism is to take fetishised categories at face value, to take fetishised categories without question into one's own thought. Nowhere has this been more disastrous in the tradition of orthodox Marxism than in the assumption that the state could be seen as the centre point of social power. A Marxism that is blind to the question of fetishism is inevitably a fetishised Marxism.[11]

The core of orthodox Marxism is the attempt to enlist certainty on our side. This attempt is fundamentally misconceived: certainty can only be on the other side, the side of domination. Our struggle is inherently and profoundly uncertain. This is so because certainty is conceivable only on the basis of the reification of social relations. It is possible to speak of the 'laws of motion' of society only to the extent that social relations take the form of relations between things.[12] Non-fetishised, self-determining social relations would not be law-bound. The understanding of capitalist society as being bound by laws is valid to the extent, but only to the extent, that relations between people really are thing-ified. If we argue that capitalism can be understood completely through the analysis of its laws of motion, then we say at the same time that social relations are completely fetishised. But if social relations are completely fetishised, how can we conceive of revolution? Revolutionary change cannot possibly be conceived as following a path of certainty, because certainty is the very negation of revolutionary change. Our struggle is a struggle against reification and therefore against certainty.

The great attraction of orthodox Marxism remains its simplicity. It provided an answer to the revolutionary dilemma: a wrong answer, but at least it was an answer. It guided the revolutionary movement to great conquests that, at the end of the day, were not conquests at all, but dreadful defeats. If, however, we abandon the comforting certainties of orthodoxy, what are we left with? Is our scream not then reduced to the childishly naïve and self-deceptive appeal to the idea of justice? Do we not return, as Luxemburg mockingly warned, 'to that lamentable Rosinante on which the Don Quixotes of history have galloped towards the great reform of the earth, always to come home with their eyes blackened'? No, we do not. We return, rather, to the concept of revolution as a question, not as an answer.

8 The Critical-Revolutionary Subject

I

Who are we, we who criticise?

In the course of the argument, we have moved from the earlier description of 'we' as a disparate compound of the author and readers of this book to talking of 'we' as the critical subject. But who, then, are we, the critical subject?

We are not God. We are not a transcendent, trans-historical Subject who sits in judgement on the course of history. We are not omniscient. We are people whose subjectivity is part of the mire of the society in which we live, flies caught in a web.

Who are we, then, and how can we criticise? The most obvious answer is that our criticism and our scream arise from our negative experience of capitalist society, from the fact that we are oppressed, from the fact that we are exploited. Our scream comes from the experience of the daily repeated separation of doing and done, of subject and object, a separation experienced most intensely in the process of exploitation but which permeates every aspect of life.

II

We, then, are the working class: those who create and have our creation (both the object created and the process of creation) snatched from us. Or are we?[1]

Most discussions of the working class are based on the assumption that the fetishised forms are pre-constituted. The relation between capital and labour (or between capitalist and working class) is taken to be one of subordination. On this basis, understanding class struggle involves, first, defining the working class and, second, studying whether and how they struggle.

In this approach, the working class, however defined, is defined on the basis of its subordination to capital: it is because it is subordinated to capital (as wage workers, or as producers of surplus value) that it is defined as working class. Indeed it is only because the working class is assumed to be pre-subordinated that the question of definition can even be posed. Definition merely adds the locks to a world that is assumed to be closed. By being *defined*, the working class is *identified* as a particular group of people. For socialists, 'working class' is then treated as a positive concept and working-class identity as something to be prized, such that the consolidation of that identity is part of the class struggle against capital. There is, of course, the problem of what to do with those people who do not fall within the definitions of working class or capitalist class, but this is dealt with by a supplementary definitional discussion on how to define these other people, whether as new petty bourgeoisie, salariat, middle class or whatever. This process of definition or class-ification is the basis of endless discussions about class and non-class movements, class and 'other forms' of struggle, 'alliances' between the working class and other groups, and so on.

All sorts of problems spring from this definitional approach to class. First, there is the question of 'belonging'. Do we who work in the universities 'belong' to the working class? Did Marx and Lenin? Are the rebels of Chiapas part of the working class? Are feminists part of the working class? Are those active in the gay movement part of the working class? And what about the police? In each case, there is a concept of a pre-defined working class to which these people do or do not belong.

A second consequence of defining class is the definition of struggles that follows. From the classification of the people concerned certain conclusions are derived about the struggles in which they are involved. Those who define the Zapatista rebels as being not part of the working class draw from that certain conclusions about the nature and limitations of the uprising. From the definition of the class position of the participants there follows a definition of their struggles: the definition of class defines the antagonism that the definer perceives or accepts as valid. This leads to a blinkering of the perception of social antagonism. In some cases, for example, the definition of the working class as the urban proletariat directly exploited in factories, combined with evidence of the decreasing proportion of the population who fall within this definition, has led people to the conclusion that class struggle is no longer relevant for understanding social change. In other cases, the definition of the working class and therefore of working-class struggle in a certain way has led to an incapacity to relate to the development of new forms of struggle (the student movement, feminism, ecologism, and so on).

Defining the working class constitutes them as a 'they'. Even if we say that we are part of the working class, we do so by stepping back from ourselves and by classifying ourselves or the group to which we 'belong' (students, university lecturers, and so on). The 'we scream' from which we started is converted into a 'they struggle'.

The framework for the definitional approach to class is the idea that capitalism is a world that is; from a left perspective it is clear that it should not be and it may be that it will not always be, but for the moment it is. This perspective certainly provides a means of describing the conflicts that exist between the two classes (conflicts over wages, over working conditions, over trade union rights, and so on). However, if the framework is the framework of an identitarian world, of a world that is, then there is no possibility of a perspective that transcends this world. The idea of revolution either must be abandoned, or the transcendent, revolutionary element must be imported in the shape of a *deus ex machina*, usually a Party. We are back with Lenin's distinction between trade union consciousness and revolutionary consciousness, with the difference that we now see that the attribution of trade union consciousness to the working class follows from the identitarian theoretical perspective (which Lenin shared) rather than from the world that is/is not. What is seen in this case is shaped more by the spectacles used than by the supposed object of vision.

III

If, on the other hand, we do not start from the assumption of the fetishised character of social relations, if we assume rather that fetishisation is a process and that existence is inseparable from constitution, then how does this change our vision of class?

Class, like state, like money, like capital, must be understood as process. Capitalism is the ever renewed generation of class, the ever renewed class-ification of people. Marx makes this point very clearly in his discussion of accumulation in *Capital*:

Capitalist production, therefore, under its aspect of a continuous connected process, of a process of reproduction, produces not only commodities, not only surplus value, but it also produces and reproduces the capitalist relation: on the one side the capitalist, on the other, the wage labourer. [1965, p. 578]

In other words, the existence of classes and their constitution cannot be separated: to say that classes exist is to say that they are in the process of being constituted.

The constitution of class can be seen as the separation of subject and object. Capitalism is the daily repeated violent separation of the object from the subject, the daily snatching of the object-creation-product from the subject-creator-producer, the daily seizure from the doer not only of her done but of her act of doing, her creativity, her subjectivity, her humanity. The violence of this separation is not characteristic just of the earliest period of capitalism: it is the core of capitalism. To put it in other words, 'primitive accumulation' is not just a feature of a bygone period, it is central to the existence of capitalism.[2]

The violence with which the separation of subject and object, or the class-ification of humanity, is carried out suggests that 'repro-duction' is a misleading word in so far as it conjures up an image of a smoothly repeated process, something that goes around and around, whereas the violence of capitalism suggests that the repetition of the production of capitalist social relations is always very much at issue.

Class struggle, then, is the struggle to classify and against being classified at the same time as it is, indistinguishably, the struggle between constituted classes.

More orthodox discussions of class struggle tend to assume that classes are pre-constituted, that the working class is effectively sub-ordinated, and to start the analysis of class struggle from there. However, the conflict does not begin after subordination has been established, after the fetishised forms of social relations have been constituted: rather it is a conflict about the subordination of social practice, about the fetishisation of social relations. Class struggle does not take place within the constituted forms of capitalist social relations: rather the constitution of those forms is itself class struggle. All social practice is an unceasing antagonism between the subjection of practice to the fetishised, perverted, defining forms of capitalism and the attempt to live against-and-beyond those forms. There can thus be no question of the existence of non-class forms of struggle. Class struggle, then, is the unceasing daily antagonism (whether it be perceived or not) between alienation and disalienation, between definition and anti-definition, between fetish-isation and de-fetishisation.

We do not struggle *as* working class, we struggle *against* being working class, against being classified. Our struggle is not the struggle of labour: it is the struggle against labour.[3] It is the unity of the process of classification (the unity of capital accumulation) that gives unity to our struggle, not our unity as members of a common class. Thus, for example, it is the significance of the Zapatista struggle against capitalist classification that gives it importance for class struggle, not the question of whether the indigenous inhabitants of the Lacandon Jungle are or are not members of the working class. There is nothing good about being members of the working class, about being ordered, commanded, separated from our product and our process of production. Struggle arises not from the fact that we are working class but from the fact that we-are-and-are-not working class, that we exist against-and-beyond being working class, that they try to order and command us but we do not want to be ordered and commanded, that they try to separate us from our product and our producing and our humanity and our selves and we do not want to be separated from all that. In this sense, working-class identity is not something 'good' to be treasured, but something 'bad', something to be fought against, something that is fought against, something that is constantly at issue. Or rather, working class identity should be seen as a non-identity: the communion of struggle to be not working class.

We are/are not working class (whether we are university professors or car workers). To say that class should be understood as class-ification means that class struggle (the struggle to classify us and our struggle against being classified) is something that runs through us, individually and collectively. Only if we were fully class-ified could we say without contradiction 'we are working class' (but then class struggle would be impossible).

We take part in class struggle on both sides. We class-ify ourselves in so far as we produce capital, in so far as we respect money, in so far as we participate, through our practice, our theory, our language (our defining the working class), in the separation of subject and object. We simultaneously struggle against our class-ification in so far as we are human. We exist against-in-and-beyond capital, and against-in-and-beyond ourselves. Humanity, as it exists, is schizoid, volcanic: everyone is torn apart by the class antagonism.

Does this mean that class distinctions can be reduced to a general statement about the schizoid character of humanity? No, because there are clearly differences in the way in which the class antagonism traverses us, differences in the degree to which it is possible for us to repress that antagonism. For those who benefit materially from the process of classification (accumulation), it is relatively easy to repress anything which points against or beyond classification, to live within the bounds of fetishism. It is those whose lives are overturned by accumulation (the indigenous of Chiapas, university teachers, coal miners, nearly everybody) in whom the element of against-ness will be much more present. It is those who are most brutally de-subjectified, whether through the stultification of endless repetition in meaningless jobs, or through the poverty that excludes anything but the fight for survival, in whom the tension of against-ness will be most tightly coiled. It remains true, however, that nobody exists purely against or against-and-beyond: we all participate in the separation of subject and object, the classification of humans.[4]

It is only in so far as we are/are not the working class that revolution as the self-emancipation of the working class becomes conceivable. The working class cannot emancipate itself in so far as it is working class. It is only in so far as we *are not* working class that the question of emancipation can even be posed. And yet, it is only as far as we *are* the working class (subjects torn from their objects) that the need for emancipation arises. We return to the contradictory result already established: we, the critical subject, are and are not the working class.

The conclusion reached is a non-sense only for identitarian thought, only if we think of 'is' and 'is not' as being mutually exclusive. The contradiction between 'is' and 'is not' is not a logical contradiction, but a real one. It points to the fact that we really are/are not reified; we really are/are not identified; we really are/are not class-ified; we really are/are not de-subjectified; in short, we really are/are not. It is only if we understand our subjectivity as a divided subjectivity, and our self as a divided self, that we can make sense of our scream, of our criticism.

The concept of fetishism, as we have seen, is incompatible with a belief in the innocent subject. Power-over reaches into us, turning us against ourselves. The working class does not stand outside capital: on the contrary it is capital that defines it (us) as working class. Labour stands opposed to capital, but it is an internal opposition. It is only as far as labour is something more than labour, the worker more than a seller of labour power, that the issue of revolution can even be posed. The concept of fetishism implies inevitably that we are self-divided, that we are divided against ourselves. The working/anti-working class/anti-class is self-divided: oppressed yet existing not only in but also against-and-beyond that oppression, not only against-and-beyond but also in that oppression. The struggle between fetishism and anti-fetishism exists within all of us, collectively and individually. There can be no question, therefore, of a non-fetishised vanguard leading the fetishised masses. By virtue of the fact of living in an antagonistic society, we are all both fetishised and in struggle against that fetishism.

We are self-divided, self-alienated, schizoid. We-who-scream are also we-who-acquiesce. We who struggle for the reunification of subject and object are also we who produce their separation. Rather than looking to the hero with true class consciousness, a concept of revolution must start from the confusions and contradictions that tear us all apart.

This is quite consistent with Marx's approach. His understanding of capitalism was based not on the antagonism between two groups of people but on the antagonism in the way in which human social practice is organised.[5] Existence in capitalist society is a conflictual existence, an antagonistic existence. Although this antagonism appears as a vast multiplicity of conflicts, we have argued (and it was argued by Marx) that the key to understanding this antagonism and its development is the fact that present society is built upon an antagonism in the way that the distinctive character of humanity, namely doing, is organised. In capitalist society, doing is turned against itself, alienated from itself; we lose control over our creative activity. This negation of human creativity takes place through the subjection of human activity to the market. This subjection to the market, in turn, takes place fully when the capacity to work creatively (labour power) becomes a commodity to be sold on the market to those with the capital to buy it. The antagonism between human creativity and its negation thus becomes focused in the antagonism between those who must sell their creativity and those who appropriate that creativity and exploit it (and, in so doing, transform that creativity into labour). In shorthand, the antagonism between creativity and its negation can be referred to as the conflict between labour and capital, but this conflict (as Marx makes clear) is not a conflict between two external forces, but an internal conflict between doing (human creativity) and alienated doing.

The social antagonism is thus not in the first place a conflict between two groups of people: it is a conflict between creative social practice and its negation, or, in other words, between humanity and its negation, between the transcending of limits (creation) and the imposition of limits (definition). The conflict does not take place after subordination has been established, after the fetishised forms of social relations have been constituted: rather it is a conflict about the subordination of social practice, about the fetishisation of social relations. All social practice is an unceasing antagonism between the subjection of practice to the fetishised, perverted, defining forms of capitalism and the attempt to live against-and-beyond those forms.

Class struggle is a conflict that permeates the whole of human existence. We all exist within that conflict, just as the conflict exists within all of us. It is a polar antagonism which we cannot escape. We do not 'belong' to one class or another: rather, the class antagonism exists in us, tearing us apart. The antagonism (the class divide) traverses all of us. Nevertheless, it clearly does so in very different ways. Some, the very small minority, participate directly in and/or benefit directly from the appropriation and exploitation of the work of others. Others, the vast majority of us, are, directly or indirectly, the objects of that appropriation and exploitation. The polar nature of the antagonism is thus reflected in a polarisation of the two classes,[6] but the antagonism is prior to, not subsequent to, the classes: classes are constituted through the antagonism.

IV

What of the workers in the factories, the industrial proletariat? Are they not central to the concept of class struggle? Is work not central to the whole understanding of the antagonism of capitalist society?

The central site for the separation of doing and done is production. The production of the commodity is the production of the separation of subject and object. Capitalist production is the production by the workers of surplus value, a surplus which, although produced by the workers, is appropriated by the capitalist. By producing a surplus as surplus value, the workers are producing their own separation from the object produced. They are, in other words, producing classes, producing their own class-ification as wage labour: 'Does an operative in a cotton-factory produce nothing but cotton goods? No, he produces capital. He produces values that give fresh command over his labour, and that, by means of such command, create fresh values' (Marx 1965, p. 578).

In production, then, the worker in producing an object produces at the same time her own alienation from that object and thereby produces herself as wage labourer, as de-subjectified subject. Capitalist production involves the ever renewed separation of subject and object. It also involves the ever renewed bringing together of subject and object but as alienated subject and object. The relation between subject and object is an unhinged relation, with value as its (un)hinge. The category of value faces both ways. On the one hand, the fact that value is the product of abstract labour points to capital's absolute dependence upon labour and its abstraction. On the other hand, value conceptualises the separation of the commodity from labour, the fact that it acquires an autonomous existence quite independent of the producer. Value, then, is the process of subordinating the strength of the worker to the domination of her autonomised product.

But the separation of the worker from the means of production is just part (although a central part) of a more general separation of subject and object, a more general distancing of people from the possibility of determining their own activity. The notion of the separation of the worker from the means of production directs our minds to a particular type of creative activity, but in fact this very distinction between production and doing in general is part of the fragmentation of doing that results from the separation of doing and done. The fact that the de-subjectification of the subject appears simply as the separation of the workers from the means of production is already an expression of the fetishisation of social relations. The separation of the worker from the means of production (in the classic sense) is part of, generates and is supported by, a more general process of de-subjectifying the subject, a more general abstracting of labour. Hence value production, surplus value production (exploitation) cannot be the starting-point of the analysis of class struggle, simply because exploitation implies a logically prior struggle to convert creativity into labour, to define certain activities as value producing.

Exploitation is not just the exploitation of labour but the simultaneous transformation of doing into labour, the simultaneous de-subjectification of the subject, the dehumanisation of humanity. This does not mean that creativity, the subject, humanity exist in some pure sphere waiting to be metamorphosed into their capitalist forms. The capitalist form (labour) is the mode of existence of doing/creativity/subjectivity/humanity, but that mode of existence is contradictory. To say that doing exists as labour means that it exists also as anti-labour. To say that humanity exists as subordination means that it exists also as insubordination. The production of class is the suppression(-and-reproduction) of insubordination. Exploitation is the suppression(-and-reproduction) of insubordinate creativity. The suppression of creativity does not just take place in the process of production, as usually understood, but in the whole separating of doing and done that constitutes capitalist society.

Thus: labour produces class, but labour presupposes a prior classification. Similarly, production is the sphere of the constitution of class, but the existence of a sphere of production, that is the separation of production from human doing in general, also presupposes a prior classification.

The answer, then, to our question about the centrality of work is surely that it is not labour that is central but doing, which exists in-against-and-beyond labour. To start uncritically from labour is to enclose oneself from the beginning within a fetishised world, such that any projection of an alternative world must appear as pure fancy, something brought in from outside. To start from labour is to reduce one's concept of class struggle, to exclude from sight the whole world of antagonistic practice that goes into the constitution of doing as labour.

But even if one adopts the broad concept of class struggle proposed here, is there not some sense in which the production of surplus value is central, some sense in which the struggles around production are the core of struggle for emancipation? There might possibly be a case for establishing such a hierarchy if it could be shown that the direct producers of surplus value play a particular part in the attack against capital. It is sometimes argued that there are key sections of workers who are able to inflict particular damage on capital (such as workers in large factories or transport workers). These workers are able to impose with particular directness the dependence of capital upon labour. However, such groups of workers are not necessarily direct producers of surplus value (bank workers, for example), and the impact of the Zapatista uprising on capital (through the devaluation of the Mexican peso and the world financial upheaval of 1994–95, for example) makes it clear that the capacity to disrupt capital accumulation does not depend necessarily on one's immediate location in the process of production.

V

It is not possible to define the critical-revolutionary subject for the critical-revolutionary subject is the indefinable. The critical-revolutionary subject is not a defined 'who' but an undefined, indefinable, anti-definitional 'what'.

Definition implies subordination. It is only on the basis of an assumed subordination that it is possible to define a subject. The definition of a critical-revolutionary subject is an impossibility, since 'critical-revolutionary' means that the subject is not subordinate, is in revolt against subordination. An approach that starts not from subordination but from struggle is necessarily anti-definitional. Insubordination is inevitably a movement against definition, an overflowing.[7] A negation, a rejection, a scream.

There is no reason to restrict the scream to a limited group of people. Yet the scream is a scream-against. The stronger the repression, the stronger the scream. Constantly changing, any attempt to define the scream is immediately overcome by the changing shape of the scream itself.

Our starting-point and constant point of return is our scream. This is where the question of the critical-revolutionary subject must begin. The scream is not a scream in the abstract. It is a scream against: a scream against oppression, against exploitation, against dehumanisation. It is a scream-against that exists in all of us to the extent that we are all oppressed by capitalism, but the intensity and force of the scream-against depends on the intensity and force of that which is screamed against.[8] The scream is not the scream of some, but not of others: it is the scream of all, with different degrees of intensity.

The scream-against is in the first place negative. It is a refusal, a negation of subordination. It is the scream of insubordination, the mumble of non-subordination. Insubordination is a central part of everyday experience, from the disobedience of children, to the cursing of the alarm clock which tells us to get up and go to work, to all sorts of absenteeism, sabotage and malingering at work, to open rebellion, as in the open and organised cry of '¡Ya basta!' Even in the apparently most disciplined and subordinated societies, insubordination is never absent: it is always there, always present as a hidden culture of resistance (on this see Scott 1990).

Often our scream is silent, the 'internal bleeding of stifled volcanoes' (Johnson 1975, p. 36). The scream of insubordination is heard at most as a low mumble of discontent, a grumble of non-subordination. Non-subordination is the simple, unspectacular struggle to shape one's life. It is people's reluctance to give up the simple pleasures of life, their reluctance to become machines, the determination to forge and maintain some degree of power-to. This sort of non-subordination is not necessarily overtly or consciously oppositional, but it remains a powerful obstacle to the voracious expansion and intensification of power-over that the existence of capital entails.

The scream of insubordination is the scream of non-identity. 'You are', says capital to us all the time, classifying us, defining us, negating our subjectivity, excluding any future that is not a prolongation of the present indicative. 'We are not', we reply. 'The world is so', says capital. 'It is not', we reply. We do not need to be explicit. Our very existence is negation, not-ness. Negation at its simplest, darkest: not 'We do not like this, or that', but simply 'We are not, we negate, we overflow the bounds of any concept.' It appears that we are, but we are not. That, at its most fundamental, is the driving force of hope, the force that corrodes and transforms that which is. We are the force of non-identity existing under the fetishised aspect of identity: 'Contradiction is non-identity under the aspect of identity' (Adorno 1990, p. 5).

What is it that is at the core of rebellious theory? What is the substance of hope? 'The working class,' say some, 'we can see it, we can study it, we can organise it, that is the substance of hope, this is where we can start to work politically.' 'Call it the working class,' we reply, 'but we cannot see it, study it, organise it, for the working class as revolutionary class is not: it is non-identity.' It seems an empty answer. Our training tells us to look for a positive force as the substance of hope, but what we have found is more like Fichte's 'dark void': non-identity, a god who says not 'I am who am', but 'We are not who we are, and we are who we are not.' That is what is disturbing about this whole argument: we want a positive force to hold on to, and all that this argument seems to offer is the negative void of non-identity.

There is no positive force to hold on to, no security, no guarantee. All positive forces are chimeras which disintegrate when we touch them. Our god is the only god: ourselves. We are the sun around which the world revolves, the only god, a god of negation. We are Mephistopheles, 'the spirit that always negates'.[9]

Yet there is a problem here. The fact that the scream is a scream-against means that it can never be a pure scream. It is always tainted by that which it is a scream against. Negation always involves a sub-sumption of that which is negated. That can be seen in any struggle against power: a merely negative response to power reproduces power within itself simply by reproducing, negatively, the terms in which power has set the conflict. The dragon that raises its head to threaten us in almost every paragraph of this book pops up again: we seem to be caught in an endlessly recursive circle.

There is indeed an endlessness in negation, but it is not the end-lessness of a circle. It is rather the endlessness of the struggle for communism: even when the conditions for a power-free society are created, it will always be necessary to struggle against the recrudes-cence of power-over. There can be no positive dialectic, no final synthesis in which all contradictions are resolved. If capitalism is to be understood as a process rather than as a state of being, even when human potential is so clogged up, how much more must this be true of a society in which human power-to is liberated.

But there is more to be said than that. We are not caught in an endlessly recursive circle simply because our existence is not recursive or circular. Our scream-against is a scream-against-oppression, and in that sense it is shaped by oppression; but there is more than that, for the scream-against-oppression is a scream against the negation of ourselves, of our humanity, of our power-to create. Non-identity is the core of our scream, but to say 'We are not' is not just a dark void. To negate Is-ness is to assert becoming, movement, creation, the emancipation of power-to. We *are* not, we do not be, we become.

'We are not' becomes, therefore, 'We are not yet', but only if 'not-yet' is understood not as certain future, secure homecoming, but as possibility, as a becoming with no guarantees, no security. If we are not yet, then our not-yet-ness already exists as project, as overflow-ing, as pushing beyond. The reign of the positive present indicative is broken and the world is seen to be full of negative subjunctive in which the distinction between present and future is dissolved. Human existence is not just an existence of negation but an existence of not-yet-ness, in which negation, by being negation of the negation of our humanity, is at the same time a projection towards that humanity. Not a lost humanity, nor an existing humanity, but a humanity to be created. This not-yet-ness can be seen not just in overt political militancy, but in the struggles of everyday living, in the dreams we have, in our projections against the denial of our projections, in our fantasies, from the simplest dreams of pleasure to the most path-breaking artistic creations (see Bloch 1986). Not-yet-ness is a constant drive against an is-ified reality, the revolt of the repressed Pleasure Principle against the Reality Principle. Not-yet-ness is the struggle to de-congest time, to emancipate power-to.

Is our scream of non-identity simply an assertion of humanism? Is the 'dark void' of non-identity simply an assertion of human nature? The problem with humanism is not that it has a concept of humanity, but that humanists usually think of humanity positively, as something already existing, rather than starting from the understanding that humanity exists only in the form of being denied, as a dream, as a struggle, as the negation of inhumanity. If a notion of humanity underlies the argument here, it is a notion of humanity as negation negated, as power-to enchained. To struggle for humanity is to struggle for the liberation of negation, for the emancipation of potential.

It is the movement of power-to, the struggle to emancipate human potential, that provides the perspective of breaking the circle of domination. It is only through the practice of the emancipation of power-to that power-over can be overcome. Work, then, remains central to any discussion of revolution, but only if it is understood that the starting-point is not labour, not fetishised work, but rather work as doing, as the creativity or power-to that exists as, but also against-and-beyond labour. Unless work is understood in this sense, transcendence is an impossibility, other than through the divine intervention of an external force.

The scream-against and the movement of power-to (the two axes of this book) are inextricably entwined. In the process of struggle-against, relations are formed which are not the mirror-image of the relations of power against which the struggle is directed: relations of comradeship, of solidarity, of love, relations which prefigure the sort of society we are struggling for. Similarly, the attempt to develop human potential (to emancipate power-to) is always a struggle-against, since it must come into open or concealed conflict with the constant expansion of power-over which is capital. The scream-against and the struggle for emancipation cannot be separated, even when those in struggle are not conscious of the link. The most liberating struggles, however, are surely those in which the two are consciously linked, as in those struggles which are consciously prefigurative, in which the struggle aims, in its form, not to reproduce the structures and practices of that which is struggled against, but rather to create the sort of social relations which are desired.

The unity of scream-against and power-to can perhaps be referred to as dignity,[10] following the language of the Zapatista uprising. Dignity is the refusal to accept humiliation, oppression, exploitation, dehumanisation. It is a refusal which negates the negation of humanity, a refusal filled, therefore, with the project of the humanity currently negated. This means a politics that projects as it refuses, refuses as it projects: a politics dense with the dream of creating a world of mutual respect and dignity, filled with the knowledge that this dream involves the destruction of capitalism, of everything that dehumanises or de-subjectifies us.

9   The Material Reality of Anti-Power

'Romantic' – 'Noble, but not very realistic' – 'We have to deal with the reality of class struggle, not abstractions about anti-power.'

How can we possibly change the world without taking power? The idea is an attractive dream, and we all like attractive dreams, but what is their reality? How can we dream after the experience of the twentieth century, when so many dreams have failed, when so many dreams have ended in misery and disaster?

Where is this anti-power that is the hope of humanity? What is the material reality of anti-power? Because if it has no material reality, then we are deluding ourselves. We all want to dream that a different type of society is possible, but is it really? The revolutionaries of the early part of the twentieth century built their dreams upon the mass organisations of the proletariat, but those organisations no longer exist or, if they do, they are not the stuff of dreams.

We have thrown out a lot of bathwater. And how many babies? A defined subject has been replaced by an indefinable subjectivity. Proletarian power has been replaced by an undefined anti-power. This sort of theoretical move is often associated with disillusion, with abandoning the idea of revolution in favour of theoretical sophistication. That is not the intention here. But where, then, is this anti-power?

I scream. But am I alone? Some of the readers scream as well. We scream. But what indication is there of the material force of the scream?

II

The first point is that anti-power is ubiquitous.

The television, the newspapers, the speeches of politicians give little indication of the existence of anti-power. For them, politics is the politics of power, political conflict is about winning power, political reality is the reality of power. For them, anti-power is invisible.

Look more closely, however. Look at the world around us, look beyond the newspapers, look beyond the political parties, beyond the institutions of the labour movement and you can see a world of struggle: the autonomous municipalities in Chiapas, the students in the Universidad Nacional Autónoma de México, the Liverpool dockers, the wave of international demonstrations against the power of money capital, the struggles of migrant workers, the struggles of the workers in all the world against privatisation. Readers can make their own list – there are always new struggles. There is a whole world of struggle that does not aim at all at winning power, a whole world of struggle against power-over. There is a whole world of struggle that sometimes goes no farther than saying 'No!' (sabotage, for example) but that often, in the course of saying 'No!', develops forms of self-determination and articulates alternative conceptions of how the world should be. Such struggles, if they are reported at all in the mainstream media, are filtered through the spectacles of power, visible only in so far as they are considered to impinge upon power politics.[1]

The first problem in talking of anti-power is its invisibility. It is invisible not because it is imaginary, but because our concepts for seeing the world are concepts of power (of identity, of the indicative). To see anti-power, we need different concepts (of non-identity, of the Not Yet, of the subjunctive).

All rebellious movements are movements against invisibility. Perhaps the clearest example of that is the feminist movement, where much of the struggle has been to make visible that which was invisible: to make visible the exploitation and oppression of women, but more than that, to make visible the presence of women in this world, to rewrite a history from which their presence had been largely eliminated. The struggle for visibility is also central to the current indigenous movement, expressed most forcefully in the Zapatista wearing of the balaclava: we cover our face so that we can be seen, our struggle is the struggle of those without face.

Yet there is an important distinction to be made here. The problem of anti-power is not to emancipate an oppressed identity (women, indigenous) but to emancipate an oppressed non-identity, the ordinary, everyday, invisible no, the rumblings of subversion as we walk in the street, the silent volcano of sitting in a chair. By giving discontent an identity, 'We are women', 'We are indigenous', we are already imposing a new limitation upon it, we are already defining it. Hence the importance of the Zapatista balaclava, which says not just 'We are the indigenous struggling for our identity to be recognised', but, much more profoundly, 'Ours is the struggle of non-identity, ours is the struggle of the invisible, of those without voice and without face.'

The first step in struggling against invisibility is to turn the world upside down, to think from the perspective of struggle, to take sides. The work of radical sociologists, historians, social anthropologists, and so on, has made us aware of the ubiquity of opposition to power, in the workplace, in the home, on the streets. At its best, such work opens a new sensitivity, often associated with struggles against invisibility and consciously starting from those struggles (the feminist movement, the gay movement, the indigenous movement, and so on). The issue of sensitivity is well posed by an Ethiopian proverb quoted by Scott at the beginning of his book: 'When the great lord passes the wise peasant bows deeply and silently farts.' In the eyes, ears and nose of the lord, the peasant's fart is completely imperceptible. For the peasant herself and for other peasants, and for those who start from the peasant's antagonism towards the lord, the fart is, however, all too evident. It is part of a hidden world of insubordination: hidden, however, only to those who exercise power and to those who, by training or for convenience, accept the blinkers of power.

That which is oppressed and resists is not only a *who* but a *what*. It is not only particular groups of people who are oppressed (women, indigenous, peasants, factory workers, and so on), but also (and perhaps especially) particular aspects of the personality of all of us: our self-confidence, our sexuality, our playfulness, our creativity. The theoretical challenge is to be able to look at the person walking next to us in the street or sitting next to us in a bus and see the stifled volcano inside them. Living in capitalist society does not necessarily make us into an insubordinate, but it does inevitably mean that our existence is torn by the antagonism between subordination and insubordination. Living in capitalism means that we are self-divided, not just that we stand on one side of the antagonism between the classes, but that the class antagonism tears each of us apart. We may not be rebellious, but inevitably rebellion exists within us, as stifled volcano, as projection towards a possible future, as the present existence of that which does Not Yet exist, as frustration, as neurosis, as repressed Pleasure Principle, as the non-identity which, in the face of the repeated insistence of capital that we are workers, students, husbands, wives, Mexicans, Irish, French, says 'We are not, we are not, we are not, we are not what we are, and we are what we are not (or not yet).' That is surely what the Zapatistas mean when they say they are 'ordinary people, that is to say, rebels';[2] that is surely what they mean by dignity: the rebellion that is in all of us, the struggle for a humanity that is denied us, the struggle against the crippling of the humanity that we are. Dignity is an intensely lived struggle that fills the detail of our everyday lives. Often the struggle of dignity is non-subordinate rather than openly insubordinate, often it is seen as private rather than in any sense political or anti-capitalist. Yet the non-subordinate struggle for dignity is the material substratum of hope. That is the point of departure, politically and theoretically.

Probably no one has been as sensitive to the force and ubiquity of the suppressed dream as Ernst Bloch, who in the three volumes of the *Principle of Hope* traces the multiple forms of projection towards a better future, the present existence of the Not Yet, in dreams, fairy tales, music, painting, political and social utopias, architecture, philosophy, religion: all testimony to the presence in all of us of a negation of the present, a pushing towards a radically different world, a struggle to walk erect.

Anti-power does not exist only in the overt, visible struggles of those who are insubordinate, the world of the 'Left'. It exists also – problematically, contradictorily (but then the world of the Left is no less problematic or contradictory) – in the everyday frustrations of all of us, the everyday struggle to maintain our dignity in the face of power, the everyday struggle to retain or regain control over our lives. Anti-power is in the dignity of everyday existence. Anti-power is in the relations that we form all the time, relations of love, friendship, comradeship, community, cooperation. Obviously, such relations are traversed by power because of the nature of the society in which we live, yet the element of love, friendship, comradeship lies in the constant struggle which we wage against power, to establish those relations on a basis of mutual recognition, the mutual recognition of one another's dignity.

The invisibility of resistance is an ineradicable aspect of domination. Domination always implies not that resistance is overcome but that resistance (some of it at least) is underground, invisible. Oppression always implies the invisibility of the oppressed. For one group to become visible does not overcome the general problem of visibility. To the extent that the invisible becomes visible, to the extent that the stifled volcano becomes overt militancy, it is already confronted with its own limits and the need to overcome them. To think of opposition to capitalism simply in terms of overt militancy is to see only the smoke rising from the volcano.

Dignity (anti-power) exists wherever humans live. Oppression implies the opposite, the struggle to live as humans. In all that we live every day, illness, the educational system, sex, children, friendship, poverty, whatever, there is a struggle to do things with dignity, to do things right. Of course our ideas of what is right are permeated by power, but the permeation is contradictory; of course we are damaged subjectivities, but not destroyed. The struggle to do right, to live morally, is one that preoccupies most people much of the time. Of course, the morality is a privatised, immoral morality which generally steers clear of such questions as private property and therefore the nature of relations between people, a morality which defines itself as 'do right to those who are close to me and leave the rest of the world to sort itself out', a morality which, by being private, identifies, distinguishing between 'those who are close to me' (family, nation, women, men, whites, blacks, decent-looking, 'people like us') and the rest of the world, those living beyond my particular moral pale. And yet: in the daily struggle to 'do right', there is a struggle to recognise and be recognised and not just to identify, to emancipate power-to and not just bow to power-over, an anger against that which dehumanises, a shared (if fragmented) resistance, a non-subordination at least.

It may be objected that it is quite wrong to see this as anti-power since, in so far as it is fragmented and privatised, such 'morality' functionally reproduces power-over. Unless there is consciousness of the interconnections, unless there is political (class) consciousness, it may be argued, such private morality is totally harmless to capital, or actually contributes actively to the reproduction of capital by providing the basis for order and good behaviour. All this is so, and yet: any form of non-subordination, any process of saying 'We are more than the objectified machines that capital requires', leaves a residue. Ideas of what is right, however privatised, are part of the 'hidden transcript' (Scott 1990) of opposition, part of the substratum of resistance that exists in any oppressive society. The Ethiopian peasant's fart certainly does not blow the passing lord off his horse, and yet: it is part of the substratum of negativity which, though generally invisible, can flare up in moments of acute social tension. This substratum of negativity is the stuff that social volcanoes are made of. This layer of inarticulate non-subordination, without face, without voice, so often despised by the 'Left', is the materiality of anti-power, the basis of hope.

III

The second point is that anti-power is not only ubiquitous: it is also the motor force of power.

This has not been the predominant emphasis either in the Marxist tradition or in left thought in general. On the whole Marxism has focused its analysis on capital and its development, and left thought in general usually prefers to highlight oppression, to stir up indignation against the evils of capitalism. There is a tendency to treat the oppressed as just that, victims of oppression. This emphasis may stir us to indignant action, but it tends to leave open completely the question of how oppressed victims can possibly liberate themselves – other, of course, than through the enlightened intervention of saviours like ourselves.

Within the Marxist tradition, this emphasis on domination rather than struggle has been attacked most articulately by the current which developed, initially in Italy, from the 1960s onwards, variously referred to as 'autonomist Marxism' or '*operaismo*'. The point was sharply formulated in an article by Mario Tronti first published in 1964, 'Lenin in England', that was to do much to shape the approach of 'autonomist' Marxism:

> We too have worked with a concept that puts capitalist development first, and workers second. This is a mistake. And now we have to turn the problem on its head, reverse the polarity and start again from the beginning: and the beginning is the class struggle of the working class. [1979a, p. 1]

Tronti immediately takes the reversal of the polarity a step further. Starting from the struggle of the working class means not simply adopting a working-class perspective, but, in complete reversal of the traditional Marxist approach, seeing working-class struggle as determining capitalist development: 'At the level of socially developed capital, capitalist development becomes subordinated to the working class struggles; it follows behind them and they set the pace to which the political mechanisms of capital's own reproduction must be tuned' (1979a, p. 1).

This is the core of what Moulier refers to as '*operaismo*'s ... Copernican inversion of Marxism' (1989, p. 19). This, according to Asor Rosa,

> ... can be summed up in a formula which makes the working class the dynamic motor of capital and which makes capital a function of the working class ... a formula which in itself gives an idea of the magnitude of the inversion of perspectives which such a position implies politically. [quoted by Moulier 1989, p. 20]

The attraction of the inversion of the traditional approach is obvious, but how is the working class to be understood as the 'dynamic motor' of capitalism? As Tronti himself says in the same article: 'this is not a rhetorical proposition. Nor is it intended just to restore our confidence ... an urgent practical need is never sufficient basis for a scientific thesis' (1979a, p. 1).[3]

The autonomist reinterpretation of Marxism has its roots in the upsurge of factory struggle in Italy in the 1960s, which led to a re-reading of *Capital*, putting particular emphasis on a part which had generally been neglected by 'Marxist economists', namely the long analysis in Volume I of the development of the labour process in the factories. In this discussion, Marx shows that capital is constantly forced to struggle with the 'refractory hand of labour'[4] and that it is this struggle which determines changes in factory organisation and technical innovation. Thus, for Marx, automation is 'animated by the longing to reduce to a minimum the resistance offered by that repellent yet elastic natural barrier, man' (1965, p. 403). Consequently, 'it would be possible to write quite a history of the inventions, made since 1830, for the sole purpose of supplying capital with weapons against the revolts of the working class' (1965, p. 436).

Taking as its focus first the struggles in the factories, the autonomist analyses show how all the organisational and technical innovations introduced by management can be understood as a response designed to overcome the force of insubordination on the part of the workers. Labour insubordination can thus be seen as the driving force of capital.

This provides a way of analysing the history of struggle. The workers develop a form of struggle; management introduce a new form of organisation or new machinery in order to reimpose order; this in turn gives rise to new forms of insubordination, new forms of struggle, and so on. One can speak of the struggle as having a certain composition. By analogy with Marx's idea that capital at any point is characterised by a certain technical and value composition, depending on the relation between constant capital (that part of the capital represented by machinery and raw materials) and variable capital (that part of the capital which corresponds to wages), the autonomists developed the concept of class composition to denote the relation between labour and capital at any particular moment. The movement of struggle can thus be seen as a movement of class composition. The forms of struggle at any particular time are expressions of the composition of the working class; when management introduce changes to restore order, they aim to bring about a de-composition of the class; this de-composition gives rise in turn to the development of new forms of struggle, or a re-composition of the class. The history of struggle can thus be described in terms of the movement of composition, de-composition and re-composition.

The concept is developed not only in relation to struggles in particular factories or industries but as a way of understanding the dynamic of struggle in capitalism as a whole. Thus, it is argued, working-class struggle in the period up to the First World War was characterised by the particular place within production of the skilled worker. This gave to the working-class movement a specific form of organisation (skill-based trade unionism) and a particular ideology (based on the notion of the dignity of labour). The de-composing response by management was the introduction of Taylorism, designed to de-skill the skilled worker and deprive him[5] of control of the labour process. This gives rise in turn to a re-composition of the working class as mass worker, with new forms of struggle, new forms of organisation (the general trade unions) and a new ideology (the rejection of work). The de-composing response by capital is seen by some autonomist theorists (Negri, in particular) as coming now not at the level of factory management but at the level of the state, with the development of Keynesianism and the Welfare State (Fordism, as it is often called) as a way of both recognising the growing strength of labour and at the same time integrating it into the maintenance of order (through social democracy) and into the dynamic of capitalism (through demand management). This gives rise, in Negri's analysis, to a socialisation of capital, the transformation of society into a 'social factory' and the emergence of a new class composition, the 'social worker' ('*operaio sociale*'). The strength of this new composition is expressed in the struggles of the late 1960s and 1970s which go far beyond the factory to contest all aspects of the capital's management of society. It is the strength of these struggles which forces capital to abandon the Keynesian-Fordist form of management and develop new forms of attack (neo-Liberalism, or what Hardt and Negri now refer to as 'empire').[6]

Class composition thus takes us beyond the analysis of factory struggles to become the key concept for understanding capitalist development. Thus, Moulier characterises the notion in broad terms:

> We must remember that the notion of 'class composition' is a concept which aims to replace the too static, academic and in general reactionary concept of 'social classes'. Class composition comprises simultaneously the technical composition both of capital and of waged labour, which refers to the state of development of the productive forces, to the degree of social cooperation and division of labour. But this level of analysis is not separable from the political composition which is its ultima ratio. We can find in it all that characterises the collective subjectivity of needs, desires, the imaginary and their objective translation into the forms of political, cultural and community organisation. [1989, pp. 40–1, n. 47][7]

The notion of class composition takes us significantly beyond the mere observation that resistance to capitalism is ubiquitous. It suggests a basis for speaking of the developing force of this resistance, a basis for trying to understand the specificity and the force of the current forms of struggle. It proposes a way in which we can see our scream not just as an ever-present feature of oppression, but as a scream that has a particular historical resonance.

There is, however, already a problem here that suggests a divergence between the autonomist approach described here and the approach developed in this book. Certainly the initial impulse is very much the same: the insistence by Tronti that the beginning is the struggle of the working class and the insistence here that the starting-point is the scream. There is, however, a distinction that becomes clear when the concept 'class composition' is used not just as a category for analysing the movement of struggle but as a way of characterising a period of capitalism.

The first indication of the divergence is the reversal of signs. Starting from the scream, we have argued here that anti-capitalist theory must be understood as negative theory, that the movement of struggle is a movement of negation. Most autonomist theory, however, presents the movement of struggle as a positive movement. The reversal of the polarity undertaken by autonomist theory transfers the positive from the side of capital to the side of the struggle against capital. In orthodox Marxist theory, capital is the positive subject of capitalist development. In autonomist theory, the working class becomes the positive subject: that is why the positive concepts of class composition and class re-composition are on the side of the working class, while the negative concept of de-composition is placed on the side of capital. In the reversal of the polarity, identity is moved from the side of capital to the side of labour, but it is not exploded or even challenged. This is wrong. Subjectivity in capitalism is in the first place *negative*, the movement against the denial of subjectivity. A truly radical reversal of the polarity involves not just transferring subjectivity from capital to the working class but also understanding that subjectivity as negative instead of positive, as the negative subjectivity of the anti-working anti-class. In the beginning is the scream, not because the scream exhausts itself in negativity, but because the only way in which we can construct relations of dignity is through the negation of those relations which deny dignity. Our movement, then, is in the first place a negative movement, a movement against identity. It is we who de-compose, we are the wreckers. It is capital which constantly seeks to compose, to create identities, to create stability (always illusory, but essential to its existence), to contain and deny our negativity. We are the source of movement, we are the subject: in that, autonomist theory is right. But our movement is a negative one, one that defies classification. What unites the Zapatista uprising in Chiapas or the Movement of the Landless (MST) in Brazil with the struggle of Internet workers in Seattle, say, is not a positive common class composition but rather the community of their negative struggle against capitalism.

The conceptualisation of 'class composition' as positive provides the basis for a slide from seeing the concept as a means of understanding the movement of struggle to using it as a way of classifying periods of development, as a way of describing how capitalism 'is'. Instead of analysing particular struggles in terms of the overall movement of capital's dependence upon labour (not Lukács's perspective of totality but certainly his *aspiration* towards totality), there is a tendency to project from particular struggles (the struggles in Fiat in the early 1970s, say) and see them as being typical of a certain stage of capitalist development. In these cases the concept of 'class composition' is used to construct an ideal type or paradigm, a heading under which all struggles are to be classified. The struggles in the Italian car factories then become a measure for other struggles, rather than being understood in terms of their place in the general movement of capital's dependence upon labour. This procedure leads easily (though not necessarily) to crude generalisations, to the construction of categories as Procrustean beds into which struggles arising from very different conditions must be forced to fit.

The same point can be made in different terms. The great merit of the autonomist approach is that it insists on seeing the movement of capitalist rule as being driven by the force of working-class struggle, on seeing capital as a 'function of the working class'. There are, however, two possible ways in which this affirmation can be understood. The weaker version would be to say that capital can be understood as a function of the working class because its history is a history of *reaction* to working-class struggle, in much the same manner as one might see, say, the movements of a defending army at war to be a function of the movements of the attacking army, or, possibly, the development of the police to be a function of the activities of criminals. The stronger version would be that capital is a function of the working class for the simple reason that capital is nothing other than the *product* of the working class and therefore depends, from one minute to another, upon the working class for its reproduction. In the first case, the relation between the working class and capital is seen as a relation of opposition, an *external* relation; in the second case, the relation is seen in terms of the generation of one pole of the opposition by the other pole, as an *internal* relation.

If the relation between the working class and capital is seen as an internal relation, then struggle is necessarily negative: it is a struggle against that which encloses us, a struggle in and therefore against, a struggle that also projects beyond, but from a position of negation. It is a struggle not just against an external enemy (capital) but also against ourselves, simply because our existence within capital means that capital is in us. If, however, the relation between working class and capital is seen as an external one, then our struggle will be seen as a positive one. If we stand outside capital, then the issue is how to increase our positive force, our autonomy. But that implies that the subject of struggle is also positive and that the enemy is an external one. Thus, although it appears to be a more radical position, this approach actually restricts the meaning of revolutionary struggle. The struggle is to transform that which is outside us, whereas in the negative approach, the struggle is to transform everything, ourselves included.

Both of these elements (the external and the internal interpretation) are present in the autonomist tradition. In many cases, however, it is the external, 'reaction' interpretation which predominates.[8] Thus, the dynamic of capitalist development is understood as a reaction or response to the power of the working-class movement. The development of capital is then understood as the defensive reaction by capital to the strength of the working-class movement revealed in moments of open revolt. Keynesianism, for example, in Negri's analysis (1988b) is a response to the revolution of 1917, which made clear that capital could survive only by recognising and integrating the working class movement. Such analyses are often immensely suggestive, but the point being made here is that capitalist development is understood as a process of reaction, that the relation between labour and capital is understood as an external relation.

The reversal of the polarity between capital and labour, essential though it be as a starting-point, ends in these cases by reproducing the polarity in a different form. The traditional Marxist analysis emphasises the logical development of capital and relegates class struggle to a 'but also' role; autonomist theory liberates class struggle from its subordinate role, but, in so far as it sees the relation as one of reaction, still leaves it confronting an external logic of capital. The difference is that the logic of capital is understood now not in terms of 'economic' laws and tendencies, but in terms of a political struggle to defeat the enemy. It is easy to see how, in the analyses of some autonomists (such as Negri) the law of value, the key category in the Marxist-economic interpretation of capitalist development, is seen as being redundant (Negri 1988b). In the face of the power of the working-class movement, capital develops into Integrated World Capitalism (Guattari and Negri 1990), and its sole logic is the logic of maintaining power. As is perhaps inevitable, the 'reaction' understanding of the labour-capital relation leads to a mirror-image view of capitalism: the greater the power of the working-class movement, the more monolithic and totalitarian the response of the capitalist class. Autonomist theory has been crucial in reasserting the nature of Marxist theory as a theory of struggle, but the real force of Marx's theory of struggle lies not in the reversal of the polarity between capital and labour, but in its dissolution. As Bonefeld puts it, 'the difficulty inherent in 'autonomist' approaches is not that 'labour' is seen as being primary but that this notion is not developed to its radical solution' (1994, p. 44).

The positivisation of autonomist theory has been developed most systematically by Negri. In *The Savage Anomaly* (Negri 1991), Negri turns to the study of Spinoza in order to provide a positive foundation for a theory of struggle. In this work, he insists, through his discussion of Spinoza, that social development, or, more precisely, 'the genealogy of social forms', 'is not a dialectical process: it implies negativity only in the sense that negativity is understood as the enemy, as an object to destroy, as a space to occupy, not as a motor of the process'. The motor of the process is positive: 'the continuous pressure of being toward liberation' (1991, p. 162). His concern is to develop the concept of revolutionary power (the *potentia* of the multitude) as a positive, non-dialectical, ontological concept. Autonomy is implicitly understood as the existing, positive drive of the *potentia* of the multitude, pushing *potestas* (the power of the rulers) onto ever new terrains.

To treat the subject as positive is attractive but it is inevitably a fiction. In a world that dehumanises us, the only way in which we can exist as humans is negatively, by struggling against our dehumanisation. To understand the subject as positively autonomous (rather than as potentially autonomous) is rather like a prisoner in a cell imagining that she is already free: an attractive and stimulating idea, but a fiction, a fiction that easily leads on to other fictions, to the construction of a whole fictional world.

The implications of the positivisation of the concept of struggle are developed most clearly in the latest major work by Negri, *Empire* (co-authored with Michael Hardt: Hardt and Negri 2000). In this they analyse the current terrain onto which the *potentia* of the multitude has pushed capital. Empire is seen as the new paradigm of rule:

> In contrast to imperialism, Empire establishes no territorial centre of power and does not rely on fixed boundaries or barriers. It is a decentred and deterritorialising apparatus of rule that progressively incorporates the entire global realm within its open, expanding frontiers. Empire manages hybrid identities, flexible

hierarchies, and plural exchanges through modulating networks of command. The distinct national colours of the imperialist map of the world have merged and blended in the imperial global rainbow. [2000, pp. xii–xiii]

There is a change in sovereignty, 'a general passage from the paradigm of modern sovereignty toward the paradigm of imperial sovereignty'. In the latter, it is no longer possible to locate sovereignty territorially in the nation state, or indeed in any particular place. Even the United States, although it plays a particularly important part in the network of power, is not the locus of power in the same way that the imperialist powers of the earlier age were. One implication of this would seem to be that it no longer makes sense to think of revolutionary transformation in terms of the taking of state power.[9]

In this new paradigm, there is no longer any place of rule, and consequently no longer any inside or any outside, no longer any possible external standpoint. Empire is an all-embracing system of rule, the latest reformulation of what Negri had earlier characterised as the 'social factory' (see, for example, Negri 1980) or 'integrated world capitalism (IWC)' (see Guattari and Negri 1990). This does not mean that all possibility of resistance or change has been obliterated. On the contrary, Hardt and Negri insist that Empire is to be understood as a reaction to the struggles of the multitude: 'The history of capitalist forms is always necessarily a *reactive* history' (2000, p. 268). Thus:

> ... the multitude is the real productive force of our social world, whereas Empire is a mere apparatus of capture that lives only off the vitality of the multitude – as Marx would say, a vampire regime of accumulated dead labour that survives only by sucking off the blood of the living. [2000, p. 62]

Within Empire, the driving force continues to be the multitude. Empire has as its material basis the development of 'immaterial labour', the intellectual, communicative and affective labour characteristic above all of the development of the service sector of the informational economy. The important thing about this immaterial labour is the degree to which it is immanently and immediately cooperative, thus creating a new subjectivity:

The immediately social dimension of the exploitation of living immaterial labour immerses labour in all the relational elements that define the social but also at the same time activate the critical elements that develop the potential of insubordination and revolt through the entire set of labouring practices. [2000, p. 29]

The inherently cooperative nature of this type of labour 'annuls the title of property' (2000, p. 410) and creates the basis for an absolute democracy, a communist society.

It is clear that the argument of Negri and Hardt pushes in a direction similar to the argument in this book in two crucial respects. First, they emphasise the centrality of oppositional struggle (whether we call it the power of the multitude or anti-power) as the force which shapes social development; second, they argue that it is important to focus on revolution, but that revolution cannot be conceived in terms of the taking of state power.

Their argument is immensely rich and suggestive, yet their approach is very different indeed from the approach that has been adopted here. This leaves us with a dilemma. Are we to say that method does not matter, that there are many different ways of reaching the same conclusion? But if we adopt that position, then much of the previous argument about fetishism and critique falls. If, however, we say that method does matter, precisely because method is part of the struggle against capitalist domination, then what are we to say of Hardt and Negri's argument?

Let us look at the matter more closely.

The difference in approach can be seen as centred in the issue of paradigm. It is in the concept of 'paradigm' that Negri's positive concept of class struggle and of class composition becomes focused. The argument of Hardt and Negri focuses on the shift from one paradigm of rule to another. This shift is characterised primarily as a shift from imperialism to Empire, but it is also variously described as a move from modernity to postmodernity, from discipline to control, from Fordism to post-Fordism, from an industrial to an informational economy. What interests us here is not the name, but the assumption that capitalism can be understood in terms of the replacement of one paradigm of rule by another, one system of order by another: 'The US world police acts not in imperialist interest but in imperial interest. In this sense the Gulf War did indeed, as George Bush claimed, announce the birth of a new world order' (2000, p. 180).

Hardt and Negri are not alone, of course, in this paradigmatic approach. Another approach which relies heavily on the notion of a shift from one paradigm to another and which has had great influence in recent years is the regulationist school, which analyses capitalism in terms of a shift from a Fordist to a post-Fordist mode of regulation. The paradigmatic approach has obvious attractions as a method of trying to understand the current changes in the world. It permits one to bring together many apparently disparate phenomena into a coherent whole. It allows one to paint an extremely rich and satisfying picture in which all the millions of pieces of the jigsaw click into place. This is immensely stimulating, for it suggests a whole series of correspondences that were not obvious before. It is also very attractive to academics because it suggests a whole world of research projects which can be completed with no jagged edges.

The problem with a paradigmatic approach, however, is that it separates existence from constitution. It rests on a notion of duration. Society is painted as being relatively stable *during* a certain period, and in this period we can recognise certain solid parameters. A paradigm creates a space in which we can say the world *is* so. A paradigm identifies. It may be argued that identification is necessary for thought: that is so, but, unless the identification bears its own negation, so that it is no more than the recognition of a fragile and evanescent moment torn by its own contradictions (us), then a world of order is created, a stability that reifies. A paradigm paints an orderly world of correspondence. The negative impulse which is the starting-point becomes converted into a positive science. The working-class refusal (Tronti 1979b) is slotted into a world of order. Although Hardt and Negri insist that order must be understood as the response to disorder, it is in fact difficult for them to avoid the predominance of order that a paradigmatic approach implies. As the title of the book implies, their tale is told through an account of order, not through disorder. Although they insist that refusal is the driving force of domination, refusal is in fact relegated to a subordinate place: it is only in the closing pages of the book (2000, p. 393) that the authors say, 'Now that we have dealt extensively with Empire, we should focus directly on the multitude and its potential political power.'

The paradigmatic approach takes classification to extremes. There is an eagerness to capture the new, to classify it, label it, make it fit into the paradigmatic order. There is almost indecent haste to declare the old order dead and proclaim the new: 'The King is dead! Long live the King!' As soon as one system of rule is in crisis, the new system of rule is proclaimed: 'At this point the disciplinary system has become completely obsolete and must be left behind. Capital must accomplish a negative mirroring and an inversion of the new quality of labour power: it must adjust itself so as to be able to command once again' (2000, p. 276). The adjustment to the new command is assumed as reality, not just seen as a project: this is the substance of the new paradigm, this is Empire.

The desire to make everything fit, to see the new paradigm as established, leads easily to an exaggeration that often seems quite unreal. Thus, 'autonomous movement is what defines the place proper to the multitude. Increasingly less will passports or legal documents be able to regulate our movement across borders' (2000, p. 397). Or: 'there are no time-clocks to punch on the terrain of biopolitical production; the proletariat produces in all its generality everywhere all day long' (2000, p. 403).

The paradigmatic approach shades into functionalism. In a world of correspondences, everything is functional, everything contributes to the maintenance of a coherent whole. Thus, for Negri and Hardt (as earlier for Negri),[10] crisis is not so much a moment of rupture as a force of regeneration in capitalism, a 'creative destruction'. Thus, 'as it is for modernity as a whole, crisis is for capital a normal condition that indicates not its end but its tendency and mode of operation' (2000, p. 222). Or:

> the crisis of modern sovereignty was not temporary or exceptional (as one would refer to the stock market crash of 1929 as a crisis), but rather the norm of modernity. In a similar way, corruption is not an aberration of imperial sovereignty but its very essence and modus operandi. [2000, p. 202]

Although the project of the book is very clearly one of rupture, the method adopted seems to absorb the possibility of rupture, to integrate movement into a photograph. A paradigmatic approach inevitably involves a freezing of time.

The functionalism extends to the understanding of sovereignty and the state. The authors interpret Marx's view of the state as a functionalist one. Referring to Marx and Engels's characterisation of the state as the executive that manages the interests of capitalists, they comment:

... by this they mean that although the action of the state will at times contradict the immediate interests of individual capitalists, it will always be in the long-term interest of the collective capitalist, that is, the collective subject of social capital as a whole. [2000, p. 304][11]

Thus, the system of modern states succeeded in 'guaranteeing the interests of total social capital against crises' (p. 306), while in the postmodern age of Empire, 'government and politics come to be completely integrated into the system of transnational command' (p. 307). The political and the economic come to form a closed system, an 'integrated world capitalism'.

It is entirely consistent with this paradigmatic approach that Hardt and Negri are very explicitly anti-dialectical and anti-humanist in their approach. Hegel is repeatedly dismissed as the philosopher of order rather than seeing him as being also the philosopher who made subversive movement the centre of his thought. Dialectics is understood as the logic of synthesis[12] rather than as the movement of negation. It is quite consistent with this that the authors insist on the continuity between animals, humans and machines. They see themselves as carrying on 'the antihumanism that was such an important project for Foucault and Althusser in the 1960s' and quote with approval Haraway's insistence upon 'breaking down the barriers we pose among the human, the animal and the machine' (2000, p. 91). Postmodernism gives us the opportunity to 'recognise our posthuman bodies and minds, [to] see ourselves for the simians and cyborgs we are' (2000, p. 92). In the new paradigm, 'interactive and cybernetic machines become a new prosthesis integrated into our bodies and minds and a lens through which to redefine our bodies and minds themselves. The anthropology of cyberspace is really a recognition of the new human condition' (2000, p. 291). The problem with this approach, surely, is that neither ants nor machines revolt. A theory that is grounded in revolt has little option but to recognise the distinctive character of humanity.

Surprisingly, perhaps, given their general project, Hardt and Negri have no concept of capital as class struggle. It is not that they do not attach importance to class struggle; it is rather that they do not understand capital as class struggle. There is a tendency to treat capital as an economic category, reproducing in this (as in other points) the assumptions of the Marxist orthodoxy which they so rightly attack. Capital does not seem to be understood as the struggle to appropriate the done and turn it against the doing. Thus, in apparent contradiction of their insistence on understanding the shift of paradigm as a response to class struggle, they assert that '*in addition to* looking at the development of capital itself, we must *also* understand the genealogy from the perspective of class struggle' (2000, p. 234; emphasis added) – thus implying that the development of capital and class struggle are two separate processes. The actual analysis of 'the development of capital itself' is in terms of under-consumptionism rather than the antagonism between capital and labour. The barriers to capitalist development all 'flow from a single barrier defined by the unequal relationship between the worker as producer and the worker as consumer' (2000, p. 222). In order to explain the movement from imperialism to Empire, they follow Rosa Luxemburg's under-consumptionist theory that capitalism can survive only through the colonisation of non-capitalist spheres:

> At this point we can recognise the *fundamental contradiction of capitalist expansion*: capital's reliance on its outside, on the non-capitalist environment, which satisfies the need to realise surplus value, conflicts with the internalisation of the non-capitalist environment, which satisfies the need to capitalise that realised surplus value. [2000, p. 227; emphasis added]

According to the authors, capital finds a solution to the exhaustion of the non-capitalist world by turning from the formal subsumption of the non-capitalist sphere to the real subsumption of the capitalist world. It is after this explanation of the passage from imperialism to Empire that it is pointed out that 'we must *also* understand the genealogy from the perspective of class struggle' (2000, p. 234; emphasis added).[13]

The consequence of understanding class struggle and capital as being separate, and of seeing the 'fundamental contradiction of capitalist expansion' as being something other than capital's dependence upon the subordination of labour, is that there is no understanding of the way in which the insubordination of labour constitutes the weakness of capital (especially in capitalist crisis). In this book, as in all of Negri's analyses, there is a clash of Titans: a powerful, monolithic capital ('Empire') confronts a powerful, monolithic 'multitude'. The power of each side does not appear to penetrate the other. The relation between the two sides of the capitalist antagonism is treated as an external one, as is indicated, indeed, by the authors' choice of the word 'multitude' to describe the opposition to capital, a term which has the grave disadvantage of losing all trace of the relation of dependence of capital upon labour.

It would be quite wrong to take Negri as standing for all autonomist authors (or indeed to try to classify autonomism as a homogeneous 'school'). What Negri draws out and takes to its extreme is the positive understanding of class struggle that is present in many autonomist writings, and, by doing so, he makes its problems manifest. It is this positivisation of the initial autonomist impulse that prevents that impulse from being taken to its radical conclusions (despite appearances).

Politically, the emphasis on the power of the working-class movement has an obvious appeal. Nevertheless, the understanding of labour and capital in terms of an external relationship leads to a paradoxical (and romantic) magnification of the power of both. The failure to explore the internal nature of the relation between labour and capital leads the autonomist analysis to underestimate the degree to which labour exists *within* capitalist forms. The existence of labour within capitalist forms, as will be argued more fully later, implies both the subordination of labour to capital *and* the internal fragility of capital. To overlook the internal nature of the relation between labour and capital thus means both to underestimate the containment of labour within capital (and hence overestimate the power of labour against capital) *and* to underestimate the power of labour as internal contradiction within capital (and hence overestimate the power of capital against labour). If the inter-penetration of power and anti-power is ignored, if the issue of fetishism is forgotten, then we are left with two pure subjects on either side; we are left with the subject as 'a strong ego in rational control of all its impulses, the kind taught in the whole tradition of modern rationalism, notably by Leibniz and Spinoza, who found here, at least, a point they could agree upon' (Adorno 1990, p. 294).[14] On the side of capital stands Empire, the perfect subject, and on the side of the working class stands: the militant. Autonomism – and this is both its attraction and its weakness – is a theorisation of the world from the unmediated perspective of the militant. Appropriately, Hardt and Negri's discussion of Empire ends with a paean to the militant: 'the militant is the one who best expresses the life of the multitude: the agent of biopolitical production and resistance against empire'

(2000, p. 411). And the example of communist militancy which they propose in the closing paragraph of the book (2000, p. 413) is the perfect embodiment of the Pure Subject: St Francis of Assisi![15] An attractive image, perhaps, for the dedicated militant, but hopelessly out of touch with the experience of those of us who live enmired in the filthy impurities of daily fetishisation and who, in spite of and precisely because of that, struggle for revolution.

To understand the force of anti-power we must go beyond the figure of the militant. The scream with which we started the book is not the scream of the militant, but the scream of all the oppressed. It is necessary to go beyond the force of overt militancy to ask about the force of all who refuse to subordinate themselves, the force of all who refuse to become capitalist machines. It is only when grounded in the ubiquity of resistance that revolution becomes a possibility.

10 The Material Reality of Anti-Power and the Crisis of Capital

I

In the previous chapter we argued that anti-power is both ubiquitous and the driving force of power. Now we must take a further step in understanding the materiality of anti-power.

The third point in understanding the reality of anti-power is that capital depends absolutely upon labour for its existence, that is, upon the transformation of human doing into value-producing labour.

This, surely, is the specific contribution of Marx to oppositional thought, that which takes Marxism beyond other forms of radical thought. The radical negation of society typically starts as an external negation, as us-against-them: women against men, blacks against white, poor against rich, multitude against Empire. Our negativity meets their positivity in external, and potentially eternal, confrontation. It is clear that the rich oppress us, that we hate them and fight against them, but the approach tells us nothing of our power or their vulnerability. In general, radical theory tends to focus on oppression and the struggle against oppression, rather than on the fragility of that oppression. Feminist theory, for example, has been extremely forceful in throwing light on the nature of gender oppression in society: what it has not developed so fully is a theory of the vulnerability or historicity of that oppression.

Against this 'us-against-them' of radical theory, Marx cries out: 'But there is no 'them', there is only us. We are the only reality, the only creative force. There is nothing but us, nothing but our negativity.'

The essential claim of Marxism, that which distinguishes it from other varieties of radical theory, is its claim to dissolve all externality. The core of its attack against 'them' is to show that 'they' depend on us because 'they' are continually created by us. We, the powerless, are all-powerful.

The critique of the 'them-against-us' externality of radical theory is not some abstruse theoretical point but the core of the Marxist understanding of the possibility of revolutionary transformation of society. It is through understanding that 'they' are *not* external to us, that capital is *not* external to labour, that we can understand the vulnerability of capitalist domination. To move beyond the externality of 'them-against-us' is at the same time to go beyond a radical theory of oppression to the concern of Marxism: understanding the *fragility* of oppression, and understanding that fragility as the force of our scream.

We have spoken much of the way in which power permeates anti-power, the damaged, alienated character of our insubordination. But the opposite is equally true. Fetishism is a two-faced process. It points not just to the penetration of opposition by power, but also to the penetration of power by opposition. To say that money, for example, is the thing-ification of social relations means equally that the antagonism of social relations enters into the 'thing' which money presents itself as being. To talk of money as disciplining social relations is equally to talk of social relations as subverting money. If power penetrates its negation, anti-power, it is equally true (and possibly more interesting) that anti-power penetrates its antithesis, power.

II

The permeation of power by anti-power is the stuff of crisis theory.

The idea that a theory of crisis is important to support the struggle against capitalism has been a central argument of the Marxist tradition: the importance of Marxism lies in giving support to the struggle for communism by showing that a transition from capitalism to communism is materially possible, that is to say, that the struggle for communism is founded in the material contradictions of capitalism and that these contradictions are concentrated in capitalist crisis. Marxists have always looked to crisis for reassurance that we are not alone in our struggle.

There are, however, two ways of understanding this 'we are not alone'. The orthodox understanding of crisis is to see crisis as an expression of the objective contradictions of capitalism: we are not alone because the objective contradictions are on our side, because the forces of production are on our side, because history is on our side. In this view, our struggle finds its support in the objective development of the contradictions of the capitalist economy.[1] A crisis precipitated by these contradictions opens a door of opportunity for struggle, an opportunity to turn economic crisis into social crisis and a basis for the revolutionary seizure of power. The problem with this approach is that it tends to deify the economy (or history or the forces of production), to create a force outside human agency that will be our saviour. This idea of crisis as the expression of the objective contradictions of capitalism complements the conception that sees revolution as the seizure of power, instead of seeing in both crisis and revolution a disintegration of the relations of power.

The other way of understanding the 'we are not alone' is to see crisis as the expression of the strength of our opposition to capital. There are no 'objective contradictions': we and we alone are the contradiction of capitalism. History is not the history of the laws of capitalist development but the history of class struggle (that is, the struggle to classify and against being classified). There are no gods of any sort, neither money nor capital, nor forces of production, nor history: we are the only creators, we are the only possible saviours, we are the only guilty ones. Crisis, then, is not to be understood as an opportunity presented to us by the objective development of the contradictions of capitalism but as the expression of our own strength, and this makes it possible to conceive of revolution not as the seizure of power but as the development of the anti-power which already exists as the substance of crisis.

In any class society, there is an instability deriving from the ruler's dependence on the ruled. In any system of power-over, there is a relation of mutual dependence between the 'powerful' and the 'powerless'. It appears to be a one-way relation in which the dominated depend on the dominator, but in fact the dominator's very existence as dominator depends on the dominated. In any society based on exploitation, a certain instability arises from the fact that the maintenance of the relations of exploitation, and hence the position of the ruling class, depends on the work of the exploited. In any class society there is an asymmetry between exploiting and exploited class: although there is clearly a sense in which each class depends on the other, the exploited class depends on the exploiting class only for the reproduction of its status as exploited, whereas the exploiting class depends on the work of the exploited class for its very existence.[2]

The social instability inherent in any class society takes different forms in different forms of society. The notion of capitalist crisis is based on the idea that capitalism is characterised by a particular instability, which finds vent in periodic upheaval. It is necessary, therefore, to go beyond the instability resulting from the general dependence of ruling classes on the work of the exploited, to ask: what is it about the particular capitalist form of dependence of the ruling class on the work of the exploited class that makes capitalism as a system of domination peculiarly unstable?

What is peculiar in the relation of dependence of capital upon labour that makes capitalism inherently unstable?

Freedom. The answer is both obvious and slightly disturbing. It is the freedom of the worker that is the peculiar feature of the relation between capital and labour. It is the freedom of the worker that distinguishes capitalism from earlier class societies.

This freedom is, of course, not the freedom dear to the liberal imagination, but freedom in a 'double sense':

> For the conversion of his money into capital ... the owner of money must meet in the market with the free labourer, free in the double sense, that as a free man he can dispose of his labour-power as his own commodity, and that on the other hand he has no other commodity for sale, is short of everything necessary for the realisation of his labour-power. [Marx 1965, p. 169]

Where the liberal notion of freedom sees only the first aspect, Marxists have tended, in opposition to liberal theory, to emphasise the second aspect, the 'reality' of freedom in capitalist society, the fact that the worker has no option but to sell her labour power. The exclusive emphasis on the second aspect, however, suggests an image of the worker as victim, as object, and misses completely the importance of freedom as an expression of the anti-power of the opposition to capital.

To emphasise also the first aspect, the freedom of the worker 'to dispose of his labour-power as his own commodity' is not in any sense to suggest a liberalisation of Marxism. It is important to bear in mind that all class societies rest on the subordination of insubordinate workers, and hence on violence: what distinguishes capitalism from other class societies is the form which this subordination takes, the fact that it is mediated through freedom.

Marx does not examine 'the question why this free labourer confronts [the owner of money] in the market', but notes that

... one thing, however, is clear – Nature does not produce on the one side owners of money or commodities, and on the other men possessing nothing but their own labour-power. This relation has no natural basis, neither is its social basis one that is common to all historical periods. It is clearly the result of a past historical development ... This one historical condition comprises a world's history. [Marx 1965, pp. 169–70]

If feudalism and capitalism are seen as different historical forms assumed by the relation of domination, then the essence of the transition from feudalism to capitalism is the freeing of the serfs and the dissolution of the personal power of the feudal lords, the creation of the 'free labourer' who confronts the owner of money (also newly created) in the market. The 'freeing of the serfs' is not the simple transition from bondage to freedom suggested in liberal accounts. The 'freeing' is rather a dis-articulation of the relation of domination.

Under feudalism, the relation of domination was a personal one: a serf was bound to a particular lord, a lord was limited to exploiting the serfs that he had inherited or could otherwise subjugate. Both sides of the class divide were bound: the serf was tied to a particular lord and a particular place, the lord was tied to a particular group of serfs. If the lord was cruel, the serf could not decide to go and work for another lord. If the serfs were lazy, unskilled or insubordinate, the lord could not simply fire them. The result was revolt on the one hand, the pursuit of other ways of expanding wealth and power on the other. The personal bondage of feudalism proved inadequate as a form of containing and exploiting the power of labour. Serfs fled to the towns, the feudal lords accepted the monetisation of the relation of domination.

The transition from feudalism to capitalism was thus a movement of liberation *on both sides of the class divide*. Both sides fled from the other: the serfs from the lords (as stressed by liberal theory), but also the lords from the serfs, through the movement of their monetised wealth. Both sides fled from a relation of domination which had proved inadequate as a form of domination. Both sides fled to freedom.

Flight to freedom is thus central to the transition from feudalism to capitalism. But there are, of course, two different and opposing senses of freedom here (a dualism which is the central contradiction of liberal theory). The flight of the serfs was a flight from subordination to the lord, the flight of those who, for one reason or another, no longer accepted the old subordination, the flight of the insubordinate. The flight of the lords was just the opposite: when they converted their wealth into money, it was a flight away from the inadequacy of subordination, a flight from insubordination. On the one side, the flight *of* insubordination, on the other side the flight *from* insubordination: viewed from either side, it was the insubordination of labour that was the driving force of the new mobility of the class relation, the mutual flight of serf and lord.

The flight of-and-from the insubordination of labour, the mutual repulsion of the two classes did not, of course, dissolve the class relation. For both serf and lord, the flight to freedom came up against the reassertion of the bond of mutual dependence. The freed serfs found that they were not free to stop work: since they did not control the means of production, they were forced to work for a master, someone who did control the means of production. To survive, they had to subordinate themselves again. However, this was not a return to the old relation: they were no longer tied to one particular master, but were free to move, to leave one master and go and work for another. The transition from feudalism to capitalism involved the de-personalisation, dis-articulation or liquefaction of the relations of domination. The relation of exploitation was not abolished by the dissolution of the ties of personal bondage, but it underwent a fundamental change in form. The particular bond that tied the serf to one particular master was dissolved and replaced by a mobile, fluid, dis-articulated relation of subordination to the capitalist class. The flight of insubordination entered into the very definition of the new class relation.

On the other side of society, the erstwhile lords who converted their wealth into money also found that freedom was not all they had imagined, for they were still dependent on exploitation, and therefore on the subordination of the exploited, the workers, their former serfs. Flight from insubordination is no solution for the lords turned capitalists, for the expansion of their wealth depends on the subordination of labour. They are free to abandon the exploitation of any particular group of workers (for whatever reason – laziness, inappropriate skills, whatever) and either establish direct links of exploitation with another group of workers or simply participate through non-productive investment in the global exploitation of labour. Whatever form their particular relation to the exploitation of labour takes, the expansion of their wealth can be no more than a part of the total expansion of wealth produced by the workers. Just as in the case of their former serfs, flight to freedom turns out to be flight to a new form of dependence. Just as the serfs' flight from subordination leads them back to a new form of subordination, the lords' flight from insubordination leads them back to the need to confront that insubordination. The relation, however, has changed, for capital's flight from insubordination is central to its struggle to impose subordination (as, for example, in the ever-present threat of factory closure or bankruptcy). The flight from insubordination has become a defining feature of the new class relation.

The insubordination of labour is thus the axis on which the constitution of capital as capital turns. It is the centrifugal mutual repulsion of the two classes, the flight of and from subordination, that distinguishes capitalism from previous class societies, that gives a peculiar form to the exploitation of work on which capitalism, like any class society, is based. The restlessness of insubordination enters into the class relation as the movement of labour and capital.

From the start, the new class relation, the relation between capitalists and workers (or, more accurately, since it is a de-personalised relation, between capital and labour) is a relation of mutual flight and dependence: flight of-and-from insubordination, dependence on re-subordination. Capital, by its very definition, flees from insubordinate labour in pursuit of more and more wealth, but can never escape from its dependence upon the subordination of labour. Labour, from the start, flees from capital in pursuit of autonomy, ease, humanity, but can escape from its dependence upon and subordination to capital only by destroying it, by destroying the private appropriation of the products of labour. The relation between capital and labour is thus one of mutual flight and dependence, but it is not symmetrical: labour can escape, capital can not. Capital is dependent on labour in a way in which labour is not dependent upon capital. Capital, without labour, ceases to exist: labour, without capital, becomes practical creativity, creative practice, humanity.

The rise of capitalism thus involves the de-personalisation or, better, dis-articulation, dis-jointing or dis-location of the relations of domination. The dissolution of the ties of personal bondage does not abolish the relation of domination but it dis-articulates it. Both serf (now worker) and lord (now capitalist) remain as antagonistic poles of a relation of domination-and-struggle, but that relation is no longer the same. The insubordination of labour has entered into the relation as restlessness, mobility, liquidity, flux, fluidity, constant flight.[3] The relation has been dis-articulated; it has been ruptured and recomposed in dis-articulated form. The dis-articulation of the class relation is the form in which the power of labour is contained, subjected to the continuing exploitation of the ruling class. The dis-articulation of the class relation is simultaneously the form assumed by the ruling class's dependence on labour. That is the meaning of capitalist freedom.

The key to the dis-articulation of the class relation is its mediation through money, or the exchange of commodities. The freedom of the serf from personal bondage is the commodification of her labour power, the acquisition by the labour power of a value-form. The means by which the worker can move from one master to another is by offering her labour power for sale and receiving in return a wage, the monetary expression of the value of the labour power. The means by which the capitalist participates in the global exploitation of labour is through the movement of his capital, in the form of money. Value, or money, is inseparable from what liberal theory refers to as freedom: the dis-articulation of social relations.

The dis-articulation of the relation of exploitation/domination brings with it a dis-articulation of all social relations. The existence of labour power as a commodity implies a generalisation of commodity relations in society, the mediation of social relations in general through the exchange of commodities, through money.

The dis-articulation of class relations is simultaneously the dis-articulation of work itself. Work, from being a general concept denoting creative activity, becomes defined as work performed as a result of the sale of labour power to the capitalist: a process of labour subject to the direction of the capitalist. Other forms of practical activity come to be seen as non-work (as expressed in the distinction commonly made between working and non-working mothers, or in the notion that someone who is not employed is 'out of work'). The same dis-articulation implies also a dis-articulation of the relation between worker and the content of work. Where the serf lived by performing a certain type, or certain types, of work, the capitalist worker lives by selling her labour power: the sale of the labour power as a commodity, that is, the mediation of money, introduces a relation of indifference between the worker and the work performed. The dis-articulation of class relations is, in other words, simultaneously the abstraction of labour.

The abstraction of labour implies also a separation between the exploiter and the content of exploitation. Whereas the well-being of the lord depended on the performance of certain types of work by his serfs, the mediation of money makes it a matter of absolute indifference to the capitalist what type of work is performed by his employees – his well-being depends not on the quality of the work done but on the quantitative expansion of value.

The dis-articulation of the class relation is also the dis-articulation of production and consumption: where the serfs produced most of what they consumed, capitalist workers produce only marginally for their own consumption – the relation between production and consumption is mediated through money. The mediation of money implies both a temporal and spatial separation of production and consumption.

Similarly, the mediation of the class relation through money/value, implies also a dis-articulation of the economic and the political. Where the feudal relation is indistinguishably a relation of exploitation and domination, indistinguishably economic and political, the fact that the capital relation is mediated through the sale and purchase of labour power implies a separation between exploitation (the economic) and the maintenance of the social order necessary for the process of exploitation (the political). By the same token, there is a redefinition of territoriality, a separation between the a-territorial process of exploitation, characterised by the mobility of labour and capital, and the territorial organisation of coercion through the definition of national states (and their citizens).

The list could be continued indefinitely. The dis-articulation of the class relation implies a general fragmentation of social relations, the refraction of relations through things. The dis-articulation is fetishism, in other words. Fetishism is indeed a two-faced process. Previously we saw fetishism as the penetration of power into opposition. Now we see that it is equally the penetration of opposition into power: the peculiar fetishism of capitalist social relations which penetrates all of us so deeply is at the same time the penetration of freedom into the form of domination.

The question that interests us here is how this dis-articulation (or fetishisation) of the class relation introduces a new instability into the world. If the distinguishing feature between capitalism and previous forms of class domination is the dis-articulation of the class relation ('freedom', 'fetishism'), then the peculiarly crisis-ridden nature of capitalism must be explained in terms of this dis-articulation.

Most obviously, the dis-articulation of social relations introduced a new chaos into the world. It created a chaotic, dis-articulated world in which nothing fits neatly with anything else. There is no necessary match between people offering to sell their labour power and people wanting to buy it; there is no necessary match between consumption and production; there is no necessary match between the political and the economic. That is precisely what dis-articulation ('freedom') means. A world of non-correspondence[4] was born, in which order is established, if at all, only through disorder, in which social connections are established through social disconnection. The orderly world of feudalism had collapsed, the ties of personal bondage had proved inadequate to contain and exploit the power of work. Class domination had been maintained, but only through the dis-articulation of the class relation. The power of labour had been contained, but at a terrible price. The cost of subjugating the power of labour was to introduce chaos into the very heart of the society. That same fetishism which we previously saw as the penetration of anti-power by power is simultaneously the irruption of anti-power into the very core of the functioning of power. The existence of power-to against and in capital takes form as the uncontrollable force of value.

This seems upside-down. We are not accustomed to thinking of value in these terms. It is more common to think of value as establishing order (the 'law of value'), as being the social bond in a society of autonomous producers. This is correct, but only if the emphasis is on the critique of liberal theory. The notion of the 'law of value' says in effect: 'Despite appearances, the apparently autonomous producers are bound together by a social connection which operates behind their backs – the law of value.' If, on the other hand, we start not from the appearance of fragmented individualism, but from the historical irruption of the insubordination of labour into the very definition of subordination, then value expresses the fragmentation wreaked by this irruption upon the more cohesive domination of feudalism. The law of value is simultaneously the lawlessness of value. Value is the political-economic expression of the presence of the contradictory flight of-and-from insubordination within subordination itself, just as freedom is its categorial expression in liberal political theory. Freedom, value and mobility are inseparable expressions of the same dis-articulation of class relations.

The category of value, then, expresses the power of insubordination, the containment of doing as labour and the terrible cost of that containment. The labour theory of value proclaims first the exclusive, all-constitutive power of labour under capitalism. It is therefore simultaneously a theory of class (cf. Clarke 1982) – if labour is all-constitutive, then conflict can only be understood in terms of the control over, or exploitation of, labour.

Second, the theory of value proclaims the subjugation of doing, the fact that human, creative doing is reduced in capitalism to the dehumanising process of abstract labour, of value-production. As Marx says of the fact that 'labour is represented by the value of its product and labour-time by the magnitude of that value': 'these formulae .. bear it stamped upon them in unmistakeable letters that they belong to a state of society, in which the process of production has the mastery over man, instead of being controlled by him' (1965, pp. 80–1). The fact that the product of doing takes the form of value is an expression of the containment of the power of doing. When the work of the serfs is freed from subordination to the lord, it does not become free creative activity, but is held in leash by the requirements of value production. Unhooked from personal bondage to the lord, the former serf is nevertheless bound through the articulation of value to exploitation by capital.

Third, value announces the cost to the ruling, exploiting class of the containment of doing. It makes clear that this form of the subjugation of work means that social relations are established 'behind the backs of the producers', that society is subject to no social control. In capitalism, the ruling class, if it can be called such, rules only in the sense that it tries to contain (and benefit from) the chaos of value. Value rules, as chaos, as the dis-articulation of social relations, as the cracked (in all senses of the word) sociality of doing. Value is the expression of the power of doing-contained, as disorder, as contradiction.[5]

In *Capital*, this loss of social control is expressed through the successive derivation of the dis-located, dis-articulated, crazy (*verrückt*) forms of social relations. Each form of social relations expresses not only a connection but a disconnection, a dis-articulation, dis-location. Each step in the progressive fetishisation of social relations traced in *Capital* not only makes society more opaque, it also makes it more dis-located, more prone to disorder. Each time the argument moves from one form to another, the point is made that the particular existence of each form (of price as a form distinct from value, for example) means that there is no necessary correspondence, that each form involves a dis-location, the introduction of unpredictability. Marx says of the relation between commodities and money: 'Commodities are in love with money, but 'the course of true love never did run smooth" (Marx 1965, p. 107). At each step, the derivation of each form of social relations is a tale of uncertain love. Against the fragmentation of social relations, Marx traces their inner unity, traces the process by which that inner unity (labour) assumes fragmented forms: important in Marx's discussion is not only the inner unity, but the real fragmentation, dis-location, of the forms assumed by labour. Too often Marxism is reduced to a functionalism in which it is assumed that the cogwheels of capitalist domination mesh together perfectly. Nothing could be further from Marx's analysis. Capitalism is crucially a society of non-correspondence, in which things do not fit together functionally, in which the law of value is inseparable from the lawlessness of value, a society based on the maintenance-in-dis-articulation of class domination, the leashed unleashing of the power of doing.

The dis-articulation of society is the possibility of social dis-integration, the possibility of crisis. Crisis is simply the extreme expression of social dis-articulation: the extreme manifestation of the non-correspondence of labour and capital, of production and consumption, of the sale and purchase of labour-power and other commodities, of the political and the economic. In that (still limited) sense, the crisis-ridden nature of capitalism is already given in the dis-articulation of the class relation.

III

If crisis is the extreme manifestation of the dis-articulation of social relations, then any theory of a tendency towards (or 'inevitability' of) crisis must begin by asking why the dis-articulation of social relations should take extreme forms. If crisis is not viewed as simply endemic in capitalism (an endemic dis-location of social relations) but is seen as the periodic intensification of dis-articulation, then it is necessary to go beyond the argument so far and ask how, in a society in which there is no inevitability, one can yet talk of a tendency towards crisis as the key to understanding the fragility of capitalism.

The problem is not just to understand crisis as a crisis of social relations, rather than as an economic phenomenon. It is not simply a question of seeing crisis as a periodic intensification of class antagonism or of intensified social change (and hence central to any understanding of social movement). This is important, but the issue at this point of the argument is how it is possible to talk of a tendency to crisis (or even inevitability of crisis) without having recourse to external, objective forces.

Any non-deterministic theory of crisis must locate the tendency to crisis in the dynamic of struggle. There must be something about the relation of struggle in capitalism, something about the relation between capital and labour, that leads it to recurrent crisis. This is not a question of seeing crisis as the consequence of a wave of struggle or militancy (as, in different ways, neo-Ricardian and autonomist analyses do),[6] but of seeing the tendency to crisis as embedded in the form of the class antagonism.

It was argued above that the distinguishing feature of the capitalist form of class antagonism was the dis-articulation of the class relation (expressed in freedom, value, mobility, and so on), and that this dis-articulation is expressed in all aspects of social relations. Now, if crisis is seen as this social dis-articulation taken to extreme, that already suggests the question: what is it about the dis-articulation of class relations that makes it tend to extreme forms?

So far the dis-articulation of social relations has been discussed in terms of the distinction between capitalism and previous forms of class society, as though the dis-articulation had been completed at the dawn of capitalism. In an antagonistic society such as capitalism, however, there are no states of being, only processes of movement. Dis-articulation, then, is not a description of the state of class relations, but a dynamic of struggle. Dis-articulation does not simply refer to the liberation of the serfs from the feudal lords and the liberation of the lords from their serfs, but can be seen as the continuing centrifugal dynamic of antagonism, as workers fight against their dependence on capital and capital fights against its dependence on labour. It is the centrifugal dynamic of struggle which is the core of capitalism's tendency to crisis. Both labour and capital constantly strive to liberate themselves from their mutual dependence: that is the source of capitalism's peculiar fragility.

The centrifugal nature of the struggle against capital is relatively easy to see. Our struggle is clearly a constant struggle to get away from capital, a struggle for space, for autonomy, a struggle to lengthen the leash, to intensify the dis-articulation of domination. This takes a million different forms: throwing the alarm clock at the wall, arriving late for 'work', back pain and other forms of absenteeism, sabotage, struggles over tea breaks, for the shortening of the working day, for longer holidays, better pensions, strikes of all sorts.

Migration is a particularly important and obvious form of flight, as millions of people flee from capital, in hope.[7] Struggles over wages can also be seen as struggles for greater autonomy from capital, for, although an intensification of work is often part of the deal for higher wages, money is identified with 'freedom', in its capitalist sense, with the capacity to lead a life less subject to external dictates. The struggle to get away from capital is obviously not confined to the place of employment: struggles over health or housing, struggles against nuclear power, attempts to establish anti-capitalist forms of living or eating all are attempts to get away from the domination of value. The struggle by labour (or, better, *against* labour) is a constant struggle for autonomy from capital, whether understood in terms of collective revolt or as the individual exploitation of opportunities. The struggle for autonomy is the refusal of domination, the NO which reverberates in one form or another not only through places of employment but through the whole of society.[8]

That capital's struggle is also for autonomy is perhaps less obvious. It would seem that the opposite is true. Capital's struggle is against the autonomy of doing. Where we seek to loosen the ties of capitalist domination, capital seeks to tighten them; where we seek to extend insubordination, capital must subordinate; where we seek to escape, capital must contain; where we seek to arrive late, capital imposes the clock. It would seem that capital's struggle is constantly against the dis-articulation of society, and that therefore the extreme manifestations of dis-articulation (that is, crises) are a matter of contingency, dependent purely on the particular outcome of the struggle between dis-articulation and articulation.

Yet the matter is not so simple. Certainly, capital's survival depends on exploiting labour. What is distinctive about capitalism, however, is the form of exploitation, the mediation of the relation of exploitation through money (value, freedom, mobility). Capital's struggle to bind labour is mediated through the dis-articulation of the social relation. The form in which capital imposes its discipline on labour is through actual or threatened flight from labour. The worker who arrives late is faced with dismissal: not with the lash or the gallows, but with the movement of capital away from her. The labour force that goes on strike or does not work at the pace required by capital is normally faced not by the machine-gun but by the closure of the factory and the conversion of the capital into money. The workers who raise the hand of insubordination are faced with dismissal and replacement by machinery – the flight of capital from variable capital through money to constant capital. The joy of capitalism, from capital's point of view, is that it is not bound to the subordination of any particular worker or group of workers, but only to the subordination of labour in general. If one group of workers proves unsatisfactory, capital can simply spit them out, turn itself into money and go in search of more subordinate ('flexible') workers. Capital is an inherently mobile form of domination.[9]

The paradox of capitalism is that both workers and capital struggle constantly, in different ways, to liberate themselves from labour. There is, in the peculiar form of the antagonism between capital and work, a centrifugality: the two poles of the antagonistic relation repel each other. There is a mutual repulsion between humanity and capital (obvious enough, but all-important). If one thinks of the dis-articulated bond of capitalism in terms of a dog-owner walking a dog on a long leash, then the peculiarity of capitalism is that both owner and dog tend to run away from each other.

To take the analogy a step further, crisis comes not when owner and dog run in opposite directions, but when the unity of the relation asserts itself through the leash. Dog and owner may have forgotten about their attachment, but eventually it asserts itself, independently of their will. It is the same with capital: no matter how much labour and capital may wish to forget about their mutual relationship, eventually it asserts itself. Behind all the forms that the relationship may take lies the fact that capital is nothing but objec-tivised labour.

The process of social dis-articulation does not in itself constitute a crisis. Hippies can opt out, workers can turn up late for work, students can fritter away their time in the study of Marx, capital can turn to financial speculation or handling drugs: all that does not matter too much as long as the production of capital (that is, the objectivisation of doing) itself is not threatened.[10] The dis-articula-tion of social relations means that the reproduction of capital depends on one particular type of social practice – the production of surplus value. It is when the dis-articulation of social relations threatens the production of surplus value (expressed through money as profit) that the underlying unity of social relations asserts itself.

In this sense, those theories of crisis which are based on Marx's analysis of the tendency of the rate of profit to fall can be seen as more relevant than under-consumption or disproportionality theories. Where the latter focus on expressions of the extreme dis-articulation of social relations (the lack of correspondence between production and consumption, or between different sectors of production), they do not address directly the relation between the classes, the relation of 'free' mutual repulsion which is the source of non-correspondence. The contradiction of this mutual repulsion is, on the other hand, the core of Marx's theory of the tendency of the rate of profit to fall.

A crucial form of capital's struggle for autonomy from living labour is the replacement of living labour by dead, past labour, by machinery. In its struggle to maximise surplus-value production, 'capital is constantly compelled to wrestle with the insubordination of the workmen' (Marx 1965, p. 367), to struggle with 'the refractory hand of labour' (1965, p. 437). Capital's response to the insubordination of labour is to dissociate itself from living labour, to replace the insubordinate worker by the docile machine and to use the machine to impose order ('Arkwright created order', Marx quotes Ure as saying (1965, p. 368)). The replacement of worker by machine is, of course, not necessarily a direct response to insubordination: mediated through money, it may take the form of a response to the costs of maintaining subordination, that is, it may simply be seen as cost-saving. Either way, the result is the same: capital's struggle to maximise surplus value, which can be produced only by living labour, takes the form of a flight from living labour, the expulsion of living labour and its replacement by dead labour.

The flight from labour (peculiar to capitalism) comes into conflict with the rulers' dependence upon labour (common to all class societies). Paradoxically, capital's flight from labour intensifies its dependence upon labour. Capital's flight from labour means that the reproduction of the material basis of its domination (value) depends on the exploitation of a relatively decreasing number of workers (this is what Marx refers to as a rising organic composition of capital). For capital to reproduce itself, there must be an ever intensifying exploitation of labour, which in turn presupposes an ever intensifying subjugation of humanity. If the intensification of exploitation is not sufficient to counteract the effects of capital's flight from labour, the consequences for the reproduction of capital will manifest themselves as a fall in the rate of profit. What is expressed in the tendency of the rate of profit to fall is precisely the contradiction, peculiar to capitalism, between capital's flight from labour and its dependence upon labour. Crisis confronts capital with its dependence upon labour, upon the doing which it denies. In that sense, crisis is no more than the expression of the unsustainability of fetishism.

So far we have explained crisis in terms of the force of the scream, the force of the flight from labour. But we have seen that the scream is the cry of a frustrated power-to. Is it possible to see crisis also as the expression of the force of power-to, and therefore as creating the basis for a different type of society?

Orthodox Marxism certainly gives a more positive interpretation of crisis, presenting it as the conflict between the forces of production and the relations of production. The development of the forces of production are understood as creating a positive basis for the construction of a communist society and as coming increasingly into conflict with their capitalist integument. Is it possible to sustain such a positive argument?

It is clear that the 'forces of production' cannot develop positively, as though they existed in some social vacuum. The phrase 'forces of production', if we forget all the mechanistic and positivistic overtones arising from the orthodox tradition, refers simply to the development of human power-to. Our human capacity to fly through the air, say, is very much greater now than it was in the times of Leonardo da Vinci: that is because of the development of human power-to or, if you will, the forces of production. Yet it is clear that there is never any neutral development of such power-to. Power-to exists at all times in and against its capitalist form, power-over. Use value exists in and against value. There is at all times a tension of in-and-against between our social doing and the fact that the sociality of our doing is mediated through value. It cannot be otherwise. In that sense, there is at every moment a clash between the development of the forces of production (our power-to) and its capitalist integument. There is, then, no positive development of our power-to-do that could simply be taken over by a self-determining society.

At the same time, it is important to see that the flight-from-labour that we have seen as the core of the contradictory character of capital, manifested in its tendency to crisis, is not necessarily (or indeed normally, if one leaves aside the case of suicide) a flight from doing. The worker who phones in to say she is sick because she wants to spend the day with her children is struggling to give priority to one form of doing over another. Even the poster that depicts a woman lying in bed and saying 'I didn't go to work yesterday. I won't go today. Live for pleasure, not for pain' shows the struggle against capitalism not just as a negative struggle but as a struggle for a different type of social doing (live for pleasure, not for pain). There are more subtle ways too in which people are engaged in fighting for alternative ways of doing: even when they simply try to do their jobs well, as in teachers trying to teach their students, nurses trying to help their patients, designers trying to design good products, producers trying to produce good products – even then, people are fighting for the development of use value against value, and thus for the emancipation of the sociality of doing. Value (the pressure to contribute to profitability or to satisfy one of the innumerable bureaucratic imitations of value) is then regarded as a disturbance, as something to be resisted. From the point of view of capital, the focus on use value rather than value is just as much a form of insubordination as absenteeism or sabotage.

There is, then, the development in capitalism of a basis for a different type of social organisation, but it lies not in machines or in the things that we produce but in the social doing or cooperation that develops in constant tension with its capitalist form. Since there is nothing that exists outside capitalist social relations, it is clearly mistaken to think of crisis in terms of a contradiction between capitalist social relations and something else. The contradiction can only be a contradiction internal to the social relations of doing. It is this internal contradiction that manifests itself in crisis: the contradiction between doing and its capitalist form, that is to say, the flight from labour to doing.

IV

Crisis involves an intensification of conflict. The mutual repulsion of humanity and capital both imposes the necessity for capital constantly to intensify its exploitation of labour and makes it difficult for it to do so. A crisis can be said to exist when the insubordination or non-subordination of doing hinders the intensification of exploitation required for capitalist reproduction to such an extent that the profitability of capital is seriously affected. Through the process of crisis, capital seeks to reorganise its relation with labour in such a way as to restore profitability. This involves the mobilisation of what Marx calls the counter-tendencies to the tendency to the rate of profit to fall: raising the rate of exploitation, eliminating a number of the capitals that would otherwise participate in the share-out of total social surplus value, restoring to some degree the proportional part played by living labour by cheapening the elements of constant capital and reducing the unproductive use of surplus value. This involves not just a reorganisation of the labour process itself but of all those conditions which affect the process of exploitation, that is to say, the whole of society. This 'mobilisation of the counter-tendencies' typically involves bankruptcies, unemployment, wage cuts, curtailment of trade union rights, an intensification of work for those still in employment, an intensification of competition between capitals and of conflict between states, cuts in state expenditure on education, health and social welfare, a consequent change in the relation between old and young, between women and men, children and parents, a change too in the relation between different aspects of ourselves, and so on.

The whole process of crisis involves a direct confrontation between capital and labour, between capital and the insubordination and non-subordination of life. This confrontation means risks for capital: the confrontation could lead not to greater subordination but to more overt insubordination and an intensification of capital's difficulties. The dangers of confrontation are even more clear from the perspective of particular capitals or particular states which run the risk of losing in the intensified competition and conflict which crisis implies. In other words, capital as a whole, and also particular capitals and particular states, may have an interest in avoiding or modifying the confrontation with the forces of insubordination.

To return to the metaphor of the dog and its master, crisis can be seen as the point in their mutual repulsion at which the leash tightens, cuts into the dog's neck and the master's hand. It is clear that dog and master cannot continue on their previous course. Yet still there is nothing predetermined about the outcome. If the dog is sufficiently strong and determined or has gathered sufficient momentum, it will either break the leash or knock the master off his feet. Alternatively, the master may have sufficient strength and skill to bring the dog to heel. In his struggle to subordinate the dog, the master has an important trick up his sleeve: he can extend the leash. This is both an acknowledgement of the dog's strength and a manoeuvre to tire the dog into submission. Once the dog is sufficiently tired and weakened, the owner can, if necessary, beat the dog to bring it to heel and shorten the leash.

The loosening of the leash, the avoidance of conflict with the aim of winning the conflict is the expansion of credit. Crisis (and hence the materiality of anti-power) cannot be understood without discussing the role of the expansion of credit.

As profits fall, companies in difficulties seek to survive by borrowing money. Governments with economic and social problems seek to avoid confrontation with their populations by borrowing. Workers too seek to alleviate the effects of incipient crisis by borrowing. The increased demand for loans combines with the problems caused by insubordination in production to make it attractive for capitals to lend their money rather than to invest it in production. The onset of crisis gives rise to an expansion of credit and debt. Accumulation becomes more and more fictitious: the monetary representation of value becomes more and more detached from the value actually produced. Capitalism becomes more fictitious, more make-believe: workers make believe that their income is greater than it is; capitalists make believe that their businesses are profitable; banks make believe that the debtors are financially sound. All make believe that there is a greater production of surplus value than is actually the case. All make believe that there is a greater subordination of labour, a greater subordination of life to capital than is really so. With the expansion of credit and debt, all our categories of thought become more fictitious, more make-believe. In a peculiar, fetishised way, the expansion of credit expresses the explosive force of the subjunctive, the longing for a different society.

Classically, the expansion of credit reaches a point, however, at which, as a result of the avoidance of confrontation with insubordination, the relative decline in the surplus value produced makes it impossible to maintain the fiction. More and more debtors begin to default in their repayments, creditors (such as banks) start to collapse and the crisis is precipitated in its full intensity, with all the social confrontation that that involves. There is a massive destruction of fictitious capital and a massive destruction of the fictitious expectations and living standards of most people. Such a destruction of a make-believe world can be seen, for example, in the stock market crash of 1929.

This classic process of crisis will, however, be modified if there is some 'lender of last resort' who is able to keep on lending, to maintain the expansion of credit in such a way as to avoid the credit collapse. Credit then becomes much more elastic, the world of make-believe more fantastic. The leash seems to be infinitely extendable, giving both dog and master the illusion of freedom.

V

The seventy years or so since the crash of 1929 have seen a change in the shape of crisis. Credit has become much more elastic, the role of the lender of last resort much more prominent. The constant expansion of credit and debt is now a central part of capitalist development.[11]

The extent to which the reproduction of capitalism now depends on the constant expansion of debt is the clearest indication of capital's incapacity to adequately subordinate life into labour. The insubordination of life has entered into the very core of capital as chronic financial instability.

The point was made clearly by the US politician Bernard Baruch, when Roosevelt abandoned the Gold Standard in 1933 in order to meet social pressures for more flexible economic and social policies: 'It can't be defended except as mob rule. Maybe the country doesn't know it yet, but I think we may find we've been in a revolution more drastic than the French Revolution. The crowd has seized the seat of government and is trying to seize the wealth. Respect for law and order is gone.'[12] The mob had been allowed into the very heart of capital. The government had given in to social discontent by adopting policies that would undermine the stability of the currency.

That was the essence of the debates of the interwar period surrounding the restoration and then the abandonment of the Gold Standard. While Keynes and those of like mind argued that it was necessary to adapt capitalist rule to incorporate the new strength of labour (manifested above all in the wave of revolutionary activity associated with October 1917)[13] by accepting a new, expanded role for the state and more flexible monetary policies, their opponents argued that to do so would undermine the long-term stability of money and therefore of capitalism. Baruch and his friends (the 'old-world party', as Keynes called them) were, of course, right, but in the short term they lost the argument: the mob was allowed into the heart of money and monetary stability was undermined.

The problems that arise for capital from this type of development became clear in the 1960s and early 1970s. The constant expansion of credit implies above all a weakening of the discipline of the market, a weakening of the social discipline imposed by the law of value. By postponing or modifying crisis, it makes possible the survival of inefficient capitals and, even worse from the point of view of capital, the survival of inefficient and insubordinate workers. It also implies the autonomisation of financial markets from commodity markets. Credit feeds on credit. In order to avoid defaulting in the repayment of loans and interest, debtors need to borrow more. An increasing proportion of credit granted is recycling credit, credit granted just for the purpose of repaying loans (or, often, the interest on loans). The more elaborate the structure of credit becomes, the more difficult it becomes to maintain, but also the more difficult to undo. A full-scale 'credit crunch' (the destruction of fictitious capital) would not only cause massive social hardship but also threaten the existence of the banking system, and, with it, the existing structure of capitalism.

The criticisms which had been voiced by the opponents of Keynes in the 1920s and 1930s arose with force again in the 1970s, when they formed the basis of the monetarist assault on the assumptions of the post-war development of capitalism. The monetarist critique of Keynesianism was directed against the fictitious character of capitalist development ('funny money', as they called it) and against the social indiscipline which the modification of the market promoted. The monetarist prescription was essentially to reverse the Roosevelt–Keynes mistake and throw the mob out of money. Baruch's argument was now repeated in the form of an argument about the need to limit democracy (and the role of the state): the undermining of monetary stability was discussed in terms of the 'economic consequences of democracy'.[14] More recently, the argument has taken the form of advocating greater independence for central banks from government (and therefore formal-democratic) influence.[15] In each case, the struggle of capital has been to get the mob out of money. In each case, it has failed, simply because the integration of labour through the expansion of debt and the avoidance of crisis has taken such proportions that the measures required to restore capitalism to financial stability would be so drastic as to threaten the existence of capitalism itself.

The attempt by the United States, British and other governments, to impose market discipline through tightening the money supply (that is, restricting the expansion of credit), in the years 1979 to 1982, not only caused considerable social hardship and economic destruction, but also threatened to destroy the international banking system. The restriction of credit by raising interest rates in the United States created a situation in which it became extremely difficult for some of the biggest debtors (such as the Mexican, Argentine and Brazilian governments) to repay their debts or even to pay the interest due. When the Mexican government threatened in 1982 to default on its payments, thus precipitating the so-called 'debt crisis' of the 1980s, it became clear that the attempt to eliminate the expansion of credit threatened the survival not only of the debtors but also of the creditors, in this case the world's major banks.

The attempt to precipitate the massive destruction of fictitious capital through tight monetary policies had proved impossible to implement. The reproduction of capital required a new and massive expansion of credit. The problem for capital was how to provide the credit needed for the reproduction of capital without allowing this credit expansion to undermine the discipline needed for the exploitation of labour. The solution attempted was the so-called 'supply-side' economics of the 1980s: the combination of measures to discipline labour with an unprecedented expansion of credit.[16] The dangers involved in such a development were signalled by a number of critics of this 'voodoo economics' in the mid-1980s (see, for example, Kaufmann 1986; Congdon 1988; Magdoff and Sweezy 1987). Although the critics were correct in pointing to the instability entailed by the expansion of debt, the stock market crash of 1987, of which they had warned, simply increased the pressures to expand credit in order to avoid a worse crisis. The response of the governments was the same: the expansion of credit and the introduction of measures to avoid at all costs a massive destruction of fictitious capital.[17]

The response to the recession of the early 1990s was the same 'Keynesian' response, especially on the part of the United States and Japanese governments: to reduce the rates of interest to stimulate borrowing, to create money through credit. In this case, however, a lot of the money borrowed in the United States (on the basis of the 3 per cent interest rate set by the Federal Reserve)[18] was not invested in the US but in the international money markets, and especially in the so-called emerging markets, where there were high profits to be won. The most important of the emerging markets was Mexico, where the inflow of capital in the form of money contributed to the opening of a huge abyss between the reality of the process of accumulation and its appearance, the abyss that was revealed in the devaluation of the peso in December 1994.[19]

The result of the constant postponement of crisis through the expansion of debt has been an ever growing separation between productive and monetary accumulation. Money has been expanding at a far faster rate than the value it represents. In other words, despite the very real restructuring of the productive process that has taken place over the last twenty years or so, the survival of capitalism is based on an ever increasing expansion of debt. Many statistics can be used to tell what is basically the same story. Public debt, for example, which was the central theme of the monetarist attack against Keynesianism, continues to expand: the OECD calculates that the net public debt of its member states increased from 21 per cent of the gross domestic product in 1978 to 42 per cent in 1994.[20] The net debt of the European governments grew from less than 25 per cent of GDP in 1980 to more than 55 per cent in 1994.[21] According to IMF figures for the member states of the Group of Seven, domestic credit as a proportion of gross domestic product rose from 44.48 per cent in 1955 to 104.54 per cent in 1994. The world bond market (which is closely tied to the financing of government budget deficits) tripled in size between 1986 and 1997.[22] The growth in world money transactions has been far faster than the growth in world trade: while yearly transactions in the London Eurodollar market represented six times the value of world trade in 1979, by 1986 they were about 25 times the value of world trade and 18 times the value of the world's largest economy (Walter 1993, p. 197). Well over a trillion dollars are exchanged daily on the world's foreign exchange markets, and this figure has been increasing about 30 per cent a year since the early 1990s. The late 1980s and the 1990s saw a massive rise in the expansion of debt through securitisation – the development of new forms of property in debt, particularly the so-called 'derivatives': the derivatives markets grew at the rate of 140 per cent a year from 1986 to 1994 (International Monetary Fund 1995, p. 18). In Wall Street, price-earning ratios on shares reached record highs.[23]

The separation between real and monetary accumulation is crucial for understanding the instability, volatility, fragility and unpredictability of capitalism today. Since the whole financial structure of capitalism is so heavily based on credit and debt, any default or threat of default by a major debtor (such as Mexico) can cause great upheaval in the financial markets: the urgency with which the international package to support the peso was put together at the beginning of 1995 was related to fears that the Mexican government could default on the payment of its debt. More generally, the autonomisation of the financial markets which the non-destruction of fictitious capital supports implies the possibility of creating ever more sophisticated financial instruments of doubtful validity; it also implies the increasingly rapid movement of greater and greater quantities of money on the world's financial markets, and therefore a radical change in the relation between individual states and world capital.

All this does not mean that world financial collapse is imminent. It does, however, mean that a chronic financial instability has become a central feature of contemporary capitalism, and that the possibility of a world financial collapse has become a structural characteristic of capitalism, even in periods of rapid accumulation.[24]

This has two crucial consequences for the understanding of crisis today. First, it means that attempts to administer the crisis by political means acquire a new importance. Both nationally and internationally, the confrontation with insubordination is selectively directed. Rather like a bank manager faced with bad debts, both states and international agencies like the International Monetary Fund, the World Bank and the Group of Seven discriminate between debtors. Depending on their position and the possible consequences of overt coercion, debtor states are dealt with more or less leniently. In all cases, debt is used as a means of imposing social discipline, subordination to the logic of capital, although not always with success.[25]

In spite of all the praise of the market by the people who operate and support this process of debt administration, the administration of debt is very far from being the free operation of the market. Just the contrary: the administration of debt which now plays such an important part in the world arises simply because the free operation of the market would give rise to such a level of social confrontation, to such a wave of insubordination, that the survival of capitalism would probably become impossible. What has taken its place is an administered confrontation with insubordination, with the debt administrators taking only such measures as they think are socially and politically feasible. The result is a deferred, prolonged, fragmented crisis, in which total confrontation is avoided, in which the full implications of crisis are felt only in certain countries and regions, while others continue to enjoy what is known as prosperity. The incidence of crisis is always uneven as some capitals or states gain from the intensification of conflict which crisis entails, but this disparity is arguably intensified as a result of the role played by debt administration. Drastic falls in the standard of living in some areas are accompanied in other areas by talk of a 'Goldilocks economy' and of a 'new paradigm' in which the problem of crisis has been solved.

At the heart of this administration of crisis is a problem for capital. There is only a partial confrontation with the expansion of debt and consequently with the insubordination or non-subordination which capital needs to eliminate. Capital, in order to develop with some degree of stability, needs to produce more and more surplus value, needs to exploit labour more and more effectively, needs to eliminate the insubordination and non-subordination which hinders it from doing so. The continued expansion of debt suggests that it is not succeeding in doing so. In spite of the partial confrontations, capitalism's dependence on debt continues to grow. In part this is actually stimulated by the process of debt administration itself. Big debtors (large states, large companies, large banks) come to learn through the process of administration that they are 'too big to fail', that the states and international agencies cannot allow them to collapse, because of the social and economic consequences that such a collapse would entail. Consequently, they know that, no matter how 'irresponsibly' they behave, no matter how indebted they may become in the attempt to maximise their profits at all costs, they will be bailed out by state or international agencies. The attempt to impose the discipline of the market undermines this discipline at the same time. This is the so-called problem of 'moral hazard' which is now at the heart of debt administration.

Secondly, crisis, by virtue of being administered, becomes more and not less unpredictable. It would be completely wrong to think that 'administration of the crisis' means that crisis is under control. Whereas in the time of Marx the occurrence of crisis followed a more or less predictable pattern, this is much less so today. The expansion of credit and the rise in the relative importance of the money form of capital, which is inseparable from that expansion, mean that there is an enormous increase in the speed and volume of capital movements. Rather than the unpredictability of capital being overcome, the expansion and administration of credit mean that crisis is increasingly mediated through the rapid and volatile movement of money. Hence the series of financial crises which have hit the world over the last twenty years or so: the debt crisis of 1982, the stock market crash of 1987, the savings and loans and junk bond crises and scandals of the late 1980s and early 1990s, the tequila crisis of 1994/95, the South East Asia crisis of 1997/98, the rubel crisis of 1998, the samba crisis of 1998/99, the tango crisis of 2000. In each one of these cases, the administrators have succeeded in restricting the impact of the crisis, normally with dire consequences for those affected; but in each case there has been a risk of a 'systemic crisis', of a world financial crisis.

The more the separation between real and monetary accumulation grows, the greater the gap between the real subordination of life achieved and the subordination demanded by the voracity of capital. Capital, in order to survive, becomes more and more demanding. 'Kneel, kneel! Prostrate yourselves! Sell every last drop of dignity that you possess!' is the watchword of contemporary capital. The drive to subordinate every aspect of life more and more intensely to capital is the essence of neoliberalism. Neoliberalism is the attempt to resolve crisis by the intensification and reorganisation of subordination. The separation of subject and object (the dehumanisation of the subject) is taken to new lengths by the extension of command-through-money. Just as capital in the eighteenth century established its rule through the enclosure of land (that is, the separation of people from the land), capital now is trying to overcome its crisis through the enclosure of more and more areas of social activity, imposing the rule of money where previously subordination was only indirect. The commodification of land, the increased commodification of health care and education, the extension of the concept of property to include software and genes, the cutting back of social welfare provision in those countries where it exists, the increase in stress at work: all of these are measures which attempt to extend and intensify subordination, which mark out new areas and say 'These areas are now subject to the direct rule of capital, of money.' In the same way as the enclosures of the eighteenth century meant that conduct that was previously just minding one's own business now became conduct-against-capital, conduct to be punished by law and poverty, so the enclosures of today mean that conduct previously regarded as normal begins to appear as a threat to capital. Thus, for example, the desire of the indigenous people of Chiapas to maintain their traditional patterns of life comes into conflict with the extension of property to include genetic development; in universities it becomes more difficult for students or professors to work on themes like Plato or Aristotle, because that sort of work is not considered compatible with capital's drive to subordinate intellectual work more and more to its needs; the simple pleasure of playing with children or celebrating birthdays becomes harder to maintain in the face of the intensification of stress at work. We are told in so many ways by capital to bend our lives more and more to its dictates (to the operation of the law of value), our lack of subordination becomes more and more a point of conflict, something to be punished by poverty or worse. 'Kneel, kneel, kneel!' cries capital (see Peláez and Holloway 1995). In vain: it is not enough.

In the 1930s Paul Mattick spoke of the 'permanent crisis' of capitalism;[26] it would seem that we are in a similar situation, in a prolonged crisis that is not resolved. Mattick's phrase was too optimistic: the crisis of the 1930s was not permanent, it *was* resolved, through the slaughter of about thirty million people. That is frightening.

And yet, there is nothing predetermined about the crisis. We are the crisis, we-who-scream, in the streets, in the countryside, in the factories, in the offices, in our houses; we, the insubordinate and non-subordinate who say No!, we who say Enough!, enough of your stupid power games, enough of your stupid exploitation, enough of your idiotic playing at soldiers and bosses; we who do not exploit and do not want to exploit, we who do not have power and do not want to have power, we who still want to live lives that we consider human, we who are without face and without voice: we are the crisis of capitalism. The theory of crisis is not just a theory of fear but also a theory of hope.

11   Revolution?

If crisis expresses the extreme dis-articulation of social relations, then revolution must be understood, in the first place, as the intensification of crisis.

This implies a rejection of two distinct understandings of crisis. First, it rejects the traditional concept of the crisis as an *opportunity* for revolution. This is a concept shared by Marxists of many different perspectives. The argument is that when the big crisis of capitalism comes, this will be the moment in which revolution becomes possible: economic crisis will lead to an intensification of class struggle, and this, if guided by effective revolutionary organisation, can lead to revolution. This approach understands crisis as economic crisis, as something distinct from class struggle, rather than as being itself class struggle, a turning-point in class struggle, the point at which the mutual repulsion of capital and anti-labour (humanity) obliges capital to restructure its command or lose control.

Second, this approach rejects the view that the crisis of capital can be equated with its restructuring. This view sees crisis as being functional for capital, a 'creative destruction' (to use Schumpeter's phrase) which destroys inefficient capitals and imposes discipline on the workers.[1] The crisis of one economic model or paradigm of rule leads automatically, in this view, to the establishment of a new one. The argument here is that a crisis is essentially open. Crisis may indeed lead to a restructuring of capital and to the establishment of a new pattern of rule, but it may not. To identify crisis with restructuring is to close the possibility of the world, to rule out the definitive rupture of capital. To identify crisis with restructuring is also to be blind to the whole world of struggle that capital's transition from its crisis to its restructuring has always involved.

Crisis is, rather, the falling apart of the social relations of capitalism. It can never be assumed in advance that capital will succeed in recomposing them. Crisis involves a *salto mortale* for capital, with no guarantee of a safe landing. Our struggle is against capital's restructuring, our struggle is to intensify the disintegration of capitalism.

II

The moving force of crisis is the drive for freedom, the reciprocal flight of capital and anti-labour, the mutual repulsion of capital and humanity. The first moment of revolution is purely negative.

On the side of capital, the drive for freedom involves the spewing out of nauseating workers, the insatiable pursuit of the alchemist's dream of making money from money, the endlessly restless violence of credit and debt.

On the side of anti-capital, flight is in the first place negative, the refusal of domination, the destruction and sabotage of the instruments of domination (machinery, for instance), a running away from domination, nomadism, exodus, desertion.[2] People have a million ways of saying No. The driving force is not just insubordination, the overt and militant refusal of capital, but also non-subordination, the less perceptible and more confused reluctance to conform. Often the No is expressed so personally (dying one's hair green, committing suicide, going mad) that it appears to be incapable of having any political resonance. Often the No is violent or barbaric (vandalism, hooliganism, terrorism): the depravations of capitalism are so intense that they provoke a scream-against, a No which is almost completely devoid of emancipatory potential, a No so bare that it merely reproduces that which is screamed against. The current development of capitalism is so terroristic that it provokes a terroristic response, so anti-human that it provokes an equally anti-human response, which, although quite comprehensible, merely reproduces the relations of power which it seeks to destroy. And yet that is the starting-point: not the considered rejection of capitalism as a mode of organisation, not the militant construction of alternatives to capitalism. They come later (or may do). The starting-point is the scream, the dangerous, often barbaric No.[3]

III

Capitalism's survival depends on recapturing those in flight. Workers must work and produce value. Capital must exploit them. Without that, there would be no capitalism. Without that, capital as a whole would be left in the same position as the unhappy Mr Peel:

Mr Peel ... took with him from England to Swan River, West Australia, means of subsistence and of production to the amount of £50,000. Mr Peel had the foresight to bring with him, besides, 3000 persons of the working-class, men, women and children. Once arrived at his destination, 'Mr Peel was left without a servant to make his bed or fetch his water from the river.' Unhappy Mr Peel who provided for everything except the export of English modes of production to Swan River! [Marx 1965, p. 766]

Mr Peel ceased to be a capitalist (and his money ceased to be capital) simply because the workers fled. In the West Australia of that period, there did not exist the conditions to force them to sell their labour power to capital. Because there was land available, the workers were not separated from the means of doing. Mr Peel's export of capital turned out to be a flight into emptiness. His incapacity to reunite himself with labour meant that he ceased to rule.

The recapture of the workers in flight depends on the double nature of the workers' freedom. They are free not only to sell their labour power, but also free of access to the means of doing. The answer to Mr Peel's problem, in West Australia as elsewhere, is to separate the workers from the means of doing by enclosure. People must be deprived of their freedom to do what they like: freedom is gradually enclosed, hemmed in. This is achieved by the establishment of property, the appropriation of the land and other means of living and doing, so that in the end the people have no option but to choose freely to be exploited by Mr Peel and his like.

Property is the means by which freedom is reconciled with domination. Enclosure is the form of compulsion compatible with freedom. You can live wherever you like, provided of course that it is not the property of others; you can do whatever you like, provided of course that it does not involve using the property of others. If you have no access to the means of doing, because all of it is the property of others, then of course you are free to go and offer to sell your labour power to them in order to survive. That does not mean that the owners of the means of doing are obliged to buy your labour power, because of course they have the freedom to use their property as they wish. Property restricts the flight of those without property, but it does nothing at all to restrict the flight of those who own property. Quite possibly, when the workers (or their descendants) eventually returned cap in hand to Mr Peel (or his descendants) to ask him for a job, they found that he had already invested his money in another part of the world where he would have less problem in converting it into capital.

The basic formula for the recapture of those in flight from labour is property. Those who do not want to labour are entirely free to do as they like, but since the means of doing are enclosed by property, those who do not wish to labour are likely to starve unless they change their attitude and sell their labour power (their only property) to the owners of the means of doing, thus returning to the labour from which they have fled. Hemmed in, they can try to escape by stealing, but risk being hemmed in even more by the operation of the judicial system. In some countries, they can try to escape by turning to the system of social security or public assistance, which, by and large, keeps people from starving to death on the streets, but, more and more, these systems are designed to return those in flight to the labour market. They can try to escape by borrowing, but few lenders will lend their money to those who are not using their labour power as property to be sold on the market, and even if they do succeed in borrowing, the debt collectors will soon come knocking. In some cases, those in flight set up their own businesses or even form cooperatives, but, in the relatively few cases where these survive, they do so by subordinating themselves to the discipline of the market, by integrating themselves into the forms of behaviour from which they have fled. The system of property is like a maze with no exit: all paths of flight lead to recapture. In time, the walls of the maze penetrate the person trapped within. The external limitations become internal definitions, self-definitions, identification, the assumption of roles, the adoption of categories which take the existence of the walls so much for granted that they become invisible.[4] But never entirely.

Capital is not hemmed in in the same way. On the contrary, property is its passport to movement. Property can be converted into money, and money can be moved with ease. The curtailing of the flight of capital comes through periodic crisis as mediated through the movement of the market, through the relative attraction of different investment opportunities. Above all, it is crisis, and the changing in market patterns through which the threat manifests itself, that forces capital, in flight from non-subordinate labour, to confront that labour and face up to its task of exploiting. The confrontation with labour is a confrontation with anti-labour, with labour in flight from labour. The confrontation involves the ever more intensive exploitation of those workers who have chosen freely to be exploited and the ever more profound enclosure of all the means of living and doing that, if left unenclosed, might stimulate the flight and non-subordination of the workers. Hence the twin drives of contemporary capitalism: the intensification of labour through the introduction of new technologies and new working practices, and the simultaneous extension of property to enclose more and more areas (genes, software, land). The more capital is repelled by people, the more it is forced to refashion people in its own image. The more frenetically capital flees from non-subordination ('globalisation', in other words), the more violently it must subordinate.

Capital becomes more and more repulsive. More and more, it drives us to flee. But flight seems hopeless, unless it is more than flight. The scream of refusal must also be a reaffirmation of doing, an emancipation of power-to.

IV

To break from capital, it is not enough to flee. It is not enough to scream. Negativity, our refusal of capital, is the crucial starting-point, theoretically and politically. But mere refusal is easily recaptured by capital, simply because it comes up against capital's control of the means of production, means of doing, means of living. For the scream to grow in strength, there must be a recuperation of doing, a development of power-to. That implies a re-taking of the means of doing.[5] We must understand revolution as more than the intensification of the dis-articulation of social relations.

Power-to is already implicit in the scream. Flight is rarely mere flight, the No is rarely mere No. At very least, the scream is ecstatic: in its refusal of that which exists, it projects some idea of what might exist in its place. Struggles are rarely mere struggles-against. The experience of shared struggle already involves the development of relations between people that are different in quality from the social relations of capitalism. There is much evidence that for people involved in strikes or similar struggles, the most important outcome of the struggles is often not the realisation of the immediate demands, but the development of a community of struggle, a collective doing characterised by its opposition to capitalist forms of social relations.[6] Barbarism is not as merely negative as the classic dichotomy between socialism and barbarism suggests. Struggle implies the reaffirmation of social doing, the recuperation of power-to.

But the recuperation of power-to or the reaffirmation of doing is still limited by capital's monopoly of the means of doing. The means of doing must be reappropriated. But what does that mean?

The appropriation by the working class of the means of production has always been a central element of programmes for a transition to communism. In the mainstream communist tradition, this has been understood as the appropriation by the state of the largest factories, as state ownership of at least the 'commanding heights' of the economy. In the practice of the Soviet Union and other 'communist' countries, this did little to transform doing itself or to make doing the responsibility of the doers themselves. The term 'means of production' has generally been avoided here precisely because it conjures up images that are difficult to dissociate from this tradition. The problem remains, however: if the means of doing are controlled by capital, then any flight from capital comes up against the need to survive, the need to do in a world in which we do not control the means of doing. As long as the means of doing are in the hands of capital, then doing will be ruptured and turned against itself. The expropriators must indeed be expropriated.[7]

To think in terms of property is, however, still to pose the problem in fetishised terms. Property is a noun which is used to describe and conceal an active process of separating. The substance of capitalist rule is not an established relationship between a person and a thing (property), but rather an active process of separating us from the means of doing. The fact that this separating is continuously repeated does not, for us, convert a verb into a noun. The fact that it becomes a habitual separating does not in any sense make it normal, any more than the habitual beating by a man of his wife makes that normal or converts the verb of beating into a noun, or an established fact. To think of property as a noun, as a thing, is to accept the terms of domination. Nor can we start from the means of production, for the distinction between production and doing is itself a result of the separation; nor even from the means of doing, for the very separation of means of doing from doing is a result of the rupture of doing. The problem is not that the means of production are the property of capitalists; or rather, to say that the means of production are the property of the capitalists is merely a euphemism which conceals the fact that capital actively breaks our doing every day, takes our done from us, breaks the social flow of doing which is the precondition of our doing. Our struggle, then, is not the struggle to make ours the property of the means of production, but to dissolve both property and means of production: to recover or, better, create the conscious and confident sociality of the flow of doing. Capital rules by fetishising, by alienating the done from the doing and the doer and saying 'This done is a thing and it is mine.' Expropriating the expropriator cannot then be seen as a reseizure of a thing, but rather as the dissolution of the thing-ness of the done, its (re)integration into the social flow of doing.

Capital is the movement of separating, of fetishising, the movement of denying movement. Revolution is the movement against separating, against fetishising, against the denial of movement. Capital is the denial of the social flow of doing, communism is the social movement of doing against its own denial. Under capitalism, doing exists in the mode of being denied. Doing exists as things done, as established forms of social relations, as capital, money, state, the nightmarish perversions of past doing. Dead labour rules over living doing and perverts it into the grotesque form of living labour. This is an explosive contradiction in terms: living implies openness, creativity, while labour implies closure, pre-definition. Communism is the movement of this contradiction, the movement of living against labour. Communism is the movement of that which exists in the mode of being denied.[8]

The movement of doing is a movement against the denial of its sociality. Memory is an important part of this, the communal putting together of the experience of collective movement and of opposition to its fragmentation (see, for example, Tischler 2000). The movement of the sociality of doing implies social or communal forms of organisation. 'The workers' council spells the political and economic defeat of reification', as Lukács points out (1971, p. 80). It cannot, however, be a question of reifying in turn the workers' council or soviet as a fixed model: each phase of struggle throws up its own forms of communal organisation. It is clear, for example, that the Internet is permitting the creation of new patterns in the formation of collective struggle (see Cleaver 1998). What is important is the knitting or reknitting or patchworking of the sociality of doing and the creation of social forms of articulating that doing on a basis other than value.

The movement of communism is anti-heroic. Heroes stand out from the community, draw to themselves the communal force of action. The revolutionary tradition is full of heroes, people who have sacrificed themselves for the revolution, people (mostly young men, it must be admitted) who have abandoned wives, children, friends, to dedicate themselves selflessly to changing the world, confronting physical hardship and danger, often even torture and death. Nobody would deny the importance of such figures, and yet there is something very contradictory in the notion of a heroic revolution, or indeed of a revolutionary hero. The aim of revolution is the transformation of ordinary, everyday life and it is surely from ordinary, everyday life that revolution must arise. The idea of a communist revolution is to create a society in which we are not led, in which we all assume responsibility, so our thought and our traditions must move in terms of the non-leaders, not the heroes. Militancy cannot be the axis of revolutionary thought, although certainly the work of 'militants' is crucial in any form of organising. Revolution is conceivable only if we start from the assumption that being a revolutionary is a very ordinary, very usual matter, that we are all revolutionaries, albeit in very contradictory, fetishised, repressed ways (but then the heroes of the revolutionary tradition were also contradictory, fetishised and repressed in many ways). The scream, the No, the refusal that is an integral part of living in a capitalist society: that is the source of revolutionary movement. The weaving of friendship, of love, of comradeship, of communality in the face of the reduction of social relations to commodity exchange: that is the material movement of communism. The non-subordinate are the anti-heroes of the revolution. This is most certainly not a call to be passive, but rather to take as the central principle of revolutionary organisation the Zapatista idea that we are ordinary-therefore-rebellious.

Revolution is the 'return of the repressed': 'The return of the repressed makes up the tabooed and subterranean history of civilisation' (Marcuse 1998, p. 16). Marcuse is speaking here of the movement of the pleasure principle against the reality principle, but the point has a general validity. Communism, we said, is the movement of that which exists in the mode of being denied. Communism, then, is the return of the repressed, the revolt against fetishism. To start theorising from militancy is something like pre-Freudian psychology, focusing on the manifest symptoms rather than that which exists in a state of subterranean repression, in the mode of being denied. This is surely the political importance of a theory of fetishism, that it starts from the force of the denied and the revolt against the process of denial.

That which exists in the mode of being denied is not just a project: it exists. It exists as the creativity upon which capital depends. It exists as the living blood which is the sole nourishment of the capitalist vampire. It exists as negation, as non-identity. It exists as revulsion, as flight from domination, as the substance of capitalist crisis, in much the same way as, in Freudian theory, the repressed is the substance of neurosis. It exists as the driving force of the explosion of debt. It exists as the sociality upon which private property (the negation of that sociality) depends, as the intense sociality of production which is concealed by the integument of private property, but which makes the claim of private property ever more grotesque. It exists as the movement of anti-fetishisation, as the crisis of fetishised forms. It exists, therefore, as the crisis of the labour movement itself, as crisis of its organisational forms and of its received ideas. It exists as the crisis of working class identity, of which this book is undoubtedly an expression. The force of that which exists in the mode of being denied is the crisis of all identity, that of capital and that of labour. As such it is to be welcomed: our struggle is not to establish a new identity or composition, but to intensify anti-identity. The crisis of identity is a liberation from certainties: from the certainties of capital, but equally from the certainties of labour. The crisis of Marxism is the freeing of Marxism from dogmatism; the crisis of the revolutionary subject is the liberation of the subject from knowing. That which exists in the mode of being denied exists as creative uncertainty against-in-and-beyond a closed, predetermined world.

V

Revolutionary politics (or better, anti-politics) is the explicit affirmation in all its infinite richness of that which is denied. 'Dignity' is the word that the Zapatistas[9] use to talk of this affirmation, meaning by that not just the aim of creating a society based on the mutual recognition of human dignity and dignities, but the recognition now, as a guiding principle of organisation and action, of the human dignity which already really exists in the form of being denied, in the struggle against its own denial. Dignity is the self-assertion of those who are repressed and of that which is repressed, the affirmation of power-to in all its multiplicity and in all its unity. The movement of dignity includes a huge diversity of struggles against oppression, many or most of which do not even appear to be struggles, but it does not imply a micro-political approach, simply because this chaotic richness of struggles is a single struggle to emancipate power-to, to liberate human doing from capital. It is an anti-politics rather than a politics simply because it moves against and beyond the fragmentation of doing that the term 'politics' implies, with all its connotation of orientation towards the state and distinction between public and private.

The struggle of that which exists in the form of being denied is inevitably both negative and positive, both scream and doing: negative because its affirmation can take place only against its own denial, and positive because it is the assertion of that which exists, albeit in the form of being denied. Anti-politics cannot therefore just be a question of positively doing 'our own thing', because 'our own thing' is inevitably negative, oppositional. Nor, however, can it just be negative: actions that are purely negative may be cathartic, but they do nothing to overcome the separation on which capitalist rule is based. To overcome that separation, actions must point-beyond in some way, assert alternative ways of doing: strikes that do not just withdraw labour but point to alternative ways of doing (by providing free transport, a different kind of health care); university protests that do not just close down the university but suggest a different experience of study; occupations of buildings that turn those buildings into social centres, centres for a different sort of political action; revolutionary struggles that do not just try to defeat the government but to transform the experience of social life.

Merely negative action inevitably engages with capital on capital's own terms, and on capital's terms we shall always lose, even when we win. The problem with armed struggle, for example, is that it accepts from the beginning that it is necessary to adopt the methods of the enemy in order to defeat the enemy: but, even in the unlikely event of military victory, it is capitalist social relations that have triumphed. And yet, how does one defend oneself from armed robbery (capital) without being armed? The problem of struggle is to move on to a different dimension from capital, not to engage with capital on capital's own terms, but to move forward in modes in which capital cannot even exist: to break identity, break the homogenisation of time. This means seeing struggle as a process of ever renewed experiment, as creative, as negating the cold hand of Tradition, as constantly moving a step beyond the absorbing identification that capitalism imposes. There can be no recipes for revolutionary organisation, simply because revolutionary organisation is anti-recipe.

This implies a non-instrumental concept of revolution. The orthodox Marxist tradition, most clearly the Leninist tradition, conceives of revolution instrumentally, as a means to an end. The problem with this approach is that it subordinates the infinite richness of struggle, which is important precisely because it is a struggle *for* infinite richness, to the single aim of taking power. In doing so, it inevitably reproduces power-over (the subordination of the struggles to the Struggle) and ensures continuity rather than the rupture that is sought. Instrumentalism means engaging with capital on capital's own terms, accepting that our own world can come into being only after the revolution. But capital's terms are not simply a given, they are an active process of separating. It is absurd, for example, to think that the struggle against the separating of doing can lie through the state, since the very existence of the state as a form of social relations is an active separating of doing. To struggle through the state is to become involved in the active process of defeating yourself.

How, then, do we prevent the process of fetishisation, the breaking of doing, the separating of doing and done? It is surely wrong to think in terms of a continuous process of organisation-building. Certainly there must be an accumulation of practices of oppositional self-organisation, but this should be thought of not as a linear accumulation, but as a cumulative breaking of linearity.[10] Think of discontinuities rather than continuity, flashes of lightning which light up the sky and pierce the capitalist forms of social relations, showing them for what they are: a daily repeated and never predetermined struggle to break our doing and to break us, a daily repeated struggle to make the abnormal seem normal and the avoidable seem inevitable. Think of an anti-politics of events rather than a politics of organisation. Or better: think of organisation not in terms of being but in terms of doing. The events do not happen spontaneously. Like parties, they require work and preparation: here the work of dedicated 'militants' is crucial. But the aim is not to reproduce and expand the caste of militants (the organisation) but to 'blast open the continuum of history' (Benjamin 1973, p. 264). The shift from a politics of organisation to a politics of events is already taking place: May 1968, of course, the collapse of the regimes of Eastern Europe too; more recently, the development of the Zapatista rebellion, for all its organisational formality, has been a movement through events,[11] and the wave of demonstrations against global neoliberalism (Seattle, Davos, Washington, Prague, and so on) is obviously event-centred. At their best, such events are flashes against fetishism, festivals of the non-subordinate, carnivals of the oppressed, explosions of the pleasure principle, intimations of the *nunc stans*.[12] For revolution is the explicit unification of constitution and existence,[13] the overcoming of the separation of is and is-not, the end of the dominion of dead labour over living doing, the dissolution of identity.[14]

How then do we change the world without taking power? At the end of the book, as at the beginning, we do not know. The Leninists know, or used to know. We do not. Revolutionary change is more desperately urgent than ever, but we do not know any more what revolution means. Asked, we tend to cough and splutter and try to change the subject. In part, our not-knowing is the not-knowing of those who are historically lost: the knowing of the revolutionaries of the last century has been defeated. But it is more than that: our not-knowing is also the not-knowing of those who understand that not-knowing is part of the revolutionary process. We have lost all certainty, but the openness of uncertainty is central to revolution. 'Asking we walk', say the Zapatistas. We ask not only because we do not know the way (we do not), but also because asking the way is part of the revolutionary process itself.

VI

This is a book that does not have an ending. It is a definition that negates itself in the same breath. It is a question, an invitation to discuss.

This is a book that does not have a happy ending. Nothing in this book has changed the horrors of the society in which we live. How many children have died needlessly since I started to write it? How many since you began to read it? If the book has done anything to weaken or dull the scream or to conceptualise it out of existence, it has failed. The aim has been to strengthen it, to make it more strident. The scream continues.

This is a book that does not (yet?) have a happy

Epilogue:
Moving Against-and-Beyond
Reflections on a Discussion[1]

I

Fine, but what on earth do we do?

Of all the questions and criticisms that have come up in the last two years of discussion[2] that is the one that throbs in the mind most of all.

That capitalism is a catastrophe for humanity becomes more obvious every day. Bush, Blair, Iraq, Israel, Sudan and the slaughter and the torture. Our scream has intensified over the last couple of years. 'Am raging and incandescent and very frustrated because I can't figure out where to put all this anger.' A letter from a friend expresses the frustration of millions.

The rage is silent and it is also vociferous. It is embittered, furious frustration but it is also Argentina and Bolivia and the anti-war movement with its demonstrations of millions. A movement of movements, a cacophony of movements.

The question is urgent. Iraq, Palestine, Sudan, Colombia stand as present realities and also warnings of the possible future of the whole of humanity. What can we do to stop this disaster and avoid its extension? How can we change the world? How do we find hope? To pose the question of power and revolution is not just an abstraction (a 'some day in the future') but a question of how we think and act now.

The traditional answers are in crisis. Blair and Lula, each in his own way, have proved yet again that voting for a 'left' party leads only to disillusion. The Leninist revolutionary parties do not offer any prospect of change either: not only is their history a history of repression and oppression, but even to think of the revolutionary seizure of power makes little sense when there is no revolutionary party anywhere in the world (with the exception of Nepal?) with the slightest possibility of taking power.

But then what? Violence becomes attractive or at least comprehensible. It is not hard to understand the actions of the suicide bombers. There is no doubt that millions around the world would rejoice if Bush or Blair were assassinated tomorrow. And yet that is not the way: such acts of violence do nothing to create a better world.

Not the state, not the violence of terrorism. But then where do we go?

Some readers have wanted to find an answer in this book and have felt frustrated. But there is no answer, there can be no answer.

Some critics have argued that to criticise the traditional answer to the question of revolution (take power and change society) without proposing an alternative answer is to demobilise social struggles or to promote (willingly or unwillingly) a proliferation of micro-politics which leads nowhere.[3] They are wrong: the book does not create a crisis of the traditional concept of revolution but pleads for its recognition as the basis for starting to talk seriously about revolution once again. The crisis of the traditional concept was there already: it is the refusal to recognise it that demobilises struggle, that makes it impossible to talk honestly about changing the world. The scale of the debate around the book is a reflection of the crisis of the traditional forms of anti-capitalist struggle.

But how then? The terrible question is still there. Does the absence of an answer mean that we should just sit at home and moan? For some critics, that is the implication of the argument. To reject the idea of taking state power is, for them, to reject the need for organisation.[4] Nothing could be further from the truth: to reject the idea of taking state power is to pose the question of organisation.

Questions, questions, questions, but where is the answer? The desire for an answer is in part a reaction of looking for a leader (tell us which way to go), but it also reflects the desperation of our situation: what on earth do we do?

What follows is an attempt to take the question further (but no, still not to give an answer), while at the same time responding to some of the criticisms.[5]

II

What is the alternative to struggling for control of the state?

There *is* an alternative to the state. Indeed, the state is simply the movement of suppressing that alternative. The alternative is the drive towards social self-determination.

Social self-determination does not and cannot exist in a capitalist society: capital, in all its forms, is the negation of self-determination.

Furthermore, individual self-determination does not and cannot exist in any society: our doing is so interwoven with the doing of others that the individual self-determination of our doing is an illusion.

What remains is the *drive towards* social self-determination. This begins with the refusal of determination by others: 'No, we will not do as we are told.' The starting point is refusal, insubmission, insubordination, disobedience, No. But the negativity implies a projection that goes beyond mere negativity: refusal of determination by others carries with it a drive towards self-determination. In the best of cases, the sentence then gets longer: 'No, we will not do as we are told, we shall do as we think fit: we shall do what we consider necessary, enjoyable or appropriate.' The No carries a Yes, or indeed Many Yeses, but these Yeses are rooted in the No to existing society – their foundation is a grammar of negativity.[6] The Yeses have to be understood as a deeper No, a negation of the negation which is not positive but more negative than the original negation.[7]

The No that carries many Yeses is a moving against-and-beyond. The move towards self-determination is a moving against the society which is based on the negation of self-determination and *at the same* time a projection beyond existing society – a projection in dreaming, in talking, in doing.

Against-and-beyond need to be held together. Traditional revolutionary theory assumes that the 'against' must come before the 'beyond': first we struggle against capitalism, then we go beyond it and enjoy the promised land. This argument was perhaps tenable in a movement certain of its victory. But we no longer have that certainty, and the exclusive emphasis on against-ness (on a logic of confrontation)[8] tends to reproduce the logic of that which is being confronted. Moreover, we cannot wait for a future that may never come. It is necessary to move beyond now, in the sense of creating a different logic, a different way of talking, a different organisation of doing. The drive towards self-determination cannot be understood in terms of 'first we destroy capitalism, then we create a self-determining society': the drive towards self-determination can only be just that, a moving forward of self-determination against a society which negates it. We, the moving of self-determination, set the agenda.

The 'against' can no more be separated from the 'beyond' than the 'beyond' from the 'against': the assertion of self-determination necessarily means moving against capitalism. Capital is the rule of value, of money, of thingified social relations that we do not control.

The assertion of a 'beyond' necessarily brings us into conflict with capital (in its various forms). Confrontation is inevitable even if we reject its logic. The realisation of our Yeses cannot be separated from the struggle of the No, just as the No, to have force and meaning, cannot be separated from the struggle to realise our Yeses.

This (the No to alien determination and the Yes to determination of our own lives) is not self-determination, because, in a world in which the doings of all are intertwined, the only self-determination possible is one that involves all people in the world. The only possible self-determination is conscious social determination of the social flow of doing. What exists now is not self-determination but the *drive towards* self-determination: not totality, but the *aspiration* to totality.[9] If we refer to social self-determination by the simpler term of communism, then it is clear that communism (at present, at least) can be understood only as a movement, a drive, an aspiration, and we can say with Marx, 'Communism is not for us a *state of affairs* which is to be established, an *ideal* to which reality will have to adjust itself. We call communism the *real* movement which abolishes the present state of things' (Marx and Engels 1976, p. 49).[10]

The drive towards social self-determination is a moving against-and-beyond (beyond-and-against) the barriers that confront it. There is no autonomy, no self-determination possible within capitalism. Autonomy (in the sense of self-determination) can be understood only as a project that continually takes us against-and-beyond the barriers of capitalism. Communism is a moving outwards, an unrest of life, an overflowing, a breaking and transcendence[11] of barriers, an overcoming of identities, an irrepressible project of creating humanity,[12] a flow of a river into new land, sometimes breaking against rocks, flowing around them before washing over them, sometimes making mistakes, taking unforeseen turns, but never resting, always pushing on in a cacophonous torrent of mixed metaphors. This flow cannot be programmed, it has no precise aims, it follows rather a utopian star, a star that rises from all the projects and dreams, all the projected beyonds in our against, all the Yeses contained in our No to a world of inhumanity. Rebellion cannot rest contented, but drives outwards and onwards towards revolution, the total transformation of human doing which is the only real basis of social self-determination.

We start then from the fissures, the cracks in capitalist domination. We start from the No's, the refusals, the insubordinations, the projections against-and-beyond that exist all over the place. The world is full of such fissures, such refusals. All over the place people say, individually or collectively 'No, we shall not do what capitalism (the system) tells us to do: we shall shape our lives as we think fit.' Sometimes these fissures are so tiny that not even the rebels perceive their own rebelliousness, sometimes they are groups of people involved in projects of resistance, sometimes they are as big as the Lacandon Jungle – but the more we focus on them, the more we see the world not (just) as an all-pervading system of capitalist domination but as a world riven by fissures, by refusals and resistances and struggles. Always these fissures are contradictory – easy to criticise, easy to make fun of: they must be contradictory because they are rooted in the antagonisms of capitalist society. Our movement against-and-beyond is always an in-against-and-beyond charged with the limitations and stupidities of existing society. What is important is not their present limitations but the direction of their movement, the push against-and-beyond, the drive towards social self-determination. The practical and theoretical problem is how to think and articulate and participate in this moving against-and beyond.

It is sometimes argued that in the transition from capitalism to communism, unlike the transition from feudalism to capitalism, the new form of organisation can not develop in the interstices of the old, that it must necessarily be a single transformation. It is now clear that there is no alternative: a single total transformation of world capitalism to world socialism or communism is unthinkable, so the only possible way to think about radical social transformation is intersticially. Even if one were to think in terms of taking state power, the particular states would at best be no more than that, potential gaps in the fabric of capitalist domination. The issue then is not whether one thinks of revolution in intersticial terms or not, but what is the best way of thinking about and organising these interstices. In other words, there is no alternative to starting from fissures in capitalist domination, and thinking how these rebellions can move against-and-beyond the capitalist forms of social relations.

Revolutionary theory is part of this flow of resistance against-and-beyond, a feeling the way forward, a breaking on rocks, an attempt to see in the dark: not a laying down of the correct line, but part of the movement and as contradictory as the movement itself.[13] A theory that drives towards self-determination is, whatever its contradictions, in the first place critical – a critique of that which negates self-determination, a critique of the fetishisation of social relations that hides even the possibility of self-determination from our view, a critique of the fetishising that constantly threatens to suffocate the drive to self-determination.

The drive towards self-determination is not instrumental: we do not start from an aim and deduce from that aim the path we must follow to reach that aim. It is rather a movement outwards, a path that is made in the process of walking – walking in the dark, guided only by the light provided by the utopian star of our own projections. Walking in the dark is dangerous, but there is no other possibility.[14]

Walking in the dark, guided by the light of the utopian star of our own projections and driven by the fury of our No to present inhumanity. Our movement is in one direction. We stumble, take wrong paths, revise our course, but try to go always in the same direction, towards social self-determination. Each step is a prefiguration of the goal of social self-determination. It is not a pivoted, two-stage movement. That is important, because traditional revolutionary theory is a pivoted movement, with the winning of state control as the pivot: first we must do whatever is necessary to win control of the state, then, in the second stage, we shall move out from the state to transform society – first we go in that direction, so that later we shall be able to go in the other.[15] The argument here is directed against this idea of a pivoted movement, this idea of a calculated going in that direction so that later we can go in the other. The criterion for judging an action in the traditional concept of revolution is: does this help us to attain the goal of winning state power? The approach here suggests a different criterion: does this action or form of organisation take us forward in the path towards social self-determination? Does it prefigure a self-determining society?

Capital (and the state as a form of capital) is the negation of our drive towards social self-determination. The stronger our drive, the weaker is capital. The weaker our drive, the stronger capital. *There is no middle term.*[16] There is no pivot. Our strength (the strength of our drive towards social self-determination) is *immediately* the weakness of capital (which is the negation of that drive). The question of revolution, of how we move forward from rebellion to revolution, is quite simply 'How do we strengthen our drive towards social self-determination?'

III

The moving out against-and-beyond is a moving out from everyday experience. It cannot be otherwise.

The drive to self-determination is anchored in the everyday practice of its negation. If that were not the case, the struggle for communism (or for another world) would make no sense. Self-emancipation would be impossible and the only possibility of revolution would be a revolution *on behalf of*, a revolution led by an elite which would do nothing more than lead to a restructuring of class domination. That is the difficult core of the communist bet. This is the terrible political-theoretical challenge hurled at us by the Zapatistas in their simple statement that 'We are women and men, children and old people who are quite ordinary, that is rebels, non-conformists, awkward, dreamers'[17] (*La Jornada*, 4 August 1999).

To take seriously the idea of self-emancipation (or the self-emancipation of the working class) we have to look not for a pure subject but for the opposite: for the confused and contradictory presence of rebellion in everyday life. We have to look at the people around us – at work, in the street, in the supermarket – and see that they are rebels, whatever their outward appearances. In the world of possible self-emancipation, people are not what they seem. More than that, they are not what they are. They are not contained within identities, but overflow them, burst out of them, move against and beyond them.

The rebelliousness that is in us all starts with a No, a refusal of the alien determination of what we do, a refusal of the alien imposition of limits on who we are. From this No there arises also a creative charge, the drive towards determining our own lives, a drive no less ordinary than rebellion itself. We come together to complain and protest, but more than that: at the level of everyday gossip, in the back-and-forth of friendship, in the comradeship that develops at work or school or neighbourhood, we develop forms of cooperation to resolve everyday problems. There is in everyday intercourse a subterranean movement of communism, a drive to create and construct and resolve cooperatively, in our own way, without the intervention of external authorities. Not all social relations are commodity relations: the commodity form imposes itself, but ordinary life also involves a constant process of establishing non-commodity or even anti-commodity relations. There is not an outside capital, but there is certainly an *against-and-beyond*.[18]

The movement is a contradictory process. We establish non-commodity relations, non-capitalist forms of cooperation, but always as a movement against the dominant forms and always to some extent contaminated by those forms. Yet through these contradictions we recognise forms of relating that go against the commodity or money form and that create a basis for projecting a different form of society: forms that we commonly refer to as love, friendship, comradeship, respect, cooperation, forms that rise upon a mutual recognition of shared human dignity.

Organising for revolution is then not (or not just) a question of the organisation of a particular group of people, but the organisation of a pole of a contradiction. To put it in class terms: the working class is not a group of people but the pole of an antagonistic relation.[19] The class antagonism cuts through us, collectively and individually. To think about the articulation of revolt is to think of the articulation not just of *those who* but also of *that which* drives against-and-beyond capital. All-important is the *form* of organisation. The movement of the drive towards social self-determination (the movement of communism) implies the promotion of certain forms of relating.[20] In other words, to say that capital is a form of relations means that it is a form of organising or articulating social intercourse, the social interactions between people. To see it as a contradictory form of social relations means that it contains (or seeks to contain) antagonistic forms of social relations, anti-capitalist forms of articulating social intercourse. These anti-capitalist forms are potentially the embryonic forms of a new society.[21] The birth of that society is the movement of the drive towards self-determination, the movement from rebellion to revolution.

There is no organisational model, but there are certain principles, which are developed through struggle and which are an important feature both of the current movement against capitalism and, in diverse expressions, of the whole history of anti-capitalist struggle. The organisational form which I take as the most important point of reference is the council or assembly or commune, a feature of rebellions from the Paris Commune to the Soviets of Russia to the village councils of the Zapatistas or the neighbourhood councils of Argentina. The ideas of council organisation are also present in many of the current attempts in the world to respond to the crisis of the party as a form of organisation. Necessarily, such attempts are always contradictory and experimental, always in movement. What interests us here is not an analysis of the current movements, but a distillation of tendencies present within them, a sharpening of the polar antagonism to capital.

Possibly the best way of thinking about the organisation of the drive to self-determination is in terms of movement. First a moving-against: a moving against all that separates us from the shaping of our own lives. Capital is a movement of separation: a separating of that which we have done from ourselves, the doers, a separation of the doers from one another, a separation of the collective from our control, a separation of the public from the private, the political from the economic, and so on. This separation is a movement of classification, of definition, of containment. It is by this movement of separation-containment that we are excluded from any possibility of determining our own doing.

The No to capital is a refusal of separation, of the separation of public from private, the political from the economic, citizens of one country from citizens of another, the serious from the frivolous, and so on. The moving against capital is a moving against definition, against classification. It is a coming together, an overcoming of separations, a forming of a We, but an undefined, non-identitarian We. The *drive towards* self-determination implies a constant moving, constant searching and experimenting. Once we confuse the *drive towards* self-determination with self-determination itself, as in certain interpretations of autonomy or in the idea of national self-determination, once we confuse the aspiration to totality with totality, once we think of communism not as a movement but as a state-of-being, once we think of the moving, anti-identitarian We as a new Identity, once we institutionalise and define a moving against definition, then all, all is lost. The moving against capital is converted into its opposite, an accommodation, an acceptance.[22]

Such a moving against definition is very much present in the current wave of struggle against capitalism: in the rejection of sexism and racism, the attacks on national frontiers, the organisation of demonstrations and events in a manner which transcends national forms, in the organisation of groups and meetings on a non-definitional basis. What is emphasised is not organisational definition (as in a Party), but indefinition (as in a party): not separation from the community, but integration into it. If one thinks of the movement against the war or the social centres in Italy or the neighbourhood councils in Argentina, it is clear that there is no question of formal membership. In many cases, the practices of the organisations are consciously or unconsciously woven into everyday life in such a way that there is no clear distinction between a 'political' activity and an act of friendship.[23]

The integration of rebel organisation into daily life[24] means that great importance is attached to aspects of life and personality which are systematically excluded by party or state-oriented organisations.

Affection and tenderness become central aspects of the anti-capitalist movement, as they are of other social relations.[25] This is important, for an instrumental organisation (organisations which have the aim of taking power, for example) tends to limit activities and discussion to that which will contribute to reaching the objective: everything else is regarded as frivolous and accorded a secondary importance. To think of organisation (not *the* organisation) as articulating the anti-capitalist feelings of everyday life means that there is no limit; no limit to the range of personal concerns and passions that can be included, but also no end to what is being fought for: a rolling, growing, roaring NO to all oppression – we want everything!

IV

The notion of self-emancipation, then, implies that we start from a ubiquitous rebelliousness, a ubiquitous potential for self-determination, a ubiquitous moving against-and-beyond existing limits. In this sense, a concept of self-emancipation is necessarily anti-identitarian,[26] necessarily dialectic. The aim of revolutionary theory and practice is to distil or articulate this rebelliousness, this moving against-and-beyond, refusing capital and projecting beyond it. Note that this is a quite different starting point from the Leninist concept of revolution. Lenin's workers are quite different. Lenin's workers are limited, self-contained. They struggle, but they struggle up to a certain point. 'The history of all countries shows that the working class, exclusively by its own effort, is able to develop only trade union consciousness' (1966, p. 74). They are contained within their role in society, they are defined. They can go beyond their limits only if taken by the hand by people from outside, by professional revolutionaries. There is a gap between the capacities of the working class and the social revolution which is necessary. This gap can be filled only by the party, by the leadership of a dedicated and disciplined group of militants who act on behalf of the oppressed. If we start from a limited subject, the only possible revolution is a revolution *on behalf of*, a revolution through the state.

This argument also stands opposed to the common view that, in order to avoid isolation and win over the majority, we must be moderate in our proposals. The view here is just the opposite: moderation bores and alienates everyone; it is important rather to address the radical anti-capitalism that is part of everyday experience.

Certainly, any movement must seek to articulate the common denominator of protest, but the common denominator should be seen perhaps not as a set of demands we can all agree upon, but as the scream of rage and horror that is part of the experience of all of us.

That does not mean that everyone is a radical anti-capitalist at heart, but simply that radical anti-capitalism is part of the daily experience of capitalist oppression. The problem of organisation is not to bring consciousness from outside to inherently limited subjects, but to draw out the knowledge that is already present, albeit in repressed and contradictory form. The task is like that of the psychoanalyst who tries to make conscious that which is unconscious and repressed. But there is no psychoanalyst standing outside the subject: the 'psychoanalysis' can only be a collective self-analysis. This implies a politics not of talking, but of listening, or, better, of talking-listening. The revolutionary process is a collective coming-to-eruption of stifled volcanoes. The language and thought of revolution cannot be a prose which sees volcanoes as mountains: it is necessarily a poetry, an imagination which reaches out towards unseen passions. This is not an irrational process, but it implies a different rationality, a negative rationality that starts not from the surface but from the explosive force of the repressed NO.

Note that this approach is not characterised in any way by a romantic assumption that people are 'good', but simply by the assumption that in a society based on class antagonism, we are all permeated by this antagonism, we are all self-contradictory. Certainly we are limited, as Lenin pointed out, but being limited is not a permanent condition but means rather that we drive against those limits. To think of revolution is to focus not on the limits of people but on the overcoming of those limits, the drive beyond those limits. The notion that we are all rebels, that revolution is ordinary, can only be sustained if we see people as contradictory, as self-divided subjects. We are rebels fighting for the survival of humanity in one moment, then we go to the supermarket and participate actively in processes that we know are leading to the destruction of humanity. The drive towards self-determination is not a characteristic exclusive to a particular group of people but something present in contradictory form in all of us. If we understand class as a polar antagonism, then we can see the drive to self-determination as a formulation of that polar antagonism, so that class organisation has to be seen not as the organisation of dedicated militants but as the distillation of this drive.

To put the point slightly differently, we are all composed of different, often contradictory parts. The question is how these parts are articulated. Think of an army, for example: it is not that all soldiers are inherently evil, it is rather that an army consciously articulates certain aspects of the soldiers' personality and suppresses others in order to convert them into obedient killers. So with capitalism: capitalism is a form of organisation that promotes an articulation of our contradictions which is highly destructive, socially and personally. The problem of revolutionary organisation is to promote a different articulation of these parts, an articulation which promotes the distillation of creativity and the drive to social self-determination.

The issue is not to look for a pure revolutionary subject, but to start from our contradictions or limitations and the question of how to deal with them. We can project the awareness of our limitations on to some sort of saviour (God, state, party) supposedly free of those limitations or we can think of the overcoming of those limitations as a process of collective self-emancipation, with the assumption of all the difficulties that that inevitably involves. This collective self-emancipation can be seen as a process of distillation of that which aspires to radical change.

Is there not a danger here? What if the scream against oppression takes a fascist or reactionary form,[27] what if that which is unconscious and repressed is both sexist and racist? If radical anti-capitalism is part of the daily experience of domination, it is also true that reproduction of that domination in its worst forms is also part of that daily experience. How do we guard against that? With the rise of the right in many parts of the world, and after the re-election of Bush, this is a very real problem.

What if the people do not want what we think they ought to want? This is the problem both of bourgeois democracy and of the dictatorship of the proletariat. When the movement for universal suffrage gathered force in the nineteenth century, the problem for the bourgeoisie was 'How do we ensure that the masses want what we think they should want?' The answer given was by ensuring that the masses were included by a form of articulation which simultaneously excluded them (representative democracy) and by linking the extension of the franchise to the extension of compulsory education (later to be supplemented, of course, by the impact of the mass media). The same problem arises again in a different context with the Russian Revolution: the revolution was to give power to the working class, but what if the working class did not want what the party felt it should want? The answer given by the Bolsheviks was that the party decided what was in the interests of the working class – the dictatorship of the proletariat became the dictatorship of the party and those who were not in agreement were denounced as bourgeois reactionaries. At the time Pannekoek argued that Lenin was mistaken in seeing the issue in terms of adherence to the correct line, that it should be seen rather as a question of the form of articulation of the proletarian will: if social decision-making is organised through factory councils, then the interests of the proletariat will automatically prevail without any need for arbitrary decisions by a body acting on behalf of the proletariat – since the bourgeoisie will obviously have no place in the factory councils.

I think that Pannekoek is right, that the question has to be seen in terms of the forms of articulation of decision making, rather than in terms of the imposition of a correct line by a party or by intellectuals. The problem of 'what if the people want the wrong things' cannot be solved by recourse to decisions 'on behalf of', though clearly intense discussion of what is right would be part of the process of self-determination – it is clear from the history of Stalin and the Soviet Union, or indeed from the history of bourgeois democracy, that decisions 'on behalf of' the people are absolutely no guarantee against the unleashing of terror. There is a very real problem here. We scream, but both we and our scream contain elements that point both towards an emancipated society based on dignity and in the opposite direction, towards authoritarian racist, sexist oppression. How can we who are so deeply damaged by capitalism create an emancipated society? How do we filter out the destructive elements of our own impulses (our own – and not just those of those right-wingers over there)? The only possible answer, if we put aside the idea of a body that decides on our behalf, is through the articulated discussion that constitutes self-determination and that constitutes also a process of self-education through struggle. An anti-authoritarian form of articulation will tend to filter out authoritarian expressions of the scream. This is still no guarantee of correctness, but perhaps it will at very least ensure that we die of our own poison rather than of the poison given to us by others.[28]

V

The drive towards self-determination implies therefore a critique of representation, a moving against-and-beyond representation.[29]

Representation involves definition, exclusion, separation. Definition, because representative and represented must be defined, as well as the time for which the representative acts on behalf of the represented. Exclusion, because definition excludes, but also because there are many elements of everyday life (love, tenderness) which it is hard for someone else to represent. Exclusion too because in choosing a representative, we exclude ourselves. In elections we choose someone to speak on our behalf, to take our place. We create a separation between those who represent and those who are represented and we freeze it in time, giving it a duration, excluding ourselves as subjects until we have an opportunity to confirm the separation in the next elections. A world of politics is created, separate from the daily life of society, a world of politics populated by a distinct caste of politicians who speak their own language and have their own logic, the logic of power. It is not that they are absolutely separated from society and its antagonisms, for they have to worry about the next elections and opinion polls and organised pressure groups, but they see and hear only that which is translated into their world, their language, their logic. At the same time a parallel world is created, a theoretical, academic world which mirrors this separation between politics and society, the world of political science and political journalism which teaches us the peculiar language and logic of the politicians and helps us to see the world through their blind eyes.

Representation is part of the general process of separation which is capitalism. It is completely wrong to think of representative government as a challenge to capitalist rule or even as a potential challenge to capital. Representative democracy is not opposed to capital: rather it is an extension of capital, it projects the principle of capitalist domination into our opposition to capital. Representation builds upon the atomisation of individuals (and the fetishisation of time and space) which capital imposes. Representation separates representatives from represented, leaders from led, and imposes hierarchical structures. The left always accuse the leaders, the representatives, of betrayal: but there is no betrayal, or rather betrayal is not the act of the leaders but is already built into the very process of representation. We betray ourselves when we say to someone 'You take my place, you speak on my behalf.' The drive towards self-determination is necessarily anti-substitutionist. Self-determination is incompatible with saying 'You decide on my behalf.' Self-determination means the assumption of responsibility for one's own participation in the determination of social doing.

The rejection of representation means also a rejection of leadership, of verticality. The assumption of responsibility implies a drive towards horizontality in organisational forms. It is clear that horizontal forms do not necessarily guarantee the equal participation of all in the movement: they may well serve as a cover for the opposite – the informal taking of collective decisions by a small group. Nevertheless, the drive towards self-determination implies the assumption of mutual respect and shared responsibility as organisational orienta- tions. Mutual respect, shared responsibility and also shared ignorance: the drive towards self-determination, towards the creation of a society based on the mutual recognition of dignity is necessarily a process of searching, of asking. This implies a relation of listening rather than talking, or rather a relation of listening-talking, of dialogue rather than monologue. In such a relation, no person can assume that they have the answer: the resolution of problems is a common pursuit, a movement through questioning and developing the questions. *Preguntando caminamos* (asking we walk) becomes a principle of organisation and this implies a rejection of vertical structures which inhibit the expression and discussion of questions and doubts. The moving is always a moving outwards, a moving into the unknown.

To say that representative democracy is not an appropriate model for the drive towards self-determination does not, of course, mean, that direct democracy does not have its problems.[30] There is the classic argument that direct democracy is appropriate only to a small community: how you could possibly fit millions of people into a single assembly and what meaning would it have even if you could achieve it physically? But even within a small community there are lots of practical problems concerning those people who are unable or do not wish to participate actively, the disproportionate weight that is acquired by those who are most active and articulate, and so on.

Such problems are probably inevitable, in so far as a fully developed system of direct democracy would presuppose the participation of emancipated humans. But we are not (yet) emancipated subjects: we are cripples helping one another to walk, falling frequently. There are undoubtedly some who can walk better than others: in that sense the existence of what is sometimes called a 'vanguard' probably cannot be avoided.[31] The issue is whether these half-cripples rush ahead – as a vanguard – leaving the rest of us crawling on the ground and calling to us 'don't worry, we'll make the revolution and then come back for you' (but we know they won't), or whether they try to move in step, helping the slowest.

Probably direct democracy cannot be thought of as a model or a fixed set of rules but rather as an orientation, an unending struggle to distil the drive to collective self-determination that exists in each and all of us. Where decisions have to be taken that go beyond the scope of a particular assembly, then the classic response of direct or council democracy is not representation but delegation, the insistence that the delegate must be immediately responsible to those who have chosen her as their delegate in this matter: the *mandar obedeciendo* of the Zapatistas. There is always the danger of the institutionalisation of such delegates, that they become converted in practice into representatives taking the place of those who have chosen them – that their existence as delegates becomes separated from their constitution as such. Certainly rules (or the establishment of accepted practices) on reporting back, rotation of delegates, and so on, can help to prevent this, but the core of the issue is the process of collective self-emancipation, the practice of active participation in the collective determination of the social flow of doing. These are the problems with which so many groups all over the world are currently grappling in what can only be a process of experimentation and invention.

There can be no organisational model, no rules, precisely because the drive towards self-determination is the moving of a question. What is important is not the detail but the thrust of the moving: against separation and substitution, towards the strengthening or weaving of the community, out into the unknown. What else can we do but follow the utopian star: the dream of a human world composed of projections against-and-beyond the inhuman world in which we live?

The drive towards self-determination is not specific to any one organisation or type of organisation. It is a continuum that stretches from helping someone to do something or cooking a meal for friends, through the millions of social or political projects that aim to create a better world, to such developed forms of rebellion as the Russian soviets or the neighbourhood councils of Argentina or the Zapatista communities of Chiapas. For all the discontinuities and differences, they all form part of the same moving, the same drive towards self-determination, the same drive to create a world of non-commodified relations, a world not ruled by money but shaped by love, companionship, comradeship and the direct confrontation with all the problems of living and dying.

VI

The drive towards self-determination is not compatible with the aim of taking state power. The state as a form of organisation is the negation of self-determination.

There is a terrible, explosive lie at the heart of Leninism. It is the idea that the seizure of state power is the culmination of the drive to self-determination, that the taking of state power was the culmination of the soviet movement in Russia. Just the opposite is true: the seizure of state power in Russia was the defeat of the soviets, the attempt to take state power is the opposite of the drive towards self-determination. The notion of a soviet state or 'a state of the Commune-type'[32] is an abomination, an absurdity.

The drive towards self-determination moves in one direction, the attempt to win state power moves in the opposite direction. The former starts to knit a self-determining community, the latter unravels the knitting.

A central issue for any movement of rebellion, large or small, is: do we channel our movement towards trying to win state power or influence within the state? There may be obvious material benefits to be gained from doing so, but it is important to realise that the state is not a thing, not an institution, but a form of social relations, that is, a process of forming social relations in a certain way, a process of imposing certain forms of organisation upon us. The state is a process of reconciling rebellion with the reproduction of capital. It does so by channelling rebellion into forms which are compatible with capitalist social relations. Where the drive towards self-determination is anti-definitional, the state is an attempt to turn that drive around and channel it into definitional forms. The state is incompatible with self-determination simply because it is a process of determination *on behalf of*. The existence of the state, the separation of public and private which that existence entails, is simply that: some people decide *on behalf of* others.[33] The state is a process of substitution: it substitutes itself for the community.[34]

Of course, the *on behalf of* constitutes a sort of community, the community of those on behalf of whom the state acts: its citizens. Where the drive towards self-determination knits a community based on the cooperation of different people with their different qualities and passions, their variety of active subjectivities, the state moves in to break and recompose this community on the basis of prior individualisation and abstraction: people are separated from their doing, constituted as abstract individual beings. The separation of the public from the private, the political from the economic or social, is fundamental to the state as a form of organisation: but this separation is a separation of being from doing. The state relates to people as beings not as doers, and since the beings are abstracted from their social doing, they can only be seen as abstract and individual beings (citizens). And since these beings are separated from their doing, from their moving against-and-beyond themselves, they are necessarily defined, limited beings. The community is conceived not on the base of a cooperative doing but on the basis of beings, self-contained, defined, limited. And since they are abstract, they are substitutable, and since they are limited, they must be substituted, integrated into a structure that acts on their behalf. The state, by its very existence as a form of separating being from doing, is a process of substitution, a process of demobilisation.

But are we talking here of the state or the party? Both, it makes no difference. Both state and party deal with limited beings. The notion of a drive towards self-determination implies that people are potentially unlimited, that we constantly drive beyond our own limits, our own being, our own identity: limited beings, but limited beings who constantly negate our own limitations. In other words, people are understood as doers, as creators, not as beings. It is only on this basis that we can talk of the ordinariness of revolution, that is, of revolution as self-emancipation.

Both the state and the party construct a community, but in this community there is no room for communal self-determination. Communal self-determination is excluded as dangerous in both cases: in the case of the state because it is incompatible with capitalist domination; in the case of the party because the 'masses', composed of limited beings, cannot be trusted to lead us in the right direction. Trotskyists are quite right to analyse the fate of the Russian Revolution in terms of a process of substitution: substitution of the class by the party, of the party by the leadership, of the leadership by the leader. What they do not see is that this process of substitution is already inscribed in the party form itself and in the attempt to take state power.[35]

But am I not confusing here two quite different things, the bourgeois state and the working-class (post-revolutionary) state? What I say may be true of the bourgeois state, it is argued, but not of the working-class state.[36] The answer is that the term 'working-class state' is nonsensical: it is rather like talking of working-class value or working-class capital. The state is a specific form of relations developed historically for the purpose of administering on behalf of, that is, excluding. To talk of the council as a form of state is like talking of asking friends to dinner as a form of commodity exchange, just because they are likely to bring a bottle of wine. This is a blurring of categories, a blurring that has enormous political consequences, precisely because it permits a slide from self-determination to authoritarian rule, a hidden reversal of the drive towards self-determination. To speak of post-revolutionary Russia as a 'soviet state' conceals the movement from the soviets (expressions of the drive towards self-determination) to the state (a form of organisation that excludes self-determination).

There is no room here for a 'but also'.[37] There is no room for saying 'Yes, we must build forms of self-determination, *but also* it is important to struggle through the state.' The two forms of struggle cannot exist peacefully side by side simply because they move in opposite directions: the state is an active and constant intervention against self-determination.

There is no *but also*, but is there room for a *but in spite of*? Does it in certain circumstance make sense to say: 'We are building forms of self-determination and we know that the state is a process of negating self-determination, but *in spite of* that, we think that, in this particular situation, struggling through the state can give us a way of strengthening or protecting our struggle for self-determination'? This is a question that is, initially at least, quite distinct from the question of taking state power. There are many people who quite clearly reject the notion of taking state power but nevertheless see it as important for their struggle to influence or gain control of parts of the state apparatus.

This is a difficult question. Most of us cannot avoid contact with the state. We have, as it were, a 'situational'[38] contact with the state: our situation, our condition in life brings us into contact with the state, we are forced to engage with the state in some way. This may be because of our employment, or because we depend on state unemployment subsidies or because we use public transport, or whatever. The question is how we deal with this contact and the contradictions that are inseparable from it. I work as a professor in a state institution: this channels my activity into forms which promote the reproduction of capital – authoritarian forms of teaching and grading, for example. By working in the state (or in any other employment) I am actively involved in the reproduction of capital, but, *in spite of that* I try to struggle against the state form to strengthen the drive towards self-determination. Living in capital means that we live in the midst of contradiction. It is important to recognise these contradictions rather than to brush them under the carpet with a 'but also'. It is important to understand our engagement with the state in such situations as a movement in-and-against the state, as a movement in-against-and-beyond the forms of social relations which the existence of the state implies.[39]

Can we extend this argument to extra-situational, chosen contact with the state?[40] Can we say, for example: 'We, in this social centre, are struggling for the development of a self-determining society; we know that the state is a capitalist state and therefore a form opposed to self-determination; nevertheless, in spite of this, we think that, by controlling our local council, we can strengthen our movement against capitalism'?[41] This is essentially the argument made by certain social centres in Italy and by movements in Brazil, Argentina and elsewhere.[42]

Probably the validity of such arguments for a voluntary, chosen contact with the state will always depend on the particular conditions: there is no golden rule, no purity to be sought.[43] Thus, for example, the Zapatistas in Chiapas make an important principle of not accepting any support from the state, whereas many urban pro-Zapatista groups in different parts of the world accept that they cannot survive without some form of state support (be it in the form of unemployment assistance or student grants or – in some cases – legal recognition of their right to occupy a social centre). The important thing, perhaps, is not to paint over the contradictions, not to hide the antagonistic nature of the undertaking with phrases such as 'participatory democracy', not to convert the *but in spite of* into a *but also*.[44] But the translation of 'in spite of' into 'but also' is precisely what is involved in our contact with the state. Engagement with the state is never innocent of consequences: it always involves the pulling of action or organisation into certain forms (leadership, representation, bureaucracy) that move against the drive to self-determination.[45] The crushing force of institutionalisation should never be underestimated, as experience in all the world has shown, time and time and time again.

The other point to be made is that the nature of the state itself is changing (not just of national states, but of state-hood as such). Everywhere states are becoming more directly repressive, more removed from any semblance of popular control. While the necessity to struggle in-against-and-beyond the state is always present, the idea of simply turning our back on the state (as the Zapatistas have done) becomes more and more attractive.[46] Certainly, the ever more widespread disillusionment with state-centred politics in all the world should be seen not as a problem but as an opportunity.[47]

The attempt to win state power is not compatible with the drive to self-determination. And yet many or most of the current movements of rebellion combine both strands: in the pro-Zapatista movement or the movement against neo-liberalism in general, those who think in terms of conquering state power work together with those who reject the state as a form of organisation. This seems to me to be good. Any movement for radical change will be, and should be, a dissonant mixture of positions and forms of organisation. My position is not at all one of ultra-left sectarianism: I understand my argument as an argument within a movement, not as an argument to divide or exclude. The aim is not to create a new Correct Line. It is precisely because the movement is a broad one, and because we are all confused (whatever our degree of ideological purity), that it is important to discuss clearly. The fact that those who channel their struggles towards the state combine with those who reject the state as a central point of reference should not prevent us from saying clearly that we should be aware that there is an enormous tension between the two approaches, that the two approaches pull in opposite directions.[48,49]

The argument in this section has centred on the distinction between the drive towards self-determination and a movement *on behalf of*. But it may be objected that there is nothing wrong with a movement on behalf of, that it is all that we can hope for, the only realistic way forward, the only practical way of changing the world. What is wrong with a revolution on behalf of, especially if it improves the living conditions of the poor and makes a stand against the almost universal prostration of political leaders to the dictates of US imperialism? It may not be perfect, but surely it is completely unrealistic to hope for anything better?

The problem with a revolution on behalf of is surely that it always involves suppression of the drive towards self-determination. A movement on behalf of, no matter how benevolent its intentions (at least initially), always involves a determination of the doing of others and therefore a repression of the moving towards self-determination: the people cannot be trusted to know what is good for them. Such a movement may possibly lead to improvements in the living standards of the poor (which is very important), it may lead to significant changes in the social structure (as in the Russian and other revolutions of the twentieth century), but it is inevitably repressive in the sense that it comes into conflict with self-determination, in the sense that whatever direct democracy exists is inevitably limited, subordinated to the decisions of those who know what is for the good of the people.[50] It might be argued that at least it has eliminated the worst inequalities, that at least it constitutes a stumbling block in imperialism's headlong dash to destroy humanity. Can we really hope for anything better? Yes, I think we can: it is not yet time to give up the dream of human dignity.

'All very nice, all very dainty your distinction between revolution on behalf of and revolution by, very poetic your talk of human dignity, but haven't you forgotten that when it comes to the crunch, it's a question of violence, of physical force? We can develop all the self-determining projects or revolts we like, but once they become annoying (not even threatening) for the ruling class, they send in the police and the army and that's the end. That is why we need to control the state, so that we can stop police or army repression. That's the way things are in the real world. So what's your answer to that, Professor?'[51]

I hum and I haw and I have no answer, but suggest three points. First, control of the state guarantees nothing. Control of the state on behalf of the working class (however that is understood) does not necessarily reduce the distance between the working class and the state. The state continues to be repressive and the police or army will tend to suppress any action of the working class which does not match the expectations of the state which rules on its behalf. It may well be that left-wing governments will give more leeway to autonomous projects or revolts than more right-wing governments, but the fundamental issue is not the composition of the government or the sympathies of the ruling politicians but the balance of social forces.

Second, organising as a revolutionary army which aims to overthrow capitalism in military confrontation makes little sense, both because it would be very unlikely to win against the might of military technology and because an army engaged in military conflict inevitably reproduces the hierarchies, the values and the logic of all armies. There could be nothing further removed from the drive towards self-determination than military organisation.

Third, there still remains the problem of how we protect ourselves from state violence. Probably we have to think in terms of forms of deterrence that discourage such violence. One form of deterrence is, of course, armed defence. The existence of the Zapatistas as the Ejército Zapatista de Liberación Nacional (EZLN) (the Zapatista Army of National Liberation) is one important example: they are not armed in a way that would allow them to win a full military confrontation with the Mexican army, but they are armed sufficiently for it to make it unattractive for the Mexican army to intervene with direct military force. However, 'unattractive' here cannot be understood in purely military terms, in terms of violence against violence. What makes military intervention 'unattractive' for the Mexican army is not just the armed violence that the Zapatistas could oppose to the army's violence, but above all the strength of the social connections that the Zapatistas have woven both with their own communities[52] and with the wider community in Mexico and beyond. Deterrence of state violence, therefore, cannot be understood simply in terms of armed defence (although this may be a necessary part of it) but above all in terms of the density of the web of social relations which integrate any particular movement into the surrounding society. But that brings us back precisely to our main argument: what is crucial for the self-defence of a movement for social change is the degree of its integration into society, and such integration implies organisation in a way that runs against-and-beyond the state process of separation.

VII

The drive towards self-determination moves against-and-beyond representation, against-and-beyond the state and, above all, against-and-beyond labour.

Although the issue of democracy and the organisation of assemblies attracts more attention, the central problem that underlies all attempts to develop the drive towards self-determination is the movement of doing against labour. If by labour we understand alienated labour, labour which we do not control, then clearly the drive for self-determination is a drive against labour,[53] a drive for the emancipation of socially self-determined doing, a push towards the conscious control of the social flow of doing. The drive towards self-determination is quite simply the development of our power-to-do, the drive of power-to against and beyond power-over.

Democracy, no matter how 'direct' its structures, will have relatively little impact unless it is part of a challenge to the capitalist organisation of doing as labour. That is why it is important to think not just of democracy but of communism, not just of people but of class, not just of rebellion but of revolution, meaning by that not a process of social change instigated from above by professional revolution-aries, but a social change which transforms the basic organisation of doing in society.[54] It may well be argued that a radicalisation of democracy would necessarily lead to the abolition of authoritarian command in the organisation of doing (that is, to the abolition of capital), but very often all the emphasis in radical discourse is put on democracy and none on the organisation of labour. This can give the false impression that radical democracy is possible within a capitalist society, a society in which doing is organised as labour. Moreover, and this is important, to separate the struggle for radical democracy from the struggle of doing against labour means to overlook the anger and the resistance that is part of the experience and tradition of the labour movement. If by communism we understand a self-determining society, then democracy means communism: it is simple, obvious and should be stated explicitly.

Doing exists in constant revolt against labour. Collectively or indi-vidually, we are probably all involved in some sort of struggle against the alien determination of our activity – by refusing to work, by arriving late, by sabotage, by trying to shape our lives according to what we want to do and not just according to the dictates of money, by coming together to form alternative projects for the organisation of our doing, by occupying factories or other places of work. The very existence of labour as alienated doing implies a constant tension between labour and the doing which strives against its own alienation. This does not imply the existence of some pure, a-historical doing which only needs to be emancipated, but signals rather that alienation cannot exist without its contrary, the struggle against alienation: alienated doing cannot exist without its antithesis – the struggle of doing against its alienation. This is obscured by the ambiguity of the term 'work' in English. If we take 'work' as our starting point and understand by that alienated or waged work, then this crucial tension is lost.[55]

That doing exists in constant revolt against labour is clear. The more difficult question is whether it is possible for doing to move beyond labour before there is a revolutionary abolition of capitalism. The traditional view is that, although factory seizures would certainly be part of the revolutionary process, the abolition of abstract, commodity-producing labour presupposes the abolition of the commodity-based economy and the creation of a planned economy, and this in turn presupposes the conquest of state power by revolutionaries. In fact, historical experience suggests the contrary: the failure to radically transform the labour process has been one of the most striking features of 'communist' or 'socialist' states. This failure can, of course, be ascribed to particular historical reasons in each case, but it can also be argued that there is a more fundamental reason: that there is a basic conflict between a revolution on behalf of, which inevitably involves command over those on behalf of whom the revolution is made, and the social self-determination of doing. Social self-determination cannot pass through the state, since the state, as a form of social relations, is the separation of determination from society.

To point out the difficulties of the traditional view does not, however, solve the problem of how we can envisage an unalienated doing in a society based on alienation. The problem is that social self-determination of doing implies conscious control of the social flow of doing. Can this be achieved in a partial, patchwork fashion? The creation of cooperatives or the transformation of occupied factories or workplaces into cooperatives has long been a feature of working-class struggle. The limitations of such cooperatives are clear: in so far as they produce for a market, they are forced to produce under the same conditions as any capitalist enterprise. The problem is not the ownership of the enterprise, but the form of articulation between different doings. If these doings are articulated through the market, then the doers lose control of their own doing, which becomes transformed into abstract labour.

The creation of cooperatives solves nothing unless the articulation between different groups of doers is tackled at the same time. The move towards self-determination cannot be seen simply in terms of particular activities but must inevitably embrace the articulation between those activities, the re-articulation of the social flow of doing (not just production, but production and circulation). The drive to self-determination cannot be understood in terms of the creation of autonomies, but necessarily involves a moving beyond those autonomies. Factory occupations or the creation of cooperatives are insufficient unless they are part of a movement, that is, unless they simultaneously reach beyond to the creation of new articulations between people who are beyond the particular cooperative project.

A wave of factory occupations (and the establishment of cooperatives) is part of any major movement of rebellion – Argentina being the latest and most obvious example. The question is how such a movement should be oriented, whether towards the state (in a demand for nationalisation of the enterprise, for example) or towards the establishment of a network of links between producers (and consumers) independent of the state. This has been the issue discussed in the case of many of the factory occupations in Argentina. From the point of view of transforming society and transforming the labour process, it is clear that orientation to the state, while it may preserve employment, is unlikely to lead to radical change. The only way forward would seem to be through the progressive expansion, the constant moving-beyond, of alternative doings, not as isolated, autonomous projects, but as nodes in new (and experimental) forms of articulation. It is only in this sense, as part of a movement from below, as part of a thrust not towards a state but towards a commune of communes or council of councils, or towards the creation of a new commons, that social planning can be an expression of social self-determination.[56]

This is not an argument in any sense at all for a romantic, back-to-rural-idiocy view of communism.[57] I am not arguing that we should give up computers and aeroplanes, and it is clear that such activities imply a socialisation of doing that goes far beyond the local level. The drive to self-determination can only be understood as a drive towards world communism, towards a form of organisation that promotes the development of our power-to and the conscious determination of the global social flow of doing. In classical terms it might be said that the issue is how to make the social relations adequate to the development of the forces of production. The objection that we need some form of state to control complex technological development is blind to the fact that the state is one aspect of a form of social relations (capital) which hinders technological development, hinders the unfolding of our capacities to do things, our power-to.

The most immediate problem confronted by anyone who tries, individually or collectively, to emancipate their doing from the rule of capital, is the question of survival. Rural groups (such as the EZLN) can often rely on their control of the land to assure a minimum of subsistence, but in the cities rebels do not even have access to that. Urban groups usually survive either on the basis of state subsidies (sometimes forced by the groups themselves, as in the case of the piqueteros who use the roadblocks to force the government to give money to the unemployed) or on the basis of some mixture of occasional or regular paid employment and state subsidies. Thus, many urban groups are composed of a mixture of people in regular employment, of people who are by choice or by necessity in irregular or occasional employment and of those who (again by choice or necessity) are unemployed, often dependent on state subsidies or some sort of market activity for their survival. These different forms of dependency on forces that we do not control (on capital) pose problems and limitations that should be recognised.

We are inevitably confronted, it would seem, with the issue of control of the results of our own doing (means of production). As long as capital appropriates the results of our doing (and hence the means of production), our material survival depends on subordinating ourselves to the rule of capital. At the core of the struggle of doing against labour is the struggle against property, not as a thing but as the daily re-imposed process of appropriation of the results of our doing. In any struggle against capital, refusal is the key, refusal to allow the appropriation of the results of our doing. But refusal is sustainable only if backed by the development of alternative doings in a growing network of articulation. In other words, the development of alternative forms of doing cannot be postponed until after the revolution: it is the revolution. To resist is to create alternatives in a constant moving against-and-beyond.[58] It is hard to see how else we can go forward.

VIII

Moving against-and-beyond the state, representation, labour, against-and-beyond all the fetishised forms that stand as obstacles to the drive towards social self-determination: such a moving against-and-beyond is necessarily always experimental, always a question, always unsure, always undogmatic, always restless, always contradictory and incomplete. Moving against-and-beyond is obviously anti-identitarian and anti-institutional, in the sense that it is a moving against-and-beyond anything that would contain or detain the creative flow of rebellion. This does not mean that we simply negate identities, but that any affirmation of identity (as indigenous, women, gay, whatever) be seen simply as a moment in a going-beyond the identity: we are indigenous-but-more-than-that. The same, surely, with institutions.[59] We probably need recognisable forms of organisation (councils, neighbourhood assemblies, *juntas de buen gobierno*).

However, the danger in any form of institutionalisation (or identity) is the possible separation of existence from constitution, the subordination of *we do* to *what is*. Identity and institution as concepts direct attention to what is, whereas the drive to social self-determination is a drive towards the absolute rule of *we do*. In this sense, the principles of council or communal organisation (the subordination of delegates to instant recall, the Zapatistas' *mandar obedeciendo*, and so on) seek to ensure that these forms of organisation are anti-institutional, but obviously the danger of institutionalisation is always present. In a society in which doing is subordinated to being, any attempt to subordinate being to doing means a constant struggle against the current, in which any staying still will always be a moving backwards.

The drive towards social self-determination is a struggle to transform time and slough off history. Self-determination implies liberation from identities, from institutions, from the determination of the present by the past, from the subordination of *we do* to *what is*. This means a breaking of time, a shooting of clocks. The time of capitalism is the time-in-which we live: a time that stands outside us, that measures our actions, that limits what we do. Our push is towards a society in which we-do knows no limits, in which time would become the time-as-which we live, a time which 'exists only as the rhythm and structure of what it is [people] choose to do' (Gunn 1985). The 'abstract and homogeneous progression leading from past to present to future' would be replaced with the 'temporality of freely chosen actions and projects' (Gunn, 1985). The drive towards self-determination is a push towards a society liberated from history, from the past determination of present actions: towards a post-history (or perhaps the end of pre-history, the beginning of history, but of history in a very different sense), in which actions are not determined by the past but characterised above all by an opening towards the future.

We do not live in such a society, but we struggle towards it. The drive towards self-determination is a drive against homogeneous time, a drive to liberate ourselves from history (in the sense of determination of the present by the past). There is no sense in which time-in-which (homogeneous time) leads us to its own transformation into time-as-which; there is no sense in which the past-determined history in which we live leads us automatically to the post-history (end of pre-history) that would be an opening towards the future. On the contrary, time-in-which and past-determined history are highways leading straight to the cliff over which we human lemmings seem determined to leap to our own destruction. Communism then is not the culmination of history, but the breaking of history.

This does not mean dismissing the past (the past struggles against capitalism, say), but it does mean rejecting the wallowing in the past that is such a common feature of left debate (the endless regurgitating of 'Stalinism' as an explanation of everything, for example). We must respect that past struggles against capitalism were also struggles against time, struggles to create a tabula rasa, blows against the continuum of history.[60] The past lives on in the present, but not as a series of causal chains that show the way forward, above all not as Tradition,[61] but as music, as suggestion box, as a series of constellations of struggle that change in appearance as the constellation from which we view them changes.[62] The struggle now, as before, is the struggle for an absolute present, in which existence does not become separated from constitution, a time-as-which where every moment is a moment of self-determination, a tabula rasa free from determination by the past – filled no doubt with the dreams of the past, with the past not-yet redeemed in the present, but freed of the nightmare of history.[63,64]

IX

Is a socially self-determining society, a communist society, really possible? We do not know. We say that 'another world is possible', but we do not really know if it is.

But it does not matter, it does not affect the argument. Communism (self-determination) remains as the sea to which all rivers run, as utopian star, as urgent necessity.

Communism is the sea to which all rivers run. The drive to self-determination is not a political slogan nor an academic construct, but inseparably rooted in a society that systematically negates self-determination. The argument is not normative, not that we *ought* to struggle for self-determination, but rather that 'No – we shall decide ourselves' is already given in the 'You shall do that.' If that basis does not exist, then there is little point in talking of communism or revolution. The first problem of theory is to eat carrots, to open our eyes, to see the invisible.[65]

Communism is a utopian star: not one that exists out there but that springs from our experience of negating the negation of our self-determination, of projecting that negation as a star to follow. It is, in other words, the present phantasmal existence of the not-yet. All that has been said here about the drive to self-determination, about moving against-and-beyond that which exists, is no more than sketching out a direction. It is not (and cannot be) a blueprint, a set of rules to apply in any particular situation.[66] This is no call for purity. The drive to self-determination pushes against-and-beyond the state, but in the meantime the state exists and with it the messy problem of how we deal with it. It is clear that we want to move against-and-beyond the state (that the state is not the road to changing society), but *how* we should do this will always depend on the particular situation. Similarly, the drive to self-determination pushes against-and-beyond labour, but in the meantime we have to survive and this usually means engaging in some way with the rules of labour. The utopian star is unquenchable, but the light it casts does not create a highway that we can march upon. The only paths that are open to us are the paths we make ourselves by walking.

Communism is a utopian star, but it is more than that. It is not an unreachable goal that inspires us, it is an urgent necessity.[67] It is emphatically not just a postulate to orient political practice.[68] It is clearer now than ever that human self-annihilation stands firmly on the agenda of capitalism and that possibly the only way to avoid it is to create a society in which we ourselves determine social development, a socially self-determining society. The drive to social self-determination is urgent, a frenetic search for cracks in the surface of domination, a hope against hope.[69]

Perhaps, above all, communism is wave after wave of unanswered questions, a world to be created, a world with commas, but no full stop

Notes

CHAPTER 1

1. For a particularly striking account of some of the features of what he describes as the Fourth World War, see Marcos (1998).
2. As Debord (1995, p. 14) puts it, 'In a world that *really* has been turned on its head, truth is a moment of falsehood.' See also Horkheimer (1978a) and Bloch (1964) II, pp. 18–53.
3. See Horkheimer (1972, p. 227): 'The critical theory of society is, in its totality, the unfolding of a single existential judgment.' ('Judgment on existence' would be a clearer translation.)
4. Foucault (1990, p. 60) speaks of the 'immense labor to which the West has submitted generations in order to produce ... men's subjection: their constitution as subjects in both senses of the word'.
5. All metaphors are dangerous, games to be discarded later on: the fly plays no role in constructing the spider's web, whereas we are the sole creators of the system which entraps us.
6. The phrase is Walter Benjamin's (1931).
7. On ecstatic thought, see, for example, Gunn (1987a).
8. See *The Prince*, ch. 15: 'leaving aside imaginary things about a prince, and referring only to those which truly exist ...' (Machiavelli 1995, p. 48).
9. Foucault (1990, p. 7). Foucault's argument is that 'the fear of ridicule or the bitterness of history' prevent 'most of us' from associating revolution and happiness, or revolution and pleasure. The argument here is that, on the contrary, the bitterness of history leads not to a toning down of expectations but to a more serious engagement with hope.
10. 'Romain Rolland's maxim 'Pessimism of the intelligence, optimism of the will' was made by Gramsci into something of a programmatic slogan as early as 1919, in the pages of *Ordine Nuovo*' (Gramsci 1971, p. 175, fn. 75).
11. As Ernst Bloch puts it in the foreword to his *Principle of Hope*, written largely during his exile from Nazi Germany, it is precisely in such a fearsome world that 'it is a question of learning hope' (1986, p. 3).
12. The collapse of the Soviet Union represents both a danger to Marxism and a liberation. The danger is that it will simply become a dead language, with fewer and fewer people reading *Capital* and being able to understand all the debates that presuppose a knowledge of Marx's work. The liberation is that we are at last freed of the positivisation of Marxism that the Soviet tradition represented and able to sharpen Marxism as negative thought.

CHAPTER 2

1. See any of the many editions of Luxemburg (1973) and Bernstein (1961).
2. See for example Stalin's 1905 article on 'Anarchism or Socialism', discussed by Néstor Kohan (1998, pp. 33ff).
3. Cuba is perhaps the most attractive (least unattractive) case of a state-centred revolution. Even here, however, the achievements of the revolution are far from the aspirations of the revolutionaries, not just because of external pressures (the

blockade, the dependence on and then collapse of the Soviet Union) but because of the distance between state and society, the lack of social self-determination. The implication of this argument is certainly not that the state-socialist countries that remain (such as Cuba) should simply integrate themselves directly into the world market: rather that the strength of the revolution depends on the degree to which it is integrated into society and the state ceases to be its pivot. For an interesting reflection on this from a Cuban perspective, see Acanda (2000).

4. Ever since Trotsky's *The Revolution Betrayed*, 'betrayal' has, for example, been a key category of the Trotskyist movement.

5. See Luxemburg (1973, p. 49), for example: 'From the first appearance of class societies having the class struggle as the essential content of their history, the conquest of political power has been the aim of all rising classes.'

6. In many countries the combination of nationalism and revolution is justified in the name of anti-imperialism. Whatever the justification, it always rests on the assumption that social relations are territorially constituted. For a discussion of the issue in relation to the Zapatista uprising, see REDaktion (1997), pp. 178–84.

7. 'To be raised in the house of power is to learn its ways, to soak them up ... The habit of power, its timbre, its posture, its way of being with others. It is a disease infecting all who come too near it. If the powerful trample over you, you are infected by the soles of their feet' (Rushdie 1998, p. 211).

8. It might be argued that the experience of movements that have aimed to change the world *without* taking power suggests that such attempts are also unrealistic. The argument for exploring the possibility of changing the world without taking power is based not just on historical experience but also on theoretical reflection on the nature of the state.

CHAPTER 3

1. Serrano (1995) p. 316. For a development of a similar argument, see Winocur (2001).

2. This is one of the points made by the Zapatista uprising. It is dignity, they insist, that made them revolt. See Holloway (1998).

3. It must be stressed that nothing in this text implies a lack of respect for those who have devoted their lives to the struggle to take power in order to change the world. On the contrary, the argument is that the best way to honour them is to keep alive the struggle for revolution, and that this now means breaking the link between revolution and the taking of power.

4. 'It is not necessary to conquer the world. It is enough for us to make it anew' (Primera Declaración de la Realidad, *La Jornada*, 30 January 1996).

5. The wave of anti-capitalist or anti-neoliberal demonstrations such as that in Seattle in November 1999 has provided important foci for the movement of anti-power.

6. Foucault (1975) p. 14. See Chapter 1, note 9, above.

7. Goethe (1969) p. 38: 'Im Anfang war die Tat.'

8. In the tense and tired couple, dialectical materialism, dialectics has precedence. Our thought is negative, therefore materialist. This is important, because others who have sought to move beyond the crisis of the orthodox 'dialectical materialism' and to construct a ''beyond' for the weary and arthritic tradition of revolutionary thought' (Negri 1991, p. xx) have preferred to give precedence to materialism and to blame the 'dialectic' for the horrors of Diamat. For a discussion of Negri, see Chapter 9.

9. The emphasis here is thus different from the classic justification of materialism in *The German Ideology* (Marx and Engels 1976, pp. 41–2).

10. John's words are not only of interest to biblical scholars, for they are the basis of postmodern theory with its privileging of language. See Foucault (1973) p. 306:

'with Nietzsche, and Mallarmé, thought was brought back, and violently so, towards language itself, towards its unique and difficult being. The whole curiosity of our thought now resides in the question: What is language, how can we find a way round it in order to make it appear in itself, in all its plenitude?'

11. Is there then no difference between saying 'in the beginning was the scream' and Faust's 'in the beginning was the deed'? There is a difference in that Faust's statement suggests the considered reflection of someone who stands outside the process and comes to a conclusion, whereas the emphasis on the scream is a more immediate reflection of (not 'on') experience, the cry of someone who, being lost, wants to find a way out, not the considered conclusion of someone who, being outside already, wants to explain.

12. Does this mean that humans would cease to be ecstatic in a communist society? Surely not, because communism cannot be understood as a state-of-being, but only as a process.

13. Thus, for example, Foucault, in the Foreword to the English edition of *The Order of Things* (1973, p. xii), comments that his work has been criticised for denying the possibility of change when, he says, his 'main concern has been with changes'. The problem, however, is that his method precludes him from understanding change as movement, so that it can appear only as diachronic change, as the change from one snapshot to another.

14. The question of objectification and its significance is one that will recur at various points in the argument.

15. In many languages the noun for 'power' is the same as the verb 'to be able': *poder, pouvoir, potere, Vermögen*.

16. Bublitz (1998, p. 22) presents a very similar idea: 'Creation is like a river. It goes on flowing as long as there is water in its bed. If you build barrages, dams, locks in its way, it will still be the river. If you steal its freedom, the water will still flow, push forward. But not as before, freely undulating, a process in which landscape and river shape each other in their own kind of conversation.'

17. On the rupture between conception and execution, see Sohn-Rethel (1978).

18. See Hobbes's definition of power in the *Leviathan*: 'The Power of a Man (to take it Universally) is his present means, to obtain some future apparent Good' (1991, p. 62). For a helpful discussion of contemporary discussions of power in mainstream social theory, see MacKenzie (1999).

19. Marx says of the alienated activity of the worker in capitalism: 'it is activity as suffering, strength as weakness, begetting as emasculating, the worker's *own* physical and mental energy, his personal life – for what is life but activity? – as an activity which is turned against him, independent of him and not belonging to him' (1975, p. 275).

20. Debord, who characterises capitalism as the 'society of the spectacle', says: 'Separation is the alpha and omega of the spectacle' (1995, p. 20).

21. As Hegel points out in *The Phenomenology of Spirit* (1977, pp. 111ff).

22. There is, then, no clear distinction to be made between alienation and objectification. Adorno and the late Lukács both insist on the distinction, almost, it would seem as a way of protecting themselves from the implications of their own theory (very explicitly so in the case of Lukács). See Lukács's Preface to the 1967 edition of *History and Class Consciousness* (1971, pp. xxiii–xxv); Adorno (1990, pp. 189ff).

23. As Adorno (1978, p. 498) puts it, the separation of subject and object is 'both real and illusory. True, because in the cognitive realm it serves to express the real separation, the dichotomy of the human condition, a coercive development. False, because the resulting separation must not be hypostatized, not magically transformed into an invariant' (quoted by Jay 1984a, p. 61).

24. In Marx, the fragmentation of the flow of doing is approached in two different ways. In the *1844 Manuscripts*, it is approached through a discussion of capital (the antag-

onistic relation of command). In *Capital*, it is approached through a discussion of the commodity. The two approaches are not, however, incompatible, since Marx makes clear that the full development of commodity production presupposes capitalist relations of production.

25. I use the term 'labour' to refer to alienated doing.

26. See Horkheimer and Adorno (1972, p. 230): 'All reification is a forgetting.'

27. On this see Gunn (1992, p. 14): 'Stasis *exists*, in the Marxist conception, but it exists as struggle subsisting alienatedly, i.e. *in the mode of being denied*' (original emphasis).

28. On the present existence of the not-yet, see Bloch (1986).

29. That is the core of Marx's labour theory of value.

30. The same point can be made in terms of the distinction between *puissance* and *pouvoir*, or *Vermögen* and *Macht*.

31. See Ashe (1999, pp. 92–3): 'Ever since Kant's contribution, the idea that there are certain transcendental features of subjectivity that are essential and fixed had been the foundation of much of the work in the Western tradition in philosophy ... Contemporary opponents of this view reformulate the notion of the subject as a product of culture, ideology and power. Rather than seeing subjectivity as autonomous and fixed, they view the subject as open, unstable and tenuously held together.' The problem, however, is not to deny the importance of subjectivity, but to rescue subjectivity from the idealised Subject. Or, as Adorno puts it (using the terms subject and subjectivity in reverse): 'To use the strength of the subject to break through the fallacy of constitutive subjectivity – this is what the author felt to be his task ever since he came to trust his own mental impulses' (1990, p. xx).

32. One is reminded of his fascinating analysis of Velázquez's *Las Meninas* at the beginning of *The Order of Things*: fascinating, but without movement.

33. This is surely a central contribution of Marxism to negative theory.

34. It is interesting to compare Negri's recuperation of the radical-democratic thrust of political theory (the development of the concept of 'constituent power') with Bloch's recuperation of the Not-Yet, the projection beyond existing society, as a constant theme in folklore, art and political theory. Contrast for example Bloch's enthusiastic discussion of Joachim of Fiore (1986, Vol. II, pp. 509–15) with Negri, who, coupling Joachim with Savonarola, says dismissively 'with Machiavelli, I am ill disposed toward those friars who are prophets by profession, 'in this city of ours, which is a magnet for all the impostors of the world'' (1999, p. 100). The argument in relation to Negri is developed at greater length in Chapter 9.

CHAPTER 4

1. See, for example, the scant mention of fetishism in Howard and King's two-volume *History of Marxian Economics* (1989, 1992).

2. For the moment we follow the style of Marx's translators in referring to people as men and 'he', bearing in mind, of course, that in the original German, Marx uses '*Mensch*' (person).

3. It follows too that private property is the consequence and not the cause of alienated labour, 'just as the gods are *originally* not the cause but the effect of man's intellectual confusion. Later this relationship becomes reciprocal' (1975, pp. 279–80).

4. 'The capitalist epoch is therefore characterised by this, that labour power takes in the eyes of the labourer himself the form of a commodity which is his property; his labour consequently becomes wage-labour. On the other hand, it is only from this moment that the produce of labour universally becomes a commodity' (Marx 1965, p. 170).

5. On form as mode of existence, see Gunn (1992).

6. For Lukács, the issue of fetishism is central to the whole of Marxist theory: 'It has often been claimed – and not without a certain justification – that the famous chapter in Hegel's *Logic* treating of Being, Non-Being and Becoming contains the whole of his philosophy. It might be claimed with perhaps equal justification that the chapter dealing with the fetish character of the commodity contains within itself the whole of historical materialism and whole self-knowledge of the proletariat seen as the knowledge of capitalist society (and of the societies that preceded it)' (1971, p. 171).

7. 'Perverted' is a translation of the German '*verrückt*', which means both 'crazy' and 'dislocated'. See Backhaus (1992, pp. 61–2).

8. See Negri's comment on Foucault: 'Foucault interprets the lessons of the Frankfurt School more faithfully than do its direct descendants' (1999, p. 340).

9. Gramsci's concept of the 'organic intellectual' is just one variation on this theme. See Gramsci (1971, pp. 3–23).

10. Since the totality of rocket and flares is a made totality, its unity can be understood only from the perspective of doing, not from the perspective of language.

11. See Jay (1984b, p. 109): 'This term, one not in fact found in Marx himself, meant the petrification of living processes into dead things, which appeared as an alien 'second nature'. Weber's 'iron cage of bureaucratic rationalisation', Simmel's 'tragedy of culture' and Bergson's spatialisation of durée were thus all part of a more general process.'

12. For a discussion of the historical establishment of clock time, see E.P. Thompson (1967).

13. On the revolutionary implications of the concept of memory, see Tischler (2000).

14. See Foucault (1973, p. 94): 'The entire species of the verb may be reduced to the single verb that signifies *to be*.' He is speaking here of the classical episteme, but it is possible to make a similar argument for the whole capitalist period.

15. Note that this is true even of those theories which focus on competition or political conflict. Conflict tends to be understood in such a way that it promotes the reproduction of the whole. Even where instability is emphasised, there is an overriding assumption of equilibrium. In those economic theories which do not treat crisis as something abnormal but as integral to the economy (as in the case of Schumpeter, for example), there is nevertheless the functionalist assumption that crisis should be understood as restructuring, as 'creative destruction', as bringing about the changes which are necessary for the reproduction of capitalism as a whole.

16. On the separation of constitution and existence, see Bonefeld (1995).

17. The masculine is used here to emphasise alienation.

18. For a critique of 'theory of', see Gunn (1992).

19. On the origins and changing use of the word 'theory', see Williams (1976, pp. 266–8).

20. In similar vein, see Smith (1996, p. 64): 'you might say that humans are that part of nature which is self-creating, self-conscious and social. This is not, of course, a *definition*. In fact, you cannot fit a definition – literally, placing a limit – on to something whose mode of being consists in continually making itself into something else.'

21. 'In this way, the great mass of the French nation is formed by simple addition of homologous magnitudes, much as potatoes in a sack form a sack of potatoes' (Marx 1962, p. 334).

22. 'The nature of history is precisely that every definition degenerates into an illusion: *history is the history of the unceasing overthrow of objective forms that shape the life of man*' (Lukács 1971, p. 186; original emphasis).

23. It is central to the Zapatista movement, for example, that it has never defined itself as 'indigenous', nor has it ever denied its indigenous character. Rather, there has

been a simultaneous definition and transcendence: 'we are indigenous and more than that'. See Holloway (1998).

24. On the complementarity between empirical research (the pursuit of new definitions) and classification (the theoretical cataloguing of the new material), see Horkheimer (1972).

25. For a discussion of the relation between mathematical abstraction and commodity exchange, see Sohn-Rethel (1978).

26. As Bublitz puts it (1998, p. 12): 'The reduction of our world to unshakeable logical principles is good for demonstrating that, in principle, we have to live the way we do, but no good for comprehending that this way buries our humanity.'

27. Over the last fifty years, binary logic has, of course, been elaborated with extraordinary practical impact in the development of computing.

28. This is the view of freedom espoused by both Kant and Engels: for a critique see Adorno (1990, pp. 248–9).

29. See the important essay by Ute Bublitz on 'Definition and Friendship' in Bublitz (1998).

30. In this sense, Carl Schmitt's political theory, with its focus on the distinction between friend and enemy, is simply the coherent development of the logic of identity: see Schmitt (1987). There is a world of difference betweeen this and Marx's anti-identitarian concept of class struggle.

31. Marcuse (1998) refers to the historically specific form of the reality principle as the performance principle. The same point is made in pre-Freudian terms by Paul Lafargue in the opening lines of *The Right to be Lazy:* 'In nations where capitalist civilisation reigns, the working classes are possessed by a strange madness. Flowing in the wake of this insanity are all the individual and social miseries that have tortured humanity for centuries. This madness is the love of work, the passion for work to the point of exhausting one's vitality and that of one's progeny' (1999, p. 3).

32. Foucault in his later years struggled to free himself from the theoretical and political impasse into which his earlier work had led him. For helpful accounts, see Ashe et al. (1999, pp. 88ff); Best and Kellner (1991).

33. Adorno's discussion here is rather confusing, precisely because he takes reification and alienation to refer to forms of consciousness rather than to the continuity of material and conceptual separation. Hence his statement that 'we can no more reduce dialectics to reification that we can reduce it to any other isolated category, however polemical' (1990, p. 190). This makes sense only if reification is abstracted from the material process of the separation of doing and done.

34. In the saying 'divide and rule', 'and' indicates not a separation between divide and rule, but an identification between the two: division is rule and rule is division.

35. *La Jornada*, 14 June 2000. About 300 people die each year in the attempt to cross the same frontier.

36. To the question of the state we shall return in more detail later.

37. Quoted by Jay (1984a, p. 49).

38. On structuralism and its assumption of permanent alienation, see Tavor Bannet (1989).

39. For the connection between postmodern theory and the disillusionment in the aftermath of the French events of May 1968, see Best and Kellner (1991).

CHAPTER 5

1. For examples of this approach, see Jessop (1991); for a critique, Holloway (1991c).

2. Thus, for example, Adorno (1990, p. 272) is surely guilty of identifying identification (treating the process of identification as established identity) when he says:

'The law, even in its most abstract form, has come to be; its painful abstractness is sedimented substance, dominion reduced to its normal form of identity.' The notion that identity is the normal form of dominion confuses the appearance (identity) for the substance (the struggle to identify). This has much to do with the pessimistic tone of Adorno's argument.

3. This tradition is discussed in greater detail in Chapter 7.

4. In other words, to speak of the 'aspiration towards totality' is to see 'totality' as a critical rather than an affirmative concept, as the critique of fragmentation rather than as the adoption of a standpoint of knowledge.

5. For a criticism of this argument, see Clarke (2002).

6. Adorno makes the same point (1990, pp. 377–8): 'Greyness could not fill us with despair if our minds did not harbour the concept of different colours, scattered traces of which are not absent from the negative whole.' But he immediately gives the point a pessimistic, reactionary twist quite different from Bloch by adding: 'The traces always come from the past and our hopes come from that which was or is doomed.' The different colours do not come from the past: they come from present resistance.

7. This is the core of the approach often referred to as 'Open Marxism': see Bonefeld, Gunn and Psychopedis (1992b, 1992c), Bonefeld et al. (1995).

8. Primitive accumulation, then, does not just refer to the origins of capitalism, but to the continuing brutality of the imposition of capitalist forms. See Bonefeld (1988); Dalla Costa (1995).

9. For a development of the concept of state as form-process, see Holloway (1991b); Holloway (1995b).

10. See Lukács (1971, p. 27): 'It is not the primacy of economic motives in historical explanation that constitutes the decisive difference between bourgeois and Marxist thought, but the point of view of totality.'

11. This in contrast to Hegel's famous sentence at the end of the Preface to *The Philosophy of Right*: 'The owl of Minerva spreads its wings only with the falling of the dusk' (1967, p. 13).

12. 'The vertigo which this causes is an *index veri*' (Adorno 1990, p. 33).

13. To think of Marxism as the study of capitalist reproduction as though that reproduction were not constantly at issue, is a common and gross distortion.

14. For a discussion of this in relation to the Zapatista uprising, see Holloway (1996).

15. 'The chances are that every citizen of the wrong world would find the right one unbearable: he would be too impaired for it' (Adorno 1990, p. 352).

16. For a fuller discussion of autonomist theory, see Chapter 9.

CHAPTER 6

1. Identitarian science can be seen as involving two types of activity: identification and classification. Horkheimer (1972, p. 188), compares the traditional concept of science to the work of a library. Experimental scientists and empirical researchers are in charge of acquisitions, enriching knowledge by supplying new material; theory keeps the catalogue, classifies the material, labels it with its library number. The distinction is sometimes made in terms of a distinction between 'first-order discourse' and 'second-order discourse' (or between theory and meta-theory), the former referring to the 'empirical' work of identification, the latter referring to the formation and evaluation of (classificatory) concepts.

2. In English, criticism in this sense is sometimes referred to as critique. Here the two terms are used interchangeably.

3. The work of Rubin (1973) on value is of fundamental importance in underlining the genetic aspect of Marx's method, but he fails to explain why Marx's method is polit-

ically important. See Holloway (1995a). For a fuller discussion of Rubin from a similar position, see De Angelis (1996).

4. For the moment we adopt the language of the English translation of Marx, bearing in mind that Marx himself used the gender-neutral word '*Mensch*'.

CHAPTER 7

1. See Gunn's critique of 'historical materialism' (1992).
2. This crude understanding of dialectics is surely at the basis of Negri's rejection of dialectics, for example.
3. For a helpful discussion of this period, see Chapter 2 of Smith (1996).
4. The oft cited idea of the 'organic intellectual' introduced by Gramsci makes little difference in this respect: the organic intellectual is simply one of 'the more intellectually developed proletarians' who have the task of introducing the correct line into the proletarian class struggle. See Gramsci (1971, pp. 3–23).
5. Subcomandante Marcos claims that the main lesson which the EZLN (Ejército Zapatista de Liberación Nacional) learnt from the indigenous inhabitants of the Lacandon Jungle was to listen: 'That is the great lesson that the indigenous communities teach to the original EZLN. The original EZLN, the one that is formed in 1983, is a political organisation in the sense that it speaks and what it says has to be done. The indigenous communities teach it to listen, and that is what we learn. The principal lesson that we learn from the indigenous people is that we have to learn to hear, to listen' (unpublished interview with Cristián Calónico Lucio, 11 November 1995, quoted by Holloway 1998, p. 163).
6. On the treatment of class struggle as an 'of course', see Bonefeld (1991).
7. For a critique of the work of Hirsch in this sense, see Bonefeld (1991) and Holloway (1991c).
8. Poulantzas, in particular, devoted considerable effort to providing a foundation for a Marxist political science in the structuralist idea of the 'relative autonomy of the political'. See particularly Poulantzas (1973).
9. Repeatedly, discussions which begin as a defence of Marxist categories within a disciplinary perspective lead to a questioning of the disciplinary perspective itself. The defence of the Marxist concept of value, for example, leads back to an insistence on the difference between the study of economics and the Marxist critique of economics, and on the lack of continuity between Ricardo and Marx.
10. An important and influential example of this is regulation theory, which seeks to understand capitalism in terms of a series of 'modes of regulation'. For a critique, see Bonefeld and Holloway (1991).
11. For a helpful discussion of the fetishisation of Marxism, in relation to recent Marxist debates, see Martínez (2000).
12. To reduce freedom to the insight into necessity, to knowledge of the laws of motion of society, as Engels does, is thus to treat people as objects. This, as Adorno points out, has had 'incalculably vast political consequences': see Adorno (1990, p. 249).

CHAPTER 8

1. The argument developed in this chapter is closely related to that developed by Gunn (1987c) and Bonefeld (2001).
2. What Marx calls primitive accumulation is thus a permanent and central feature of capitalism, not a historical phase. On this, see Bonefeld (1988).
3. 'The communist revolution is directed against the hitherto existing *mode* of activity, does away with *labour*, and abolishes the rule of all classes with the classes

themselves, because it is carried through by the class which no longer counts as a class in society, which is not recognised as a class, and is in itself the expression of the dissolution of all classes, nationalities, etc., within present society' (Marx and Engels 1976, p. 52).

4. Notions of class composition, de-composition and re-composition should be understood, therefore, not as the changing position of different groups but as the changing configuration of the antagonism that traverses all of us, the antagonism between fetishisation and anti-fetishisation, between classification and anti-classification. This is discussed further in Chapter 9.

5. It is very clear from the incomplete chapter on class (Chapter 52 of Volume III of *Capital*) – and indeed from the whole of *Capital* – that Marx rejected the notion of class as a definable group of people.

6. Thus, for Marx, capitalists are the personification of capital, as he repeatedly points out in *Capital*. The proletariat too first makes its appearance in his work not as a definable group but as the pole of an antagonistic relation: 'a class ... which ... is the *complete loss* of man and hence can win itself only through the *complete rewinning of man*' (Marx and Engels 1975, p. 186).

7. 'The cistern contains; the fountain overflows' (William Blake, 'Proverbs of Hell', 1973, p. 97). We are a fountain, not a cistern.

8. It is in this sense that Marx introduces the figure of the proletariat as those whose conditions of existence make them the absolute negation of capitalism, because capitalism is the absolute negation of them. 'By proclaiming the *dissolution of the hitherto existing world order* the proletariat merely states the *secret of its own existence*, for it is *in fact* the dissolution of that world order' (Marx and Engels 1975, p. 187; original emphasis).

9. '*Der Geist der stets verneint*', is how Mephistopheles describes himself to Faust (Goethe 1969, p. 40). 'Man is the only creature who refuses to be what he is' (Camus 1971, p. 17).

10. 'Then that suffering that united us made us speak, and we recognised that in our words there was truth, we knew that not only pain and suffering lived in our tongue, we recognised that there is hope still in our hearts. We spoke with ourselves, we looked inside ourselves and we looked at our history: we saw our most ancient fathers suffering and struggling, we saw our grandfathers struggling, we saw our fathers with fury in their hands, we saw that not everything had been taken away from us, that we had the most valuable, that which made us live, that which made our step rise above plants and animals, that which made the stone be beneath our feet, and we saw, brothers, that all that we had was DIGNITY, and we saw that great was the shame of having forgotten it, and we saw that DIGNITY was good for men to be men again, and dignity returned to live in our hearts, and we were new again, and the dead, our dead, saw that we were new again and they called us again, to dignity, to struggle' (Ejército Zapatista de Liberación Nacional 1994, p. 122; original emphasis). The autonomist concept of self-valorisation is perhaps the closest that the Marxist tradition comes to a concept that expresses positively the struggle against-and-beyond capital, but the term is clumsy and obscure. On self-valorisation, see Cleaver (1992).

CHAPTER 9

1. For an interesting discussion of various examples, see Stratman (n.d.).

2. Subcomandante Marcos, in a communiqué dated 1 August 1999: 'we are women and men and children and old people who are quite ordinary, that is to say, rebellious, non-conformist, uncomfortable, dreamers' (*La Jornada*, 4 August 1999).

3. For a more recent formulation, see Hardt and Negri (2000, p. 208): 'Proletarian struggles constitute – in real, ontological terms – the motor of capitalist development. They constrain capital to adopt ever higher levels of technology and thus transform the relations of domination. From manufacturing to large-scale industry, from finance capital to transnational restructuring and the globalisation of the market, it is always the initiatives of organised labour power that determine the figure of capitalist development.'

4. Marx quotes Andrew Ure: 'This invention [the self-acting mule] confirms the great doctrine already propounded, that when capital enlists science into her service, the refractory hand of labour will always be taught docility' (1965, p. 437).

5. The notion of class composition has gender implications.

6. For a recent restatement of the argument, see Hardt and Negri (2000, p. 409).

7. See also Witheford (1994, p. 90): 'The concept of 'class composition' – a gauge of each side's internal unity, resources and will, determined not merely by the technical and social division of labour, but also by cultural milieu, organisational forms and political direction. As the cohesion of the working class grows, capital must respond by offensive restructurations deploying economic, technological and state power to 'decompose' its opponent's organisation. But because capital is dependent on collective labour as the source of surplus value, it cannot entirely destroy its foe. Each offensive, however successful, is followed by a 'recomposition' of the workforce, and the appearance of new resistances by different strata of labour with fresh capacities, strategies and organisational forms. Rather than being 'made' once-over, the working class is re-made again and again in a dynamic of constant transformation with working class recomposition and capitalist restructuration pursuing each other in a 'double spiral' of ever enlarging conflict (Negri 1980, p. 174)'. See also Cleaver (1992).

8. The other interpretation, the understanding of capital as dependent upon labour because it is the product of labour, is also present in some of the autonomist discussions: see, for example, the passage in a later article by Tronti: 'If the conditions of capital are in the hands of the workers, if there is no active life in capital without the living activity of labour power, if capital is already, at its birth, a consequence of productive labour, if there is no capitalist society without the workers' articulation, in other words if there is no social relationship without a class relationship, and there is no class relationship without the working class ... then one can conclude that the capitalist class, from its birth, is in fact subordinate to the working class' (1979b, p. 10).

9. Hardt and Negri do not make this point very explicitly, but it certainly seems to be implicit in their approach. For example: 'The decline of any autonomous political shpere signals the decline, too, of any independent space where revolution could emerge in the national political regime, or where social space could be transformed using the instruments of the state. The traditional idea of counter-power and the idea of resistance against modern sovereignty in general thus becomes less and less possible' (Hardt and Negri 2000, p. 307).

10. See the discussion in Holloway (1992, p. 164).

11. For a critique of the functionalism of this interpretation, see Hirsch (1978) and Holloway and Picciotto (1978b).

12. For a critique of the understanding of dialectics in terms of synthesis, see Adorno (1990).

13. For a criticism of Hirsch's reduction of class struggle to the status of a 'but also', see Bonefeld (1991).

14. Adorno (1990, p. 294) (on Kant): 'Most likely, he conceived the intelligible character as a strong ego in rational control of all its impulses, the kind taught in the whole tradition of modern rationalism, notably by Leibniz and Spinoza, who found here, at least, a point they could agree upon.' Negri's theory (1991) is very explicitly based on Spinoza.

15. Rather than to St Francis of Assisi, perhaps communists should look to Mephistopheles, the negating devil present in all of us!

CHAPTER 10

1. There is a long debate as to how to understand these objective contradictions between the proponents of the three main variants of Marxist crisis theory, the tendency of the rate of profit to fall, disproportionality theory and underconsumption theory.
2. This is Hegel's argument in the famous passage on lordship and bondage (1977, pp. 111–19).
3. It follows that class antagonism cannot be understood simply in terms of production, but in terms of the unity of circulation and production. The view of production as primary and circulation as secondary tends to lead to a view of the working class as the class of people subordinated in production, that is, the industrial proletariat. If capital is understood in terms of the unity of production and circulation (or the unity of the flight of-and-from insubordination and the imposition of subordination), then a different picture emerges. Capital lives by subordinating and then fleeing from the insubordination which is inseparable from subordination: it sucks in labour to exploit and then spits it out as unpalatable. The antagonism which constitutes the working class is not one of subordination, but of subordination/insubordination: the working class are not subordinate victims but the insubordinate from whom capital flees and whom it must subordinate. If capital lives by sucking and spitting, the working class can accurately be characterised as the unpalatable sucked and spat of the earth.
4. Theories of society as a system of correspondence between social phenomena (regulationist theory, Negri's theories) are blind to this fundamental aspect of capitalism. For a critique of regulation theory along these lines, see Bonefeld (1991).
5. This crucial aspect of the theory of value is overlooked both by those who treat value simply as a category of Marxist economics and, more surprisingly perhaps, by others who, in spite of their criticism of orthodox Marxism, maintain a dualism between 'laws of capitalist development' and struggle.
6. For a neo-Ricardian account, emphasising the role of wage struggles, see Glyn and Sutcliffe (1972); for an autonomist account, emphasising class struggle in general, see Cleaver and Bell (1982).
7 See Hardt and Negri (2000, p. 212): 'Mobility and mass worker nomadism always express a refusal and a search for liberation: the resistance against the horrible conditions of exploitation and the search for freedom and new conditions of life.'
8. Hardt and Negri (2000) rightly attach great importance to flight (nomadism, desertion, exodus) in their discussion of the struggles against Empire: 'The deterritorialising desire of the multitude is the motor that drives the entire process of capitalist development, and capital must constantly attempt to contain it' (2000, p. 124). Later they suggest that 'whereas in the disciplinary era sabotage was the fundamental notion of resistance, in the era of imperial control it may be desertion' (2000, p. 212). They fail to see, however, that flight is given in the concept of capital, and that it is a reciprocal flight, the flight of workers and the flight of capital.
9. The way in which the notion of the mobility of capital is used in many current discussions of the 'internationalisation' or 'globalisation' of capital is one example of the separation of subordination and insubordination, structure and struggle. Capital is assumed to be basically located in one place ('US capital', 'British capital') and labour, if it features at all, appears only as a victim.
10. In the 'postmodern economy', production of surplus value may appear to be a thing of the past. The idea of making money from money has always been the dream of capital.

11. On the argument in this section, see Bonefeld and Holloway (1995) and Bonnet (2000).
12. Quoted by Schlesinger (1959, p. 202).
13. See Negri (1988b).
14. See Samuel Brittan's book of that title (1977).
15. On this, see, for example Bonefeld and Burnham (1998).
16. For a discussion of this, see Bonefeld (1995) and Bonefeld and Holloway (1995).
17. See Bonefeld, Brown and Burnham (1995, pp. 66–8): 'The crash did not result in a meltdown of the stock market. This was prevented by a huge reflation package which included the lowering of interest rates, the relaxation of controls on the money supply, and financial support for banks and other financial institutions. The reflation package helped to sustain the credit based boom. Samuel Brittan's advice was well observed: 'When a slump is threatening, we need helicopters dropping currency notes from the sky. This means easier lending policies and, if that is not enough, some mixture of lower taxes and higher government spending ... By the end of the 1980s bank loans in the US had more than doubled and in Japan they were three times their level at the beginning of the decade' (Harman, 1993, p. 15).'
18. For a discussion of this, see, for example, Grant (1996).
19. Grant (1996) wonders why the speculative boom in the United States had not led to a recession. The answer is surely that the 'Mexican' crisis was in part the collapse of the US bubble, as were later the East Asian, Russian and Brazilian crises. For a discussion of the Mexican crisis, see Holloway (2000).
20. *Financial Times*, 31 October 1994.
21. *Financial Times*, 16 January 1995. And see Walter (1993, p. 215): 'Between 1976 and mid-1987, aggregate US debt rose from $2.5 trillion to nearly $8 trillion, and the ratio of total debt to GDP rose from 136 per cent to 178 per cent ... the indebtedness of the private sector in Japan has risen substantially in recent years: the indebtedness of non-financial companies increased from 94 per cent of GDP in 1975 to 135 per cent of GDP in 1990, while that of households increased from 45 per cent to 96 per cent of disposable income over the same period.' Between 1985 and 1997, total US household debt as a percentage of disposable personal income rose from just over 60 per cent to almost 85 per cent (*Financial Times*, 2 January 1998).
22. Warburton (1999, p. 3). Also: 'The world bond market has grown from less than $1 trillion in 1970 to more than $23 trillion in 1997.'
23. For a detailed discussion of the expansion of debt in the 1990s and the dangers of financial collapse, see Warburton (1999). See also Bonnet (2000), especially Chapter 1.
24. Lipietz poses the issue strikingly in terms of an 'image which has been haunting me since the crisis began – the image of a cartoon character who has gone over the edge of a cliff and carries on walking on thin air. This seemed to me to illustrate the position of the world economy, which continues to work 'on credit' while the actual ground on which post-war growth has been based ... crumbles beneath it' (Lipietz 1985, pp. 5–7).
25. In the universities of Mexico, for example, we have very direct experience of the way in which international debt is used to impose social discipline, and also of the way in which the result of such action is to give rise to a new wave of social insubordination.
26. See Mattick (1978), originally published in 1934.

CHAPTER 11

1. This view is shared by Negri (1988c), by Hardt and Negri (2000) and by most proponents of regulation theory.

2. See the discussion of 'nomadism, exodus, desertion' in Hardt and Negri (2000, pp. 210ff).

3. Hardt and Negri (2000, pp. 215ff) discuss Benjamin's concept of the new barbarians: 'The new barbarians destroy with an affirmative violence and trace new paths of life through their own material existence' (215). This may be so, at least in some cases, but we start from the assumption that the destruction is purely negative.

4. The internalisation of enclosure, which has been discussed here in terms of fetishism, is discussed by Foucault as the passage from a disciplinary society to a society of control, and by both Foucault, and Hardt and Negri, as bio-power.

5. See Hardt and Negri (2000, p. 212): 'This refusal certainly is the beginning of a liberatory politics, but it is only a beginning. The refusal in itself is empty ... Our lines of flight, our exodus must be constituent and create a real alternative. Beyond the simple refusal, or as part of that refusal, we need also to construct a new mode of life and above all a new community.'

6. See, for example, the detailed discussion in Stratman (n.d.).

7. See Marx (1965, p. 763): 'Centralisation of the means of production and socialisation of labour at last reach a point where they become incompatible with their capitalist integument. This integument is burst asunder. The knell of capitalist private property sounds. The expropriators are expropriated.'

8. 'Communism is for us not a *state of affairs* which is to be established, an *ideal* to which reality [will] have to adjust itself. We call communism the *real* movement which abolishes the present state of things' (Marx and Engels 1976, p. 49; original emphasis).

9. And before them, Ernst Bloch (1961).

10. The movement of communism is not a linear progress but a 'hard, endangered journey, a suffering, a wandering, a going astray, a searching for the hidden homeland, full of tragic interruption, boiling, bursting with leaps, eruptions, lonely promises, discontinuously laden with the consciousness of light' (Bloch 1964, Vol. 2, p. 29).

11. See Holloway and Peláez (1998).

12. On the idea of communism as the realisation of the moment of fulfilment see Bloch (1964). This is closely related to Benjamin's concept of the *Jetztzeit* (now-time): see Benjamin (1973, p. 263).

13. Revolution can never be a single event, or a state of being, but an unending process, or an event which must constantly be renewed. The orthodox tradition (USSR, Cuba) sees revolution as an event that gives rise to an identified post-revolution, with disastrous consequences.

14. Gunn (1987a, p. 91) says of Bloch: 'No other writer within Marxism sets the stakes in revolutionary transformation so awesomely high.' But there is no other way, is there?

EPILOGUE

1. For their comments on an earlier draft of this epilogue, many thanks to Chris Wright, Dorothea Härlin, Sergio Tischler, Raquel Gutierrez, Nika Sommeregger, Néstor López, Luis Menéndez and Werner Bonefeld.

2. The book is an invitation to discuss, and, if the number of commentaries and criticisms it has received are anything to go by, then it has been a very successful invitation. With many of the criticisms I disagree, some I recognise as valid, in all cases I feel honoured by the care with which the arguments of the book have been discussed. The written comments on the book (over a hundred) can be found in the web page of the publishers of the Argentinian edition, Herramienta: <www.herramienta.com.ar>

For me an important part of the response has also been the large number of people taking part in the many public presentations of the book – over 1200 people in the main presentation in Buenos Aires in late 2002, but also over 500 in Berlin in the spring of 2004. To all who have taken up, in however hostile a manner, the book's invitation to discuss, I am immensely grateful.

3. On this see especially the excellent discussion by Alberto Bonnet (2003). See also Bonnet (2005).

4. Atilio Borón agued this explicitly in a debate in the UNAM in Mexico City in May 2004.

5. Criticisms will be addressed explicitly mainly in the notes. This epilogue is in no sense a complete response to all the criticisms nor a just reflection of the richness of the commentaries on the book. It is simply an attempt to develop the argument in a certain direction while responding to some of the points raised in the discussion. There are many commentaries that raise points that go beyond the present text – and some of the richest discussions of the book are not even mentioned in this epilogue. It is in the nature of the argument that more attention is paid here to the critical commentaries rather than to the favourable reviews.

6. For a criticism of this emphasis on negativity see the generally sympathetic discussion by Massimo De Angelis (2005) and the much more hostile review by Michael Lebowitz (2005).

7. See Adorno (1990, p. 158): 'To equate the negation of the negation with positivity is the quintessence of identification; it is the formal principle in its purest form. What thus wins out in the inmost core of dialectics is the anti-dialectical principle: that traditional logic which, *more arithmetico*, takes minus times minus for a plus.' However much we focus on the 'other world' which we hope is possible, it is important to remember that the cutting edge of the drive to another world is negativity, our refusal of the world that exists. On the enduring importance of negative theory, see the work of Johannes Agnoli (Agnoli 1999, for example) and the commentary on this book by Werner Bonefeld (2004). For a criticism of the influence of Adorno's negative dialectics on the book, see the commentaries by Peter Hudis (2003) and Rubén Dri (2002).

8. For a critique of the logic of confrontation, see Benasayag and Sztulwark (2000) and Aubenas and Benasayag (2002).

9. This distinction between totality and aspiration to totality is the explosive contradiction at the heart of Lukács's *History and Class Consciousness*. See above, Chapter 5, section III.

10. Whether the book is 'Marxist' or not does not matter, of course. Nevertheless, against the many critics who have seen it as an abandonment of Marxism, it is worth pointing to Stoetzler's (2005) acute comment that 'Holloway's book is an essentially orthodox intervention (in the sense of revisionist of the tradition by loyalty to its founding texts) concerned with transmitting – like that message in a bottle – an unredeemed theoretical achievement of the past into a contemporary "political scene" that is dominated by the busy-ness of "activists" and party/trade unionist/NGO cadres and their typically rather hectic thinking that tends to be amnesiac of its own historical conditions and contradictions.' On this, see also Fernández Buey (2003).

11. Negri (2002, p. 184) says that he refuses 'absolutely any form of transcendence'. Although he probably means something else by transcendence, it remains true that in his and in other post-structuralist approaches, there is no possibility of understanding struggle in terms of moving-against-and-beyond. The connection that is often made between this book and Hardt and Negri's *Empire* is politically and theoretically ill-founded, except in the sense that both argue for a rethinking of revolutionary theory. On the question of the connection with post-structuralism,

see Seibert (2004); on the contrast between this book and Negri's theory, see Bonefeld (2004).

12. The drive to social self-determination is no more than a rephrasing of Marx's crucial distinction between the architect and the bee (*Capital*, Chapter 7, discussed above in Chapter 3). The distinction between humans and other animals is not their present self-determination of their doing, but their (negated) potential self-determination. In that sense, self-determination (which can only be social) is the project of creating humanity.

13. Marcel Stoetzler expresses this beautifully when, after pointing to many contradictions in the argument of the book, he says 'it is perhaps part of the appeal of the book that it gives expression to real contradictions by being itself contradictory' (Stoetzler 2005).

14. The argument in this section is directed against the criticism made by Alberto Bonnet: 'An exclusively expressive politics is impossible – and with it any revolution conceived in these terms. But let us accept for the sake of argument that it were possible. Then, many thanks, but we will stay with the (supposedly) instrumental politics. We prefer it for a number of reasons that would require various pages to present, but let us stick to the key point: expressive politics is irrational politics. A politics without objectives (and expressing oneself authentically is not an objective) cannot be evaluated rationally, a politics without organisation (and an escola de samba does not count as a political organisation) cannot be democratic, and so on. Moreover, we know of some expressionist experiences in political history, but they are not exactly among the most revolutionary ...' However, it is hard to see how radical politics today can be other than expressive, in the sense of a moving outwards in a general direction (the utopian star), but not towards a precisely defined goal. As Barry Marshall puts it in his discussion of the book (2002): 'it entails a negative, questioning movement which instead of plotting a direct course of social change, moves like ripples in water, ever outward'.

15. The assumption of a two-staged pivoted movement is central to many of the criticisms of the book. See Mike Gonzalez (2003), for example, or Peter McLaren's (2003) comment that 'Holloway's cry that "we do not struggle as working class, we struggle against being working class, against being classified" really amounts to attempting to abolish capitalist relations of production by pretending that they aren't there.' It is not a question of pretending that capitalist social relations do not exist, but of pushing now against-and-beyond those relations rather than taking them as an iron cage against which we can do nothing until they are completely abolished.

16. This argument is developed in my reply to Joachim Hirsch, 'The Printing House of Hell' (Holloway 2003a).

17. 'Somos mujeres y hombres, niños y ancianos bastante comunes, es decir, rebeldes, inconformes, incómodos, soñadores.'

18. Hardt and Negri (2000) are right in arguing that there is no 'outside' to which we can appeal: we are all inside capitalism. What they do not emphasise is that being inside means (inevitably, because of the contradictory nature of capitalism) that we constantly move against-and-beyond capitalism.

19. On the question of class, see now the edited collection *Clase=Lucha* (Holloway 2004a).

20. The book has been criticised for not paying sufficient attention to the question of organisation (Wright 2002; De Angelis 2005). What should perhaps have been made more explicit in the book is that to speak of social relations is inevitably to speak of the way in which our social interactions are organised. To say, for example, that the state is a capitalist social relation is to talk of the state as a specifically capitalist form of organisation.

21. This is a point emphasised by Raúl Zibechi: see Zibechi (2003).

22. This is the answer to those who accuse the book of adopting a neo-liberal approach. Both the current wave of struggles and neo-liberal politics can be said to be reactions to the crisis of the post-war (Fordist) pattern of domination-and-resistance, but where neo-liberalism seeks to contain this crisis, anti-capitalist struggle seeks to exacerbate it. Orthodox Marxism pretends that the crisis does not even exist.

23. On this, see for example Zibechi (2003).

24. A feature of clandestine organisations is that their clandestinity makes integration into the community difficult: see for example the account of the German Rote Armee Fraktion by Margrit Schiller (2001). That this is not always the case is clear from the experience of the Zapatistas.

25. Néstor López recounts how an old lady's request to an *asamblea barrial* in Buenos Aires to help find her lost dog separated the traditional revolutionary left (who regarded such an activity as absurd) from the rest of the assembly, who organised a search – and found the dog.

26. For a defence of the importance of identity against the argument of the book, see Rajchenberg (2003), Romero (2002).

27. This is a point made by Marcel Stoetzler (2005), Gegenantimacht (2004), Carlos Figueroa (2003) and Felix Klopotek (2004). A related point is made by Aufheben (2003) who argue that I fall all too easily 'into a cheer-leading of any form of resistance'. The argument in this epilogue is that it is important to start from the scream (any scream) but to articulate that scream as drive towards self-determination.

28. This is a reference to Chico Buarque's song 'Pai'.

29. The issue of democracy is raised by Michael Löwy in his discussions of the book (2003, 2004). See my replies to him in Holloway (2003c, 2004b). See also Figueroa (2003).

30. The current wave of struggles in Argentina has unleashed a rich discussion of horizontality and the problems both of representative and direct democracy: see Bonnet (2003), Mattini (2003), Thwaites (2003, 2004), Zibechi (2003). For an excellent discussion of the practicalities and difficulties of organisation, see Colectivo Situaciones and MTD Solano (2002).

31. See the argument put forward by Thomas Seibert (2004).

32. The quote is from Lebowitz (2005), and the same phrase is used by Cruz Bernal (2002), but similar arguments are advanced by Callinicos (2003), Borón (2003, 2005) and Hearse (2003). Is this just a verbal distinction, a question of terminology? Not at all: the absorption of two opposite forms of organisation under the same concept is a blurring that plays an important role in the transformation of self-determination into its opposite. For an important discussion of the relation (or rather, lack of relation) between Leninism and revolutionary theory today, see Bonefeld and Tischler (2003).

33. The basic principle of anti-state politics is stated simply and clearly by Leticia of the Zapatista Junta de Buen Gobierno Corazón Centrico in the celebration of the eleventh anniversary of the Zapatista uprising: 'We have the intelligence and capacity to determine our own destiny' ('*Tenemos inteligencia y capacidad para dirigir nuestro propio destino*') (*La Jornada*, 2 January 2005).

34. There is no idealisation here of existing communities. By community here I understand the potential for social self-determination, the social drive towards self-determination.

35. There has been much talk in recent years of the creation of a party of a new type having a different sort of relation with movements of social protest. The most obvious examples are Rifondazione Comunista in Italy or parts of the PT in Brazil, but there are movements in the same direction in a number of countries: see Marcos Del Roio's commentary (2004). However, as Fausto Bertinotti made clear in his recent intervention in the European Social Forum, the central issue for such parties

is still the lack of revolutionary consciousness among the workers and the role of the party in bringing such consciousness to the workers.

36. This argument is put forward by Borón (2003), for example.

37. Some of the kinder reactions to the book have taken the form of 'You are quite right, but also it is important to struggle through the state'; see for example Hirsch (2003), Bartra (2003). For my reply to Hirsch's argument, see Holloway (2003a).

38. On the notion of situation, see the work of Colectivo Situaciones (2001), Benasayag and Sztulwark (2000).

39. On the notion of 'in-and-against', see London Edinburgh Weekend Return Group (LEWRG) (1979).

40. Obviously, the distinction between 'situational' and 'non-situational' contact with the state is not a clear distinction. As a professor in a public university, I have a situational contact with the state, but I was not born a professor: it was, initially at least, an extra-situational choice.

41. One of the most impressive experiences in the discussion of this book was the discussion that took place in the Centro Sociale of Garbatella in Rome, where one of the leading members of the Centro Sociale (Massimiliano Smeriglio) is also president of the local municipality (Municipio XI of Rome).

42. See Hilary Wainwright's book, *Reclaim the State* (2003).

43. This is the important and difficult point raised by Seibert (2004), Gegenantimacht (2004), Smeriglio (2004) and Bertinotti (2004) in their discussions of the book. Certainly the danger of any such contact with the state is that the 'in spite of' can very quickly become converted into a 'but also' and the drive beyond the state become lost. Any contact with the state will tend to separate leaders or representatives from the rest of the movement. On the question of elections see the commentaries of Claudio Albertani (2003) and Carlos Figueroa (2003).

44. It is precisely because of the practical difficulty of such situations that it is important to emphasise that the state is a specifically capitalist form of social relations. This can be too easily lost in analyses that point to the contradictory nature of the state: see Mabel Thwaites Rey (2004). The fact that the state (like any phenomenon in an antagonistic society) is contradictory does not mean that it (like capital, like value, like money) is not a specifically capitalist form of social relations, a form of organisation that impedes the drive towards social self-determination.

45. Armando Bartra's (2003, p. 134) metaphor of wearing a condom in our contact with the state is suggestive, but underestimates the force of institutionalisation.

46. Some critics (Mathers and Taylor 2005, and also Joachim Hirsch and Hilary Wainwright in recent discussions, for example) have argued that the book is a reversal of the position that I previously argued for (with others) in *In and Against the State*. I do not think this is the case, although I do think there is probably a shift in emphasis connected with the changing nature of the state.

47. I do not think we should call, as Rhina Roux (2003) does in her careful discussion, for a 'recovery of politics'. The point is rather to develop with self-confidence the drive towards social self-determination. This is what I understand by anti-politics.

48. The tension is clear in the development of the social forum movement, most recently in the clash between 'horizontals' and 'verticals' in the European Social Forum, London, 2004.

49. A similar point might be made in relation to Venezuela: favouring an anti-state approach to changing the world does not mean simply condemning out of hand the apparently state-led process in Venezuela, but rather being aware of the tensions and dangers inherent in the dissonant interplay of the different forms of struggle in this case: that the driving force, despite appearances is not the state but popular revolt and that the relation of the state to this revolt is contradictory, at best. For a very different view, see Tariq Ali (2004).

50. For a defence of the idea of revolution on behalf of, see the commentary by Francisco Fernández Buey (2003).

51. This is an important point raised both in public discussions of the book and by a number of critics: see, for example, Almeyra (2002), Borón (2003), Manzana (2003) and, more questioningly, Gegenantimacht (2004).

52. Luis Lorenzano (1998) rightly emphasises the importance of seeing the Zapatistas as an armed community rather than as an army.

53. To speak of the drive towards self-determination being a drive against labour does not, of course, mean that a self-determining society would be a land of Cockayne in which roast chickens fly past waiting to be plucked out of the sky: 'work' would still be necessary to ensure the reproduction of society, but it would be a society in which what we do would be determined by what we decided was necessary or desirable, with no clear distinction being made between 'necessary' and 'desirable', and therefore no clear distinction between 'work' and 'play'.

54. This has been a point of discussion in the Zapatista journal, *Rebeldía*: Rodriguez (2003), Holloway (2003d). For an interesting comment, see Huerta (2004).

55. The same argument could be made in other words by speaking not of 'doing' and 'labour', but of 'unalienated' and 'alienated' work; but the very separation of work from other forms of doing (play, for example) is surely a characteristic of alienation. For a discussion of the concept of doing see the commentaries by Wildcat (2003), Imhof (2004), Reitter (2003), Aufheben (2003), Rooke (2002).

56. For a discussion of this, see Palomino (2005).

57. In the 'real world', however (so it is objected), trains and power stations have to be run and computers constructed. Such complex activities require centralised, state-controlled coordination: see Bonnet (2003). I see no reason, however, why such activities should not be organised democratically, by a council of councils. The objection that we need a state to perform such tasks confuses the form of social relations (the state) and the function to be performed (running trains). On this, see Bonefeld (2003).

58. See the title of the book by Aubenas and Benasayag: *Résister, c'est Créer*.

59. On the supposed necessity of institutions, see Enrique Dussel (2004) and the response by Néstor López (2004) and the discussion by Belén Sopransi and Verónica Veloso (2004).

60. See Tischler (2005, p. 7).

61. In this I agree with Negri when he says 'what we need is a political critique of tradition. Oppression is founded on tradition.' (Negri 2002, p. 120). And see Marx at the beginning of the *Eighteenth Brumaire*: 'The tradition of all the dead generations weighs like a nightmare on the brain of the living.'

62. See the exciting discussion of time and constellations of struggle in Tischler (2004).

63. See Vaneigem, 'an ideology of history has one purpose only: to prevent people from making history' (1994, p. 231). And also Stephen Dedalus in Joyce's Ulysses (2000, p. 42): 'History, Stephen said, is a nightmare from which I am trying to awake.'

64. This is a very partial (and inadequate) response to those who have criticised the book for its non-historical approach. See Bensaid (2003), Romero (2002), Méndez (2003), Vega (2003), Manzana (2003), Bartra (2003), Smith (2002), Grespan (2004), Kraniauskas (2002) ... and my replies: Holloway (2003b, 2003e). A related issue is the question of objectification and alienation, which I do not discuss here but recognise as important: see Löwy (2003) and my reply to him (2003c) and also Centro Rodolfo Ghioldi (2002), and Callinicos (2005).

65. Clearly what we can see at any particular moment is part of the whole constellation of struggle, but theory pushes at the limits of visibility, strains its eyes. The problem then is whether what theory sees really exists, or whether it exists only in our imagination, but that problem can be solved only through the articulation of theory and movement.

264   Change the World Without Taking Power

66. The theorist is not a theatre director, as Nika Sommeregger pointed out in her comments on the draft of this epilogue.
67. See Eduardo Galeano: 'She is on the horizon – says Fernando Birri –. I approach two paces, she goes two paces further away. I walk ten paces and the horizon moves back ten paces. However much I walk, I shall never reach it. How does utopia help us? That's how it helps us: to walk' ('Ella está en el horizonte – dice Fernado Birri –. Me acerco dos pasos, ella se aleja dos pasos. Camino diez pasos y el horizonte se corre diez pasos más allá. Por mucho que yo comine, nunca la alcanzaré. ¿Para qué sirve la utopia? Para eso sirve: para caminar') (*Las Palabras andantes*, cited in *Chiapas*, No. 13 (2002), p. 134). Yes, but the communist horizon is much more than that.
68. This is the interpretation of Marxism proposed by Enrique Dussel, but it effectively waters down completely the critical force of Marx's argument.
69. Is this epilogue fully compatible with the argument in the book? I do not know. I hope not. It would be nice to think that I have learnt something in the last few years and that the epilogue moves against-and-beyond the book.

Bibliography

Note: Almost all contributions to the debate are available in the web page of *Herramienta*: <www.herramienta.com.ar>.

Acanda, Jorge Luis (2000) 'Sociedad Civil y Estado', paper presented to the conference on 'El marxismo: una Mirada desde la Izquierda', Havana.

Adorno, Theodor W. (1967) *Prisms: Cultural Criticism and Society* (London: Neville Spearman).

Adorno, Theodor W. (1978) 'Subject-Object', in Arato, A. and Gebhardt, G. (eds), *The Essential Frankfurt School Reader* (Oxford: Basil Blackwell), pp. 497–511.

Adorno, Theodor W. (1990) *Negative Dialectics* (London: Routledge).

Agnoli, Johannes (1999) *Subversive Theorie* (Freiburg: Ça ira).

Albertani, Claudio (2003) 'Presentation of *Bajo el Volcán* No. 6', *Herramienta* web page.

Ali, Tariq (2004) 'Venezuela: Changing the World by Taking Power', Interview, <www.venezuelanalysis.com>.

Almeyra, Guillermo (2002) 'El Dificultoso No-Asalto al No-Cielo', *Herramienta* web page.

Arato, Andrew and Gebhardt, Eike (eds) (1978) *The Essential Frankfurt School Reader* (Oxford: Basil Blackwell).

Ashe, Fidelma (1999) 'The Subject', in Ashe, F. et al. (eds), *Contemporary Social and Political Theory: An Introduction* (Buckingham: Open University Press), pp. 88–110.

Ashe, Fidelma et al. (eds) (1999) *Contemporary Social and Political Theory: An Introduction* (Buckingham: Open University Press).

Aubenas, Florence and Benasayag, Miguel (2002) *Résister, c'est Créer* (Paris: La Découverte).

Aufheben (2003) 'Review: Change the World Without Taking Power', *Aufheben* (Brighton), No. 11.

Backhaus, Hans-Georg (1992) 'Between Philosophy and Science: Marxian Social Economy as Critical Theory', in Bonefeld, W., Gunn, R. and Psychopedis, K. (eds), *Open Marxism, Volume I: Dialectics and History* (London: Pluto Press), pp. 54–92.

Bartra, Armanda (2003) 'La Llama y la Piedra: De cómo cambiar el mundo sin tomar el poder según John Holloway', *Chiapas* (Mexico City), No. 15, pp. 123–41.

Benasayag, Miguel and Sztulwark, Diego (2000) *Política y Situación: De la potencia al contrapoder* (Buenos Aires: De mano en mano).

Benjamin, Walter (1931) 'Linke Melancholie', *Die Gesellschaft*, VIII.

Benjamin, Walter (1973) 'Theses on the Philosophy of History', in *Illuminations* (New York: Schocken Books).

Bensaid, Daniel (2003) 'La Révolution sans prendre le Pouvoir?' *Contre Temps* (Paris), No. 6, pp. 45–59.

Bernstein, Eduard (1961) *Evolutionary Socialism* (New York: Schocken).

Bertinotti, Fausto (2004) Interventions in the presentation of the Italian edition of the book in Rome and in the European Social Forum in London.

Best, Steven and Kellner, Douglas (1991) *Postmodern Theory: Critical Interrogations* (London: Macmillan).

Blake, William (1973) *William Blake* (introduced and ed. by J. Bronowski) (Harmondsworth: Penguin).

Bloch, Ernst (1961) *Naturrecht und menschliche Würde* (Frankfurt: Suhrkamp).

Bloch, Ernst (1964) *Tübinger Einleitung in die Philosophie* (2 Bde) (Frankfurt: Suhrkamp).

Bloch, Ernst (1986) *The Principle of Hope* (3 vols) (Oxford: Basil Blackwell).

Bonefeld, Werner (1987) 'Marxism and the concept of Mediation', *Common Sense*, No. 2.

Bonefeld, Werner (1988) 'Class Struggle and the Permanence of Primitive Accumulation', *Common Sense*, No. 6, pp. 54–65.

Bonefeld, Werner (1991) 'The Reformulation of State Theory', in Bonefeld, W. and Holloway, J. (eds), *Post-Fordism and Social Form* (London: Macmillan), pp. 35–68.

Bonefeld, Werner (1992) 'Social Constitution and the Form of the Capitalist State', in Bonefeld, W., Gunn, R. and Psychopedis, K., (eds), *Open Marxism, Volume I: Dialectics and History* (London: Pluto Press).

Bonefeld, Werner (1994) 'Human Practice and Perversion: Between Autonomy and Structure', *Common Sense*, No. 15, pp. 43–52.

Bonefeld, Werner (1995) 'Capital as Subject and the Existence of Labour', in Bonefeld, W. et al. (eds), *Open Marxism, Volume III: Emancipating Marx* (London: Pluto Press). pp. 182–212.

Bonefeld, Werner (2001) 'Clase y Constitución', *Bajo el Volcán*, No. 2, pp. 139–165.

Bonefeld, Werner (2003) 'The Capitalist State: Illusion and Critique', in Bonefeld, W. (ed), *Revolutionary Writing* (New York: Autonomedia).

Bonefeld, Werner (2004) 'El principio esperanza en la emancipación: acerca de Holloway', *Herramienta*, No. 27; 'The Principle of Hope in Human Emancipation: on Holloway', in *Herramienta* web page.

Bonefeld, Werner, Brown, Alice and Burnham, Peter (1995) *A Major Crisis?* (Aldershot: Dartmouth).

Bonefeld, Werner and Burnham, Peter (1998) 'Counter-Inflationary Credibility in Britain, 1990–1994', *Review of Radical Political Economics*, Vol. 30, No. 1, pp. 32–52.

Bonefeld, Werner and Holloway, John (eds) (1991) *Post-Fordism and Social Form* (London: Macmillan).

Bonefeld, Werner and Holloway, John (eds) (1995) *Global Capital, National State and the Politics of Money* (London: Macmillan).

Bonefeld, Werner and Psychopedis, Kosmas (eds) (2000) *The Politics of Change* (London: Palgrave).

Bonefeld, Werner and Psychopedis, Kosmas (eds) (2005) *Human Dignity* (Aldershot: Ashgate).

Bonefeld, Werner, Gunn, Richard, Holloway, John and Psychopedis, Kosmas (1995) *Open Marxism, Volume III: Emancipating Marx* (London: Pluto).

Bonefeld, Werner, Gunn, Richard and Psychopedis, Kosmas (1992a) 'Introduction', in Bonefeld et al. (eds), *Open Marxism, Volume I: Dialectics and History* (London: Pluto Press).

Bonefeld, Werner, Gunn, Richard and Psychopedis, Kosmas (eds) (1992b) *Open Marxism, Volume I: Dialectics and History* (London: Pluto Press).

Bonefeld, Werner, Gunn, Richard and Psychopedis, Kosmas (eds) (1992c) *Open Marxism, Volume II: Theory and Practice* (London: Pluto Press).

Bonefeld, Werner and Tischler, Sergio (eds) (2003) *What is to be Done? Leninism, Anti-Leninist Marxism and the Question of Revolution Today* (Aldershot: Ashgate).

Bonnet, Alberto (2000) *Dinero y capital-dinero en la globalización* (Buenos Aires: Tesis de Maestría, Universidad de Buenos Aires).

Bonnet, Alberto (2003) 'Micropolíticas posmodernas, malgré John', *Herramienta* web page.

Bonnet, Alberto (2005) 'Hopeful voyage, unexpected port of arrival?' *Capital & Class* (London).

Borón, Atilio (2003) 'Poder, 'contrapoder' y 'antipoder'. Notas sobre un extravío teórico-político en el pensamiento crítico contemporáneo', *Chiapas*, No. 15, pp. 143–62.

Borón, Atilio (2005) 'Holloway on Power and the "State Illusion"', *Capital & Class*, London.

Braunmühl, Claudia von (1978) 'On the Analysis of the Bourgeois Nation State within the World Market Context', in Holloway, J. and Picciotto, S. (eds), *The State and Capital: A Marxist Debate* (London: Edward Arnold), pp. 160–77.

Brittan, Samuel (1977) *The Economic Consequences of Democracy* (Harmondsworth: Penguin).

Bublitz, Ute (1998) *Beyond Philosophy: Reconciliation and Rejection* (London: Universal Texts).

Callinicos, Alex (2003) 'How do we deal with the state?' *Socialist Review*, No. 272, pp. 11–13, March.

Callinicos, Alex (2005) 'Change the World Without Taking Power', *Capital & Class* (London).

Camus, Albert (1971) *The Rebel* (Harmondsworth: Penguin).

Centro Rodolfo Ghioldi (2002) *Nominalismo, Freudomarxismo y dialéctica diádica en el pensamiento de John Holloway* (Buenos Aires: Centro Rodolfo Ghioldi).

Clarke, Simon (1982) *Marx, Marginalism and Modern Sociology* (London: Macmillan).

Clarke, Simon (ed.) (1991) *The State Debate* (London: Macmillan).

Clarke, Simon (2002) 'Class Struggle and the Working Class: the Problem of Commodity Fetishism', in Dinerstein, A. and Neary, M. (eds), *The Labour Debate* (London: Ashgate).

Cleaver, Harry (1992) 'The Inversion of Class Perspective in Marxian Theory: From Valorisation to Self-Valorisation', in Bonefeld, W., Gunn, R. and Psychopedis, K. (eds), *Open Marxism, Volume II: Theory and Practice* (London: Pluto Press), pp. 106–45.

Cleaver, Harry (1998) 'The Zapatistas and the Electronic Fabric of Struggle', in Holloway, J. and Peláez, E. (eds), *Zapatista! Reinventing Revolution in Mexico* (London: Pluto Press), pp. 81–103.

Cleaver, Harry and Bell, Peter (1982) 'Marx's Crisis Theory as a Theory of Class Struggle', *Research in Political Economy*, Vol. 5.

Colectivo Situaciones (2001) *Contrapoder. Una Introducción* (Buenos Aires: Ediciones de Mano a Mano).

Colectivo Situaciones and MTD de Solano (2002) *La Hipótesis 891. Más allá de los Piquetes* (Buenos Aires: Ediciones de Mano a Mano).

Congdon, Tim (1988) *The Debt Threat* (Oxford: Blackwell).

Cruz Bernal, Isidoro (2002) 'Elegante manera de hacerse el distraído', *Socialismo o Barbarie* (Buenos Aires), No. 11.

Cunow, Heinrich (1898–99) 'Zur Zusammensbruchstheorie', *Die Neue Zeit*, Jg. XVIII, Bd 1, p. 430.

Dalla Costa, Mariarosa (1995) 'Capitalism and Reproduction', in Bonefeld et al. (eds), *Open Marxism, Volume III: Emancipating Marx* (London: Pluto Press), pp. 7–16.

De Angelis, Massimo (1996) 'Social Relations, Commodity-Fetishism And Marx's Critique Of Political Economy', *Review of Radical Political Economics*, Vol. 28, No. 4 pp. 1–29.

De Angelis, Massimo (2005) 'HOW?! An Essay on John Holloway's *Change the World Without Taking Power*', *Historical Materialism* (London).

Debord, Guy (1995) *The Society of the Spectacle* (New York: Zone Books).

Del Barco, Oscar (1980) *Esbozo de una Crítica a la Teoría y Práctica Leninistas* (Puebla: Universidad Autónoma de Puebla).

Del Roio, Marcos (2004) 'O Problema do Poder na Revolução', *Novos Rumos* (São Paulo).

Dinerstein, Ana and Neary, Michael (eds) (2002) *The Labour Debate* (London: Ashgate).

Dri, Rubén (2002) 'Debate sobre el poder en el movimiento popular', *Retruco* (Buenos Aires).

Dussel, Enrique (2004) 'Dialogo con John Holloway. Sobre la interpelación ética, el poder, las instituciones y la estrategia política', *Bajo el Volcán* (Puebla), No. 8; also *Herramienta* (Buenos Aires), No. 26.

Ejército Zapatista de Liberación Nacional (1994) *La Palabra de los Armados de Verdad y Fuego* (Mexico City: Fuenteovejuna).

Engels, Friedrich (1968) *Socialism: Utopian and Scientific* (Moscow: Progress).

Fernández Buey, Francisco (2003) '¿Cambiar el Mundo sin Tomar el Poder?' *El Viejo Topo* (Barcelona), pp. 35–40.

Figueroa, Carlos (2003) 'Pensando de nuevo la revolución, pensando de nuevo al marxismo', *Bajo el Volcán* (Puebla), No. 6, pp. 59–70.

Foucault, Michel (1973) *The Order of Things* (New York: Vintage Books).

Foucault, Michel (1975) *Discipline and Punish* (London: Allen Lane Penguin).

Foucault, Michel (1990) *The History of Sexuality. Volume 1: An Introduction* (New York: Vintage Books).

Gegenantimacht (2004) 'Wir sind Autonome, aber wir sin mehr als das ... Wie ein Prof aus Mexiko uns aus dem Herzen spricht', *Herramienta* web page.

Gerstenberger, Heide (1990) *Die subjektlose Gewalt: Theorie der Entstehung bürgerlicher Staatsgewalt* (Münster: Westfälisches Dampfboot).

Glyn, Andrew and Sutcliffe, Bob (1972) *British Capitalism, Workers and the Profits Squeeze* (Harmondsworth: Penguin).

Goethe, Johann Wolfgang (1969) *Faust*, I. Teil (Stuttgart: Reclam).

Gonzalez, Mike (2003) 'Crying out for Revolution', *International Socialism*, No. 99, pp. 133–8.

Gramsci, Antonio (1971) *Selections from the Prison Notebooks* (ed. and trans. Quintin Hoare and Geoffrey Nowell Smith) (London: Lawrence and Wishart).

Grant, James (1996) *The Trouble with Prosperity* (New York: Times Books).

Grespan, Jorge (2004) 'Um convite a discutir', *Margem Esquerda* (São Paulo), No. 3, pp. 178–86.

Guattari, Félix and Negri, Antonio (1990) *Communists Like Us* (New York: Semiotext(e)).

Gunn, Richard (1985) 'The Only Real Phoenix: Notes on Apocalyptic and Utopian Thought', *Edinburgh Review*, No. 71:1.

Gunn, Richard (1987a) 'Ernst Bloch's 'The Principle of Hope'', *New Edinburgh Review*, No. 76, pp. 90–8.

Gunn, Richard (1987b) 'Marxism and Mediation', *Common Sense*, No. 2.

Gunn, Richard (1987c) 'Notes on 'Class'', *Common Sense*, No. 2.

Gunn, Richard (1991) 'Marxism, Metatheory and Critique', in Bonefeld, W. and Holloway, J. (eds) *Post-Fordism and Social Form* (London: Macmillan), pp. 193–209.

Gunn, Richard (1992) 'Against Historical Materialism: Marxism as a First-order Discourse', in Bonefeld et al. (eds), *Open Marxism, Volume II: Theory and Practice* (London: Pluto Press), pp. 1–45.

Hardt, Michael and Negri, Antonio (2000) *Empire* (Cambridge, MA: Harvard University Press).

Harman, Chris (1993) 'Where is Capitalism Going?', *International Socialism*, No. 58, pp. 3–57.

Hearse, Phil (2003) 'Change the World? Without Taking Power?' *Fourth International Press List*.

Hegel, Georg W.F. (1967) *Philosophy of Right* (Oxford: Oxford University Press).

Hegel, Georg W.F. (1977) *Phenomenology of Spirit* (Oxford: Oxford University Press).

Hirsch, Joachim (1978) 'The State Apparatus and Social Reproduction: Elements of a Theory of the Bourgeois State', in Holloway, J. and Picciotto, S. (eds), *The State and Capital: A Marxist Debate* (London: Edward Arnold), pp. 57–107.

Hirsch, Joachim (2003) 'Macht und Anti-Macht', *Das Argument* (Berlin), No. 249, pp. 34–40.

Hobbes, Thomas (1991) *The Leviathan* (Cambridge: Cambridge University Press).

Holloway, John (1991a) 'Capital is Class Struggle (And Bears are not Cuddly)', in Bonefeld, W. and Holloway, J. (eds) *Post-Fordism and Social Form* (London: Macmillan).

Holloway, John (1991b) 'The State and Everyday Struggle', in Clarke, S. (ed.), *The State Debate* (London: Macmillan), pp. 225–59.

Holloway, John (1991c) 'The Great Bear: Post-Fordism and Class Struggle. A Comment on Bonefeld and Jessop', in Bonefeld, W. and Holloway, J. (eds), *Post-Fordism and Social Form* (London: Macmillan), pp. 92–102.

Holloway, John (1995a) 'From Scream of Refusal to Scream of Power: The Centrality of Work', in Bonefeld W. et al. (eds), *Open Marxism, Volume III: Emancipating Marx* (London: Pluto Press), pp. 155–81.

Holloway, John (1995b) 'Global Capital and the National State', in Bonefeld, W. and Holloway, J. (1995), *Global Capital, National State and the Politics of Money* (London: Macmillan), pp. 116–40.

Holloway, John (1996) 'La resonancia del zapatismo', *Chiapas*, No. 3, pp. 43–54.

Holloway, John (1998) 'Dignity's Revolt' in Holloway, J. and Peláez, E. (eds), *Zapatista! Reinventing Revolution in Mexico* (London: Pluto Press), pp. 159–98.

Holloway, John (2000) 'Zapata in Wall Street', in Bonefeld, W. and Psychopedis, K. (eds), *The Politics of Change* (London: Palgrave), pp. 173–95.

Holloway, John (2003a) 'Die Drückerei der Hölle. Eine Anmerkung in Antwort auf Joachim Hirsch', *Das Argument* (Berlin), No. 250, pp. 219–27; also 'The Printing House of Hell', *Herramienta* web page.

Holloway, John (2003b) 'Conduis ton char et ta charrue par-dessus les ossements des morts', *Contre Temps* (Paris), pp. 160–9.

Holloway, John (2003c) 'Intercambio entre Michael Löwy y John Holloway', *Bajo el Volcán* (Puebla) No. 6, pp. 13–26; also *Herramienta* (Buenos Aires), No. 23, pp.191–200.

Holloway, John (2003d) 'El Arbol de la Vida: Una Respuesta a Sergio Rodríguez', *Rebeldía* (Mexico City), No. 13, pp. 13–16; also *Herramienta* (Buenos Aires), No. 24, pp. 167–71.

Holloway, John (2003e) 'La Renovada Actualidad de la Revolución. Respuesta a Aldo Romero', *Herramienta* (Buenos Aires), No. 22, pp. 173–6.

Holloway, John (2004a) *Clase=Lucha* (Buenos Aires: Herramienta).

Holloway, John (2004b) 'Power and Democracy: More than a Reply to Michael Löwy', *New Politics* (New York), No. 36, pp. 138–41.

Holloway, John and Peláez, Eloína (eds) (1998) *Zapatista! Reinventing Revolution in Mexico* (London: Pluto Press).

Holloway, John and Picciotto, Sol (1977) 'Capital, Crisis and the State', *Capital & Class*, No. 2, pp. 76–101.

Holloway, John and Picciotto, Sol (eds) (1978a) *The State and Capital: A Marxist Debate* (London: Edward Arnold).

Holloway, John and Picciotto, Sol (1978b) 'Introduction: Towards a Materialist Theory of the State', in Holloway, J. and Picciotto, S. (eds), *The State and Capital: A Marxist Debate* (London: Edward Arnold), pp. 1–31.

Horkheimer, Max (1972) 'Traditional and Critical Theory', in *Critical Theory: Selected Essays* (New York: Seabury Press), pp. 188–243.

Horkheimer, Max (1978a) 'On the Problem of Truth', in Arato, A. and Gebhardt, E. (eds), *The Essential Frankfurt School Reader* (Oxford: Basil Blackwell), pp. 407–43.

Horkheimer, Max (1978b) 'The End of Reason', in Arato, A. and Gebhardt, E. (eds), *The Essential Frankfurt School Reader* (Oxford: Basil Blackwell), pp. 26–48.

Horkheimer, Max (1993) *Critique of Instrumental Reason* (New York: Continuum).

Horkheimer, Max and Adorno, Theodor W. (1972) *Dialectic of Enlightenment* (New York: Herder and Herder).

Howard, M.C and King, J.E. (1989) *A History of Marxian Economics, Vol. I, 1883–1929* (London: Macmillan).

Howard, M.C and King, J.E. (1992) *A History of Marxian Economics, Vol. II, 1929–1990* (London: Macmillan).

Hudis, Peter (2003) 'Rethinking the Idea of Revolution', *News & Letters* (Chicago), January–February.

Huerta, Enrique (2004) 'La Nueva Filosofía Política y Los Múltiples Espejos del Zapatismo', *Herramienta* web page.

Imhof, Werner (2004) 'Ein heilloser (?) Fall von Formblindheit', *Trend* (on-line journal), July.

International Monetary Fund (1995) *International Capital Markets: Developments, Prospects and Policy Issues* (Washington, DC: IMF).

Jay, Martin (1984a) *Adorno* (London: Fontana).

Jay, Martin (1984b) *Marxism and Totality* (Berkeley: University of California Press).

Jessop, Bob (1991) 'Polar Bears and Class Struggle: Much less than a Self-Criticism', in Bonefeld, W. and Holloway, J. (eds), *Post-Fordism and Social Form* (London: Macmillan), pp. 145–69.

Johnson, Linton Kwesi (1975) *Dread Beat and Blood* (London: Bogle L'Ouverture Publications).

Joyce, James (2000) *Ulysses* (London: Penguin).

Kaufman, Henry (1986) *Interest Rates, the Markets and the New Financial World* (London: Tauris).

Klopotek, Felix (2004) 'Holloways Mittelweg. John Holloway versucht die Synthese aus Wertformanalyse und Globalisierungskritik', *Herramienta* web page.

Kohan, Néstor (1998) *Marx en su (Tercer) Mundo: Hacia un Socialismo no Colonizado* (Buenos Aires: Biblos).

Kraniauskas, John (2002) 'Revolution is Ordinary', *Radical Philosophy*, No. 115 (September–October) pp. 40–2.

Lafargue, Paul (1999) *The Right to be Lazy* (Ardmore, PA: Fifth Season Press).

Lebowitz, Michael (2005) 'Holloway's Scream: Full of Sound and Fury', *Historical Materialism* (London).

Lenin, Vladimir Illich (1966) *Essential Works of Lenin* (New York: Bantam).

Lipietz, Alain (1985) *The Enchanted World* (London: Verso).

London Edinburgh Weekend Return Group (LEWRG) (1979) *In and Against the State* (London: CSE Books; revised version London: Pluto Press, 1980).

López, Néstor (2004) 'Discrepando con Dussel', *Herramienta* (Buenos Aires), No. 27, pp. 143–50.

Lorenzano, Luis (1998) 'Zapatismo: Recomposition of Labour, Radical Democracy and Revolutionary Project', in Holloway, J. and Peláez, E. (eds) *Zapatista! Reinventing Revolution in Mexico* (London: Pluto Press).

Löwy, Michael (2003) 'Intercambio entre Michael Löwy y John Holloway', *Bajo el Volcán* (Puebla), No. 6, pp. 13–26; also *Herramienta* (Buenos Aires), No. 23, pp. 191–200.

Löwy, Michael (2004) 'John Holloway, *Change the World Without Taking Power*', *New Politics* (New York), No. 35.

Lukács, Georg (1971) *History and Class Consciousness* (Cambridge, MA: MIT Press).

Luxemburg, Rosa (1973) *Reform or Revolution* (New York: Pathfinder).

Machiavelli, Nicolo (1995) *The Prince* (London: Penguin).

MacKenzie, Iain (1999) 'Power', in Ashe, F. et al. (eds), *Contemporary Social and Political Theory: An Introduction* (Buckingham: Open University Press), pp. 69–87.

McLaren, Peter (2003) 'Intervention' in *Marxism Digest*, <marxism-digest@lists.panix.com>, June.

Magdoff, Harry and Sweezy, Paul (1987) *Stagnation and the Financial Explosion* (New York: Monthly Review Press).

Manzana, Ernesto (2003) 'Un buen intento con un magro resultado', *Herramienta* web page.

Marcos, Subcomandante Insurgente (1998) 'Siete Piezas Sueltas del Rompecabezas Mundial', *Chiapas*, No. 5, pp. 117–43.

Marcuse, Herbert (1968) *One Dimensional Man* (London: Sphere).

Marcuse, Herbert (1998) *Eros and Civilization* (London: Routledge).

Marramao, Giacomo (1978) 'Teoría del Derrumbe y Capitalismo Organizado en las Discusiones del 'Extremismo Histórico'', *Cuadernos del Pasado y Presente*, No. 78, pp. 7–50.

Marshall, Barry (2002) 'Change the World Without Taking Power: The Meaning of Revolution Today', *Bad Reviews*, <http://eserver.org/bs/reviews/2002-12-3-04.19PM.html>

Martínez, José Manuel (2000) *Tres tesis sobre la Fetichización del Marxismo Contemporaneo* (Rosario: Tesis de doctorado, Universidad Nacional de Rosario).

Marx, Karl (1965) *Capital*, Vol. I (Moscow: Progress).

Marx, Karl (1972a) *Capital*, Vol. III (London: Lawrence and Wishart).

Marx, Karl (1972b) *Theories of Surplus Value*, Part III (London: Lawrence and Wishart).

Marx, Karl (1973) *Grundrisse* (London: Lawrence and Wishart).

Marx, Karl and Engels, Friedrich (1962) *Selected Works in Two Volumes*, Vol. I (Moscow: Progress).

Marx, Karl and Engels, Friedrich (1975) *Marx Engels Collected Works*, Vol. 3 (London: Lawrence and Wishart).

Marx, Karl and Engels, Friedrich (1976) *Marx Engels Collected Works*, Vol. 5 (London: Lawrence and Wishart).

Mathers, Andrew and Taylor, Graham (2005) 'Contemporary Struggle in Europe: "Anti-Power" or Counter-Power?' *Capital & Class*, London.

Mattick, Paul (1978) 'Sobre la Teoría Marxiana de la Acumulación y del Derrumbe', *Cuadernos del Pasado y Presente*, No. 78, pp. 86–106.

Mattini, Luis (2003) 'Autogestión productiva y asambleismo', *Cuadernos del Sur* (Buenos Aires), No. 36, pp. 102–9.

Méndez, Andrés (2003) 'Tomar el Poder, no; construir el Contrapoder', *Herramienta* (Buenos Aires), No. 22, pp. 177–3.

Moulier, Yann (1989) 'Introduction', in Negri, A., *The Politics of Subversion* (Cambridge: Polity Press), pp. 1–44.

Negri, Antonio (1980) *Del Obrero-Masa al Obrero Social* (Barcelona: Anagrama).

Negri, Antonio (1988a) *Revolution Retrieved: Selected Writings on Marx, Keynes, Capitalist Crisis and New Social Subjects 1967–83* (London: Red Notes).

Negri, Antonio (1988b) 'Keynes and the Capitalist Theory of the State', in Negri, A., *Revolution Retrieved: ...* (London: Red Notes) (1988a), pp. 5–42.

Negri, Antonio (1988c) 'Marx on Cycle and Crisis', in Negri, A., *Revolution Retrieved: ...* (London: Red Notes) (1988a), pp. 43–90.

Negri, Antonio (1989) *The Politics of Subversion* (Cambridge: Polity Press).

Negri, Antonio (1991) *The Savage Anomaly* (Minneapolis: University of Minnesota Press).

Negri, Antonio (1999) *Insurgencies: Constituent Power and the Modern State* (Minneapolis: University of Minnesota Press).

Negri, Antonio (2002) *Du Retour. Abécédaire biopolitique. Entretiens avec Anne Dufourmantelle* (Paris: Calmann-Lévy).

Palomino, Héctor (2005) 'Trabajo y Movimientos Sociales en Argentina Hoy', *Bajo el Volcán* (Puebla), No. 8, also *Herramienta* (Buenos Aires), no, 27, pp. 73–86.

Pannekoek, Anton (1977) 'The Theory of the Collapse of Capitalism', *Capital and Class*, No. 1, pp. 59–82.

Pashukanis, Evgeny (1978) *Law and Marxism: A General Theory* (London: Ink Links).

Peláez, Eloína and Holloway, John (1995) 'Learning to Bow: Post-Fordism and Technological Determinism', in Bonefeld, W. and Holloway, J. (eds), *Global Capital, National State and the Politics of Money* (London: Macmillan), pp. 135–44.

Piper, Watty (1978) *The Little Engine that Could* (New York: Putnam).

Poulantzas, Nicos (1973) *Political Power and Social Classes* (London: New Left Books).

Rajchenberg, Enrique (2003) 'John y la Identidad', *Herramienta* web page.

Red Notes (1979) *Working Class Autonomy and the Crisis: Italian Marxist Texts of the Theory and Practice of a Class Movement: 1964–79* (London: Red Notes).

REDaktion, (Hg) (1997) *Chiapas und die Internationale der Hoffnung* (Köln: ISP).

Reitter, Karl (2003) 'Wo wir stehen', *Grundrisse* (Vienna), No. 6, pp. 13–27.

Rodriguez, Sergio (2003) '¿Puede ser verde la teoría? Sí, siempre y cuando la vida no sea gris', *Rebeldía* (Mexico City), No. 8, pp. 9–17.

Romero, Aldo (2002) 'El Significado de la Revolución hoy', *Herramienta* (Buenos Aires), No. 21, pp. 173–5.

Rooke, Mike (2002) 'The Limitations of Open Marxism', *What Next* (London).

Roux, Rhina (2003) 'Dominación, Insubordinación y Política. Notas sobre el grito de Holloway', *Bajo el Volcán* (Puebla), No. 6, 37–58.

Rubin, Isaak Illich (1973) *Essays on Marx's Theory of Value* (Montreal: Black Rose Books).

Rushdie, Salman (1998) *The Satanic Verses* (London: Vintage).

Schiller, Margrit (2001) *Es war ein harter Kampf um meine Erinnerung. Ein Lebensbericht aus der RAF* (Munich: Piper).

Schlesinger, Arthur (1959) *The Age of Roosevelt: the Crisis of the Old Order, 1919–1933* (Cambridge, MA: The Riverside Press).

Schmitt, Carl (1987) *Der Begriff des Politischen* (Berlin: Duncker & Humblot).

Scott, James (1990) *Domination and the Arts of Resistance* (New Haven: Yale University Press).

Seibert, Thomas (2004) 'Welt-Veränderung-Macht. John Holloway und Thomas Seibert im Gespräch', *Arranca!* (Berlin), No. 30, pp. 9–13.

Serrano, Marcela (1995) *Antigua Vida Mía* (México: Alfaguara).

Smeriglio, Massimiliano (2004) Intervention in the presentation of the Italian edition of the book, Rome, March.

Smith, Cyril (1996) *Marx at the Millennium* (London: Pluto Press).

Smith, Cyril (2002) 'Anti-Power Versus Power', *The Commoner* (online journal); also *Herramienta* (Buenos Aires), No. 21, pp. 164–8.

Sohn-Rethel, Alfred (1978) *Intellectual and Manual Labour* (London: Macmillan).

Sopransi, Belén and Veloso Verónica (2004) 'Contra la subjetividad privatizada', *Herramienta*, (Buenos Aires) No. 27, pp. 87–105.

Stoetzler, Marcel (2005) 'On How to Make Adorno Scream: John Holloway's Concept of Revolution against Class and Identity', *Historical Materialism* (London).

Stratman, David (n.d.) *We Can Change the World* (Boston: New Democracy Books).

Tavor, Bannet Eve (1989) *Structuralism and the Logic of Dissent* (London: Macmillan).

Thompson, Edward P. (1967) 'Time, Work-Discipline and Industrial Capitalism', *Past and Present*, No. 38, pp. 56–96.

Thwaites Rey, Mabel (2003) 'La Autonomía como Mito y como Posibilidad', *Cuadernos del Sur* (Buenos Aires), No. 36, pp. 87–101.

Thwaites Rey, Mabel (2004) *La autonomía como búsqueda, el Estado como contradicción* (Buenos Aires: Prometeo).

Tischler, Sergio (2000) 'Memoria y Sujeto. Una Aproximación desde la Política', *Bajo el Volcán*, No. 1, pp. 11–24.

Tischler, Sergio (2005) 'Time of Reification and Time of Insubordination', in Bonefeld, W. and Psychopedis, K. (eds) *Human Dignity* (Aldershot: Ashgate).

Tronti, Mario (1979a) 'Lenin in England', in Red Notes, *Working Class Autonomy and the Crisis: ...* (London: Red Notes), pp. 1–6.

Tronti, Mario (1979b) 'The Strategy of the Refusal', in Red Notes, *Working Class Autonomy and the Crisis: ...* (London: Red Notes), pp. 7–21.

Vaneigem, Raoul (1994) *The Revolution of Everyday Life* (London: Rebel Press/Left Bank Books).

Vega, Cantor Renán (2003) 'La historia brilla por su ausencia', *Herramienta* (Buenos Aires), No. 22, pp. 191–6.

Wainwright, Hilary (2003) *Reclaim the State* (London: Verso).

Walter, Andrew (1993) *World Power and World Money* (London: Harvester Wheatsheaf).

Warburton, Peter (1999) *Debt and Delusion* (London: Allen Lane/The Penguin Press).

Wildcat (2003) 'Der Schrei und die Arbeiterklasse', *Wildcat-Zirkular* (Berlin), No. 65, pp. 48–54.

Williams, Raymond (1976) *Keywords* (Glasgow: Fontana).

Winocur, Marcos (2001) 'La Izquierda Que Tanto Ame, El Viento Se La Llevo', *Bajo El Volcán*, No. 3, pp. 211–34.

Witheford, Nick (1994) 'Autonomist Marxism and the Information Society' *Capital and Class*, No. 52, pp. 85–125.

Wright, Chris (2002) 'Change the World Without Taking Power', *Herramienta* web page.

Zibechi, Raúl (2003) *Genealogía de la Revuelta* (La Plata: Letra Libre).

Name Index

Subject Index